Art & Craft

Art & Craft

Thirty Years on the Literary Beat

Bill Thompson

The University of South Carolina Press

Published by the University of South Carolina Press
Columbia, South Carolina 29208

www.sc.edu/uscpress

Manufactured in the United States of America

24 23 22 21 20 19 18 17 16 15 10 9 8 7 6 5 4 3 2 1

Library of Congress Cataloging-in-Publication Data can be found at
http://catalog.loc.gov/

This book was printed on a recycled paper with 30 percent
postconsumer waste content.

For Rosemary Michaud, muse and foil, and with felicitations to Alan Kovski, Bill Petry, and the gents of the Book Club (who kept me on my toes)

CONTENTS

ILLUSTRATIONS

FOREWORD

When I first started writing, right around 1978, I wasn't part of a writer's community. There wasn't one—I didn't know any other novelist working in the lowcountry, or any writers' groups or workshops. There were only a couple of book clubs. By the time I finished my first novel and found a publisher for it, there was no bookstore!

Then a new independent bookstore opened in 1983, just in time for me, and for Harlan Greene and Padgett Powell, whose first novels appeared the same month mine did. Other writers sprang up in succession over the years; today we have maybe 60 people working and publishing, and more on the way. I'd say Charleston now qualifies as a hotbed, a place where organic matter ferments and generates heat and nurtures new seedlings. Whether our growth spurt might eventually lead to a second Charleston Renaissance, nobody knows. But it's definitely been a good time for writers.

Do writers really need community? I think so. Not so much for the critiquing and encouragement and advice on how to get an agent (although those things are welcome) but more for the laughs, the commiseration, and the happy but often shocking discovery that someone else thinks the same way you do. Writers are surprisingly similar whether they're writing fiction or poetry or history or magazine articles. We're loners by necessity; there's no job more solitary. At the same time, we need human connection, or we lose the very thing that makes us writers.

A community may well germinate organically wherever there are writers and readers, but in Charleston the process was sped up by a catalyst—Bill Thompson—whose newspaper reviews and interviews sparked our energy and made us aware of each other, generated the warmth we needed. As book review editor at The Post and Courier from 1981 to 2012, Bill Thompson was the observer who electrified the observed. And because he was a writer himself, and a really good one, he knew what we were about and what we were after.

Interestingly enough, Bill decided he would never actually review the books of local writers in the region. His reasons for this decision boil down to the fact that he was one of us. He could expect to run into us from time to time. So instead of reviewing us, he interviewed. He wrote about our habits, our dreams and fears, and occasionally the secrets we blurted out during the interview. The decision not to review was perhaps a choice he made for his own well-being, but it was also of real benefit to the community of writers. Bill Thompson was the one commentator who did not judge but instead opened a window, introduced us, interpreted us, and by that encouraged us. He was a great listener and elicitor; you'll find in these interviews more than one intimate glimpse into the writer's mind and heart, like Pat Conroy's "I'll never have confidence in the writing," Roy Blount's "Anyone can be funny. I want to make sense," or Lee Smith's "I don't want to prettify."

But Bill did review the works of writers beyond our circle of Southerners, and these were just as valuable as the interviews. The expanded horizon is crucial for writers and readers alike. As Bill says in his section on travel writing (but it clearly applies to all kinds of writers), "The vastness of the world and its cultures does not make one feel small and insignificant . . . one feels humbled, yes, yet enlarged, granted passage to a broader and keener perception."

And that's the goal for all of us, writers, readers, travelers and editors alike. A broader and keener perception, yes, plus open minds, serious transformation and whatever revelation might be possible. Bill quotes Bret Lott as saying, "My job as a writer is to try and discover," a sentiment echoed again and again by others, even the nonfiction writers. Gary Smith says, "You approach a story like a bit of an adventure, and, by giving in to it, you use it as a window to learn about so much more."

Week by week, Bill Thompson gave us that kind of window, and with this collection he opens it again, providing a view from the kind of "questing intellect" he sees in writers but also clearly owns himself. From fiction and biography to books about travel, history, crime, television, the Charleston Renaisssance, the environment—his range is wide. What's more, the essays are just plain fun to read. Bookstores may have come and gone, and the publishing industry is in a state of panic. But we are a strong writing community today, thanks in no small measure to the Thompson era. Bill got us going, and we are grateful.

Josephine Humphreys

ACKNOWLEDGMENTS

Were it not for Betsy Cantler, long-time features editor of both The News and Courier and The Post and Courier (now blissfully retired), these articles and reviews would not exist—at least not with my name attached—for it was she who entrusted me with the post of book review editor. I am forever grateful.

These may be "my" stories, but many a fellow editor and photographer at The Post and Courier contributed over the years. They have my thanks, as do the legion of staff and freelance book reviewers who infused the Sunday book page with so much verve, gravity, and humor, making me (and the paper) look good. Of the latter, I owe the greatest debt to Catherine Holmes of the College of Charleston, who almost single-handedly dispelled those disparaging generalizations about "academic" writing with an ocean of measured, insightful, and beautifully rendered reviews. She's still at it, tirelessly, and readers are lucky to have her.

I should also mention the members of the late, lamented Southern Book Critics Circle, whose comradeship made each trip to the Southern Festival of Books in Nashville a delight, and my colleagues in the National Book Critics Circle, for sustaining an admirable tradition.

A deep bow, too, must go to Jonathan Haupt of the University of South Carolina Press, who was kind enough to invite me to submit such a collection, to Jo Humphreys for her exceptionally kind foreword, to Linda Sue Lewis for her copyediting, to Ben Moïse for his sage advice, to Adam Parker for taking the baton, and to such current and former Post and Courier personnel as Libby Wilder, Brad Nettles, Becky Baulch, and Fred Smith, as well as publisher P. J. Browning, who were generous with their time and help.

Profuse thanks, as well, is owed to Wes and Judy Moore, for entrusting me with their home, and allowing me to complete this book in an enchanted surround.

I am indebted to the authors who not only produced so many wonderful books, but who also shared their thoughts, experience, and wisdom. Lastly, and above all, I salute the readers of the newspaper who have consistently supported books and reading, especially in an era of diminishing coverage and vanishing book editors.

Sine qua non.

Prologue

Just as a photographer never allows his shadow to fall across the face of a frame, a journalist should not intrude on the page, like a ghost that calls attention to itself.

A writer's style may inform and grace the material, but it should not eclipse his or her subject. Easier said than done, of course, because writers, especially young ones, risk falling in love with their own voices. The temptation to overfurnish a piece is hard to resist. After all, a young writer is trying to show what he or she can do. This is no less true of journalists than of aspiring authors. Yet dispassionate observers engender trust. The self-involved do not. When a reporter also is a critic, as I have been, he or she is at pains to keep these spheres clearly separated in the reader's mind. Articles and profiles may suggest the temperament of the interviewer, and even harbor a veiled comment now and again, usually as connective tissue between the subject's thoughts. But reviews and columns are different animals entirely. The former is entirely about an informed opinion. The latter, an alloy of commentary and reportage.

Still, many of the pieces which endure the longest are spiced with personality. It's the equilibrium that matters. So for the moment, permit me to dispense with that trusty embargo—which prohibits the word *I*—and reference the self.

In 41 years in newspapering, 32 of them at The Post and Courier in Charleston, S.C., I had the great good fortune to work in many of the most rewarding arenas: as an all-purpose feature writer covering (quite literally) anything under the sun, as a travel writer, business writer, arts writer, film critic, columnist and book review editor.

In was in this last capacity that I had the opportunity to meet and converse with some of the most distinguished novelists and nonfiction writers America has produced, as well as with numerous visitors from abroad. With that came a singular education, and a passion for books that deepened over time.

While I always was encouraged to read, I did not, like so many who one day would work at the writer's trade, grow up smitten with books. Nor did I harbor the slightest notion of being a writer myself until midway through college. I was destined to be an architect, or so I thought.

When the sea change came, and I found myself submerged in an ocean of books, it was the ancient world whose tides I found most compelling. The literature of antiquity, of origins, trumped all else. The Americas? The South? Mainly footnotes. As a Tar Heel, I knew Thomas Wolfe. I also knew Faulkner. But Welty and O'Connor were only recent acquaintances, as were many of the accomplished writers of the day, in and out of the South. As my tastes expanded, they also became increasingly cosmopolitan, owing no allegiance to any time, place or people. That penchant would be no less pronounced in professional life. As a book review editor I cast a wide net, rejecting calls to tighten the weave. From time to time a well-meaning local or area writer would ask, often with a hint of consternation, "Why do you spend so much time writing about authors from outside the state and the South? Why don't you focus exclusively on *us*?"

Certainly many in and out of newspaper work have taken that path, and with notable success. Responding to this call from writers and friends to do likewise called for diplomacy (and restraint). But in the end, I had to be candid. As an editor I wanted to keep my reviewers as engaged as their readers. And that meant variety. As a reporter covering books, I did not want to be parochial. I did not wish to read just one page of the library of literature, no matter how esteemed. Nor did I want to limit the readers of The Post and Courier's Features and Books pages to one region's ideas and perceptions. The South *would* be covered, and thoroughly, just not at the expense of the rest of the country and the world.

Three decades covering books produced many hundreds of author interviews, reviews and discussions of issues in publishing. In some cases, I conducted numerous interviews with the same author over the years, most often with writers in the Carolinas. But the majority have been one-offs, brief yet arresting encounters that have taken up permanent residence in my memory. I treasure the experience. My one-to-one conversations with these dedicated, creative people, pondering their ideas and inspirations, were their own reward, and what kept me in the game. Here I have chosen a selection of my favorites from across a range of stories.

Some are straightforward profiles tied to a newly released book at hand, others a kind of schematic diagram of the writer's process or treatments of topical issues. Still others are "philosophical" ruminations on the tension between art and commerce, stylistic invention or the interaction of character and plot on a narrative, as well as on the rewards and tribulations of the writing life. Some combine all three approaches. And I am convinced that such stories captivate readers.

Throughout I have assumed the newspaper's audience for book-related material was that of an intelligent, educated general reader. Unlike some book review editors, I never considered myself a litterateur (not that I held such folks in contempt) or one devoted to the latest academic fashion. I was simply a journalist, bibliophile and devotee of the printed word.

In my view, genuine respect for the art and craft of books also means you are a defender of excellence, of standards, of writing that seeks to do more than pummel readers with a point of view. I believe that calcified ideologies lose their intellectual freedom of movement, and that a thoughtful writer or editor should harbor an innate distrust of absolutes and certitude. While a journalist must faithfully reflect an interview subject's individual perceptions and words in an article, it is also the reporter's responsibility to ask tough questions and place matters in context.

Fortunately, outside of the political swirl, I encountered little of this rigidity. As a group, writers exhibit a questing intellect. Ideas are their lingua franca. They are asking questions, and grappling with doubts across the entire spectrum of human experience.

In at least one respect, having to wear multiple hats at The Post and Courier was beneficial. Writing about motion pictures, as I did concurrently for 19 of my years as book editor, was useful in both book and film interviews, given the intimate interaction between these art forms. This affords a reporter the chance to add a layer of richness to an article or review that might not have existed otherwise. I also applied the same standards to the writing of book reviews as I did film critiques: be demanding but fair. If a writer has made a genuine attempt at excellence, praise the attempt. Point out where, in your opinion, he or she fell short. But refrain from corrosive or incendiary prose for its own sake. Don't get too cute, and don't get personal, but by all means inform and entertain. I like to think I fulfilled those criteria.

The pieces collected in this book naturally reflect the limitations of daily newspapering, compared to magazine work, with the daily deadlines, scant space and competing responsibilities. But I hope they also reflect the vigor and joy of the work, the immense pleasure I took in doing it.

My first nine years in the business were spent as a sportswriter, where a certain latitude in pyrotechnic prose style was not only accepted but encouraged. I was one lucky guy, I thought, flitting around the country and getting paid (however modestly) to cover all those grand spectacles. I could scarcely have imagined what the next 32 years would bring. Lucky man, indeed.

I hope you enjoy the ride. I did.

Pat Conroy. Photograph by Grace Beahm

Leading Lights, or the Test of Renown

"A work that aspires, however humbly, to the condition of art should carry its justification in every line."

Joseph Conrad, *The Children of the Sea* (1897)

Fame can be a cruel mistress, but it beats obscurity. Usually.

Some authors hope for the equivalent of being a working character actor, steadily employed and recognized by filmgoers, even if the audience can't always apply a name to the face. They are welcome company. For others, nothing less than mega-stardom will do. Unlike matinee idols, however, most "big name" writers don't have to relinquish their privacy at the altar of renown. Just a portion of it.

That's the bargain, of course. The unfortunate thing about fame is that once achieved, sustaining it can become the dominant impulse, not the work. Some find that they've made a devil's pact, writing to suit the fashion of the moment, delivering content that pleases and avoiding what less discerning readers may not like.

The authors profiled in this section made no such compromise. They take chances. They are not satisfied with the commonplace, or with fleeting fancies.

They are allied with the ancients, who believed that fame was the crown of achievement, not with the aspirants of Andy Warhol's 15-minute world, whose conviction is that fame is the only thing that's worthwhile, an end in itself.

I learned early on that interviewing famous writers is no different from speaking to less exalted ones, once their radiance loses a bit of its wattage. This usually happens in five minutes or less, when one realizes they are driven by the same aims, needs and insecurities as lesser lights. But acclaim does not always equate with talent, much less execution. Some of modest gifts and desires have simply found a profitable niche and are content with that. Others are more ambitious, either financially or artistically or both. And many writers garner fame for a reason, apart from the luck of the draw and fortuitous timing. They're just that good.

Twain said fame is a vapor, a wisp. But I suspect the regard in which these writers are held will linger.

Tom Wolfe's *A Man in Full*

Could it be true? Could Tom Wolfe, maverick New Journalist of the '60s whose use of fictional techniques left editors aghast, really be nearing his 70s?

Yes. Not that there's any less vigor to his writing, as Wolfe's much-heralded second novel *A Man in Full* (Farrar, Straus & Giroux) amply demonstrates. Set in boomtown Atlanta, the 742-page broadside received a National Book Award nomination well before landing in bookstores this week.

In it, Wolfe nails our corrosive worship of conspicuous consumption and a peculiarly American brand of hubris with sufficient depth and flair to bury all that rot about him being a "one-novel wonder."

Wolfe insists, jocularly, that one of the most distinguishing features of the novel is its literal, not literary weight. A hefty three pounds, the book may have been 11 years in the making, but was written in a little more than a year.

"I once made the statement that all books are written in six months. The rest is dancing around the project," says Wolfe. "Much time was consumed in outlining the novel. As I tell my children, outlines are as much a part of the craft of writing as the writing of sentences."

Wolfe was founding father and chief practitioner of the so-called New Journalism in articles and in such books as *The Kandy-Kolored Tangerine-Flake Streamline Baby* (1965), *The Electric Kool-Aid Acid Test* (1968) and *Radical Chic and Mau-Mauing the Flak Catchers* (1970). He also championed the notion—anathema to some literateurs—that the more creative approaches to modern journalism surpassed fiction as a window to the heart, soul and rhythm of the land.

The Richmond, Va., native, who graduated from Yale with a degree in American studies, underscored the claim in 1979 with *The Right Stuff*, but by the latter part of the '80s realized he could undertake the novel without compromising his convictions. Thus was born *The Bonfire of the Vanities* (1987), his hugely successful Reagan-era satire.

"I do believe the novel can bring you the news, and there's never been a bigger need for it in this century."

It's reassuring to know that Wolfe, ever the sartorial dandy, hasn't shed his taste for the unconventional, for surprise.

"A lot of what's in the book just sort of hopped into my head," says Wolfe, deflecting mention of his reputation for intellection and hard work. "The intimidating thing about fiction is that you have all this freedom. In nonfiction, you're handed this character and this plot, and the challenge is to bring them alive."

The protagonist of *A Man in Full* is embattled Atlanta real estate developer Charlie Croker, an aging former football hero with an ambitious young wife and a wagonload of woe. His business ventures going sour, Croker is facing the loss of his 20,000-acre plantation. Despite a ton of debt and humiliating austerity measures imposed from without, he clings to a driving desire to see the name "Croker" emblazoned 50 stories on high.

"The edifice complex," Wolfe quips.

"If the ruling metaphor of contemporary life is a bad loan that's suddenly come due," writes one reviewer, "Wolfe has again noticed it first, then pushed ahead of other creditors."

He's also pushed ahead in other ways. To a large extent, Wolfe is utilizing Atlanta to deal metaphorically with such issues as evolving cultural identity. And he is just as puzzled as any why Atlanta, the very emblem of the New South, so seldom has lured the serious novelist.

"You'd think it would be an absolute natural. It's such a colorful and exciting place and in many ways such a young, new place, that you'd think there would have been 30 or 40 novels set there by now. This whole business of passing up this incredibly rich and bizarre panorama just baffles me. Not just Atlanta. What about Dallas? What do writers want?"

Some might counter that a sprawling, unfocused Atlanta is too hard to pin down. It may be a complex social structure, but otherwise recalls Gertrude Stein's "there is no there, there" comment about Oakland.

"People make that argument. They say that American society is so fragmented that if you try to do a slice of life as the novel does you just get a slice of chaos. All that really means is that it's just a little more difficult to portray the life of a city than it was in, say, Dickens's time. You just have to work a little harder. It's by no means impossible. There should be great novels about Charleston, too. The same is true of my hometown."

Like *Bonfire of the Vanities*, which was set in motion by a racial incident, *A Man in Full* cranks up when a local black football star is accused of raping the daughter of a prominent white businessman.

"One of my convictions is that if you want to write about urban America today, you can't duck race. It's a huge part of our national life. So far in fiction, it's being dealt with in a delicate, mincing fashion that is kind of pathetic. It's time to write about the subject head on. I can't believe how the majority of fiction writers today are avoiding incomparable material and essentially just sitting there sucking their thumbs.

"This idea began around the 1870s in France, where tremendous emphasis was put on the so-called psychological novel or the exquisite novel—something understood by only we precious few. And that's the state our literature is in now. Many writers are taught in college graduate writing programs that journalism today reports all the facts and so it's no use to compete with it, that in no way can the novel be used to bring the news. In a way, the opposite is true. Less is being covered in 1998 than in 1908."

It is partly for this reason that Wolfe says "A Man in Full" is his best book.

"On the other hand, if you don't think that you're in deep trouble. I did pretty much what I set out to do. Along the way came an unexpected pleasure—the treatment of Stoicism and the Stoic philosopher Epictetus—and it added something to the book that surprised me. I've written nonfiction most of my career. There won't be many surprises there apart from the discovery of material that is new and hasn't been discovered before."

Fiction or nonfiction, Wolfe still surprises us.

November 15, 1998

Norman Mailer's *Oswald's Tale*

Lee Harvey Oswald hungered for renown, the sort of global fame attendant to great achievements. He was dyslexic, but a voracious reader who aspired to write and move millions. He defected to the Soviet Union at age 19, certain it held the answer to his dreams.

It is not news that superior ability breeds superior ambition. But it was Oswald's tragedy that his abilities were mediocre.

He ventured to Russia and into the arms of the KGB, only to be consigned to the gloom of Minsk and a job in a nondescript factory. He was not interviewed. He was not debriefed. For two years, Oswald and his Russian wife were constantly observed by those who didn't quite know what to make of him: CIA plant or deranged romantic?

Had Oswald found what he so desperately sought, might he have become a different person than the man accused of the Kennedy assassination?

Norman Mailer thinks so. Thanks to unprecedented access to KGB documents, Mailer, aided by investigative reporter Lawrence Schiller, has deconstructed the Oswald we thought we knew and reconstructed the character of the man he calls "the American Ghost."

In *Oswald's Tale: An American Mystery* (Random House), Mailer's first book-length work of nonfiction in 16 years, the two-time Pulitzer Prize-winning writer explores the nature of a man accused of murdering not just a president, but an era. He does not ask, "Who killed Kennedy?" but "Who was Oswald?" He finds an individual far different from the ineffectual loner of popular myth.

"One of my fundamental literary beliefs is that whether people are good or evil, they have humanity, and that we can learn as much from evil people as from good people. And Oswald saw himself as a potentially great man, a leader who one day would change the world."

Mailer insists that the most misguided way to regard Oswald is as a dangerous recluse, because it is too simplistic. Oswald, he says, was not passive, but active, even audacious. Yet over the years American popular culture has painted him as a much-diminished character.

"I noticed that in most of the reviews of my book, even the positive ones, the reviewer said 'Yes, but Mailer's making too much of this fellow.' And I'm at a loss. Because I find him not only fascinating but adventurous. I'm not trying to celebrate him. He was a terrible liar and deceitful and killed a man I have huge regard for. Or I believe he did.

"But the fact of the matter is that he was a very enterprising kid. At the age of 19, he's a Marine who goes over to the Soviet Union and dares to defect. That in itself is bold and kind of extraordinary, especially for a young man who also exhibited great timidity. A weak man doesn't step out into the unknown. He dared to believe, for instance, that the USSR is not as bad as we painted it."

When Oswald determined to leave the USSR, he succeeded in working through the bureaucracies of the U.S. State Department, which he had earlier defied, and the KGB. He left with his wife, Marina, a Russian girl whom he had chanced to marry.

"(These are) brave acts which reveal a lot of fortitude," says Mailer. "He had instincts about dealing with bureaucracies. I was amazed to see how smart and skillful some of the moves he made were. Then he comes home and presumably kills the president. This is not a small man. The idea that people wanted to believe that he was a nerd is hard to understand. He didn't have much personality on the surface, but my God, what storms were building underneath him. The people who change history can be losers, but they're not small losers."

Discoveries in Minsk

Initially, Mailer undertook the book in hopes of finding new evidence of a conspiracy, as well as for the purpose of developing background on a planned follow-up to *Harlot's Ghost*, his 1991 novel of the CIA.

"I was always fascinated by the assassination, horrified to begin with. I felt that the inquiry the Warren Commission was making was not a good one. At one point, I tried to interest a great many of my fellow writers in forming an amateur commission to try to investigate it, but couldn't rouse enough interest.

"But I didn't know I was necessarily going to do a book on the subject until Larry Schiller came along and said that he had obtained access to the KGB files and asked if I would do the book."

Schiller had worked with Mailer on *The Executioner's Song* (1979), the latter's widely hailed dissection of Gary Gilmore, and Mailer regards his colleague as something of a wizard in obtaining obscure or guarded information.

"Of course, I was hoping I'd find a smoking gun, as everyone does when they go out on a story. I started the book in September of 1992, after talking with Larry and going over to Minsk to see what the KGB had to offer."

Mailer spent six months in Minsk, interviewing people who were Oswald's friends and co-workers, as well as those KGB officials charged with tracking Oswald's movements. Mailer and Schiller also had access to a surveillance dossier more than a foot thick.

"The Cold War had ended. The place where we interviewed most of the people not of the KGB was now part of a separate country. They hadn't talked about Oswald in 30 years but it was minted in their memory. They were the best interviews I ever had in some ways because it was all so clear to them and they'd never before talked with anyone."

Mailer says the Soviet segment (1959–1962) of *Oswald's Tale* depends "upon the small revelations of different points of view." It was not a simple matter to reconcile these views into a coherent psychological profile of the man.

"What I learned from them had more to do with the possibilities of his character than the logic of it. The startling thing was how much Oswald, in certain ways, was like other people. Yet he was anything but an ordinary fellow. Seeing ordinary features of one-half of his existence helped me see how exceptional he was in other ways. Until you see what's ordinary in people, you can never begin to understand them. The revelations I found were day-to-day in nature, in a place that was dreary, oppressive, and sad."

Mailer brackets his chronicle of Oswald's years in Minsk with an account of his difficult childhood and Marine Corps service, and the events extending from his return in June, 1962, to the Kennedy killing 17 months later. Oswald and Marina ultimately settled in Fort Worth, where they lived in poverty and obscurity—an unacceptable fate for two highly ambitious people.

The author has stated that there is a very good possibility—though it's impossible to prove—that Oswald, debriefed by the CIA and FBI upon his return to the United States, had been working for the FBI as a paid agent of COINTELPRO, a secret echelon within the FBI established, in part, to subvert organizations like the American Communist Party. Mailer asks: Would they have let someone as potentially useful as Oswald slip by? Some of Oswald's actions are difficult to explain except in terms of him being a provocateur.

Another Point of View

The American obsession with Oswald and Kennedy won't go away. Nor will the question: Did Oswald do it alone? Mailer believes that he did, but that the secondary questions concerning CIA and/or FBI connections are still immense. Even if they had nothing to do with the assassination, he believes there was a massive cover-up that paralyzed the Warren Commission.

However, the intent of *Oswald's Tale* is not to solve the case. It is to encourage the reader to re-examine. Which, in a way, is what the 72-year-old Mailer has been doing for much of his career.

It may be argued that, along with *The Naked and the Dead*, *Armies of the Night*, *Of a Fire on the Moon*, *The Executioner's Song* and other works, *Oswald's Tale* is of a piece—one chapter in an opus that affords a look at the 20th century as perceived by Mailer.

"I do have a point of view that has developed and changed but become fairly consistent over the past 30 years," says Mailer, oft called "the American Tolstoy." "There is a philosophy underlying what I write, but I'll leave that determination to literary critics, who may see patterns I don't see."

Though contemplating an autobiography, Mailer says his own image has been so distorted that it is probably beyond repair. Not that he cares.

"I don't worry about that anymore. There's a time when you're trying to get people to see you the way you want to be seen. But by the time you reach the age of 72, your feeling is that it doesn't matter anymore. And besides, once people pass 70, I think everybody tends to give them a little more slack. So it hardly matters what a biographer writes. At that point you're seen as old and semi-respectable. You can be an old reprobate. But if you're 70, you're a wonderful old reprobate."

June 4, 1995

Diane Ackerman's *An Alchemy of Mind*

Cacophony, anyone?

"The real wonder of the brain, I think, is the ease with which it can craft a fluent, persuasive, stable sense of self when there is all this uncertainty going on."

Diane Ackerman should know. She has been deflecting the din of the world, making connections and communicating fluent, persuasive thoughts for years. The respected poet, naturalist and author of literary nonfiction has brought all of her curiosity and artistic skills to bear for her latest book, *An Alchemy of Mind: The Marvel and Mystery of the Brain* (Scribner).

It's Ackerman's eighth book of nonfiction, which keeps amiable company with seven volumes of verse and three installments in her continuing series of nature books for children.

With the same elegance and attention to detail that characterized her *A Natural History of the Senses*, Ackerman explores how our celebrated "gray matter," an intricate tangle of billions of neurons, functions to make us at once unique and universal.

The mind trying to decipher its own mysteries is not unlike an artist having difficulty drawing or painting the human hand. In some ways, we're too close to the subject.

"We are the only facet of nature that we can't stand outside of and observe," says Ackerman. "So to some extent our understanding of the brain will always be a mystery that's just out of reach. But we have begun to understand an awful lot about how it operates because we are so good at self-reflection and we are such curious beasts that we want to know all the time. We have a part of the brain that's constantly asking, "Why, why, why."

The Ithaca, N.Y., resident, who earned her doctorate in English and comparative literature from Cornell University, always has been equally intrigued by mind and matter.

"I started out in physiological psychology at college and thought that was what I would go into, but when I transferred colleges the computer put me in English by mistake. At 18, you think it's fate. I decided that since I'd been writing enthusiastically all my life, I would stay in English. But I kept my fascination with the mind. And I've been writing about it in different forms in all different kinds of books about the senses or love or the dark night of the soul, or our relationship with nature."

The Conduit

Finally, she determined it was time to sit down and get up to speed on neuroscience. Quite an undertaking.

"Nothing really is available to us except through the brain. It's the only way we can know the world. In one way it imprisons us but in another it gives us so much freedom because it allows us to extend our bodies and our ideas in time and space. I've enjoyed so much thinking about how all that works and trying to find language that would both capture the scientific reality of the brain but also a sense of what the experience of having a brain and minds feels like. These books are a celebration and a kind of factual tour. I think of the mind as a comforting mirage that the brain creates so that we will feel continuous and real. Though, of course, we live from one illusion to the next."

In one chapter "The Emotional Climate," Ackerman notes that the discrepancy between "the actual world and what we choose to know about it is so vast that we often make mistakes, overreact, fill in some spaces with superstition." Our concepts may remain orderly but our emotions are still Pleistocene.

"There's a time lag of half a second between perceiving something and being conscious of it. It takes time for the perception to roll around the brain and the brain to circulate the news. So it feels like we're sensing things and knowing about them at the same time, but brain time isn't world time. We're all a little offbeat, by design. Evolution has made us willing fools who would otherwise not be able to cope with reality and be late for absolutely everything, which we are anyway. So there's this watchman in the pantry who backdates events."

Being Mammal

We've managed to elaborate the experience of being alive, with all its manifest sensations and thoughts, to a degree not experienced by any other earthy creature, so much so that Ackerman feels we miss much of the texture of "being animal, of being part of nature."

We should embrace our animal nature, not reject it, she counsels.

"I think there is a terrible loneliness at the heart of society that comes from trying to exile ourselves from nature and from the seasons, which we evolved to be part of. Our animal nature certainly has sabotaged us a lot and continues to, but it's also quite glistening and miraculous. And even though the media likes to feature the dark side of our nature, the bright side is at least as complex and unpredictable. Our capacity for generosity of spirit is great."

Ackerman says that it is also instructive to view that pivotal invention of the human animal, language, as being poetry in all its forms, and that one of the ways in which the brain functions rests with its continuous use of metaphor.

"We use countless metaphors all the time, unconsciously, because we need a hinge between feelings and ideas. Here we are, minds that inhabit a visceral body, and we rely on the abstraction of language, but we need a way to embody thought and to make ideas sensible, and be able to probe the world even when our body is resting. That, for me, seems quite miraculous. And we do it through metaphor. Thought becomes action that we can then stage right in the mind's eye.

"We do it so fast that we don't notice that we're really playing an elaborate what-if game so that we can protect our bodies. That's why it evolved. We need to hold onto thoughts."

Litmus Tests

Too often, interpretation of research into the brain has seemed to be in thrall to ideology or the academic fashion of the moment. Apart from the intellectual straitjacket this implies, don't such people miss the beauty and poetics of the thing (as well as the good, unalloyed science being done)?

"Always they miss the beauty and poetics of it. I suppose that's why I'm not a straight up-and-down scientist. I would never be happy. I am essentially an artist, a poet, who rejoices in the revelations of science. For me, nature includes all of it. I just think of myself as a nature writer, a nature poet, if what you think of as nature is the full sum of creation."

As an observer of how we apprehend the universe, one thing that disturbs Ackerman more than most is the effects of watching violence on television, in movies and in video games, and what that can do to the brain. A risk we dismiss at our peril, she maintains.

"So much of what we see is so graphic and gruesome that I don't know what effect it's going to have on our brains in the future. Are we changing our own evolution? To some extent we have been all along, when we invented civilization, agriculture, etc. We don't always play by evolution's rules. We make our own. But there is a question about whether we're living in sensory overload and how violent images, how this rapid-paced, novelty-mad society is going to affect the brain. Can it make permanent changes in our children and in ourselves, in our human nature?"

Gender, Genius

Although it can be argued that there is more difference between any two individuals throughout life than between men and women, there is evidence of differences in the brain and of our relative skills and strengths. When one eliminates the sensibility that sees all of life through the lens of gender politics, those differences can be fascinating.

"It is a delicate subject, isn't it? For the longest time we were arguing that there was no difference and, therefore, women deserved dignity, equality and respect. We were really right about the latter, and really wrong about the no differences because we've evolved different biological agendas. We are mainly alike, mostly alike. But that little way in which we are different has enormous influence on us. In subtle ways men's and women's brains are wired differently, and these things were all important to our ancestors."

Nature or nurture? Well, both, Ackerman thinks. Is anything in life not a synthesis of influences?

Also freighted are the subjects of intelligence and genius. Ability is one thing, extraordinary ability another. Talent does what it can, genius what it must.

"I've been curious, too, whether or not geniuses are truly different," Ackerman says. "There is some evidence that smarter people have more gray matter in their frontal lobes or that one part of the brain may be more developed than another. But I think they also differ greatly in how they learn to use their memory. They tend to quickly recognize patterns and better store and retrieve long-term memories when they need to. That's found to be an hereditary trait.

"People who study geniuses in the arts and sciences find that perseverance plays an absolutely crucial role, as does motivation and also the ability to play. The single greatest ability is the ability to persevere."

Passion and Play

Nothing happens in our selves or in our culture, the author asserts, without passion or play. Are artists wired differently?

"All really creative, imaginative people also seem to develop startling expertise, which probably means they are superbly good at paying attention. Or, as I prefer to think of it, the useful application of obsession. Unfortunately, artists can obsess uselessly, too. But to be able to concentrate happily for long spells is what is required in art. It's like throwing a lavish party in just one room of a big house.

"Dispositions also get inherited, just as one inherits eye color. But if you inherit a talent, it doesn't necessarily mean that you are going to use it. It just increases the likelihood. And I don't think a creative gift starts like a metaphor skill or memory skill, but maybe as a slightly different way of cognitively processing, one person being more skilled at abstract thought or being born more visual. The memories that they embed reflect those specialties.

What we like to do becomes the thing we do most often, and the thing we do most often becomes the thing we do best."

Which is to say, "practice makes perfect."

July 18, 2004

Edward Albee's *The Goat or Who Is Sylvia?*

Iconoclasts do not make good wage slaves. Take Edward Albee.

Some years ago, the playwright assayed his career thusly: "I have been both over-praised and under-praised. I assume by the time I finish writing—and I plan to go on writing until I'm 90 or gaga—it will all equal itself out. You can't involve yourself with the vicissitudes of fashion or critical response."

The principal hazard of doing so?

"You become an employee," says Albee. "You start doing what they like in order to be more popular. But you shouldn't go around trying to be as unpopular as possible either. Just be yourself."

A Cut Above

A giant of American drama, Albee is the winner of three Pulitzer Prizes and the National Medal of Arts. His most recent hit play, *The Goat or Who Is Sylvia?* captured the 2002 Tony Award for Best Play. He is perhaps best known for the corrosive *Who's Afraid of Virginia Woolf?* (1962), which returned to Broadway in 2005 to renewed acclaim and received six 2005 Tony Award nominations, including best play. Albee also earned a Tony Award for Lifetime Achievement in Theater this year.

Born in Washington, D.C., in 1928, Albee was adopted at the age of two weeks by millionaire couple Reed and Frances Albee, who named their son for his paternal grandfather, Edward Franklin Albee, a Vaudeville producer on the Keith-Albee Theater Circuit. He was raised in Westchester, N.Y., immersed in the theatrical realm from an early age.

His formative years were marked by a nonconformist's badge of honor: academic dismissals, first from prep school in 1943 at age 15 after writing a "scandalous" three-act sex farce titled *Aliqueen.* The same fate awaited him at Valley Forge Military Academy. One suspects he was serving notice that his life and career would not hew to conventional paths.

“I guess so,” Albee says. “But I think I got out of the college I did because they weren’t teaching me what I wanted to learn. So I left. Why waste your time?”

Attending Choate from 1944 to 1946, the already prolific Albee published his first poem, *Eighteen*, in the Texas literary journal Kaleidoscope. During his senior year, Albee’s first published play, *Schism*, appeared in the school literary magazine.

Albee savored the company of artists and intellectuals at Trinity College, a small liberal arts school in Hartford, Conn., where he also gained some direct theater experience, albeit as an actor. In 1947, his sophomore year, he was dismissed again, allegedly for cutting classes.

Relocating in Greenwich Village, Albee, then 20, wrote music programming for WNYC radio. In 1953, he met playwright Thornton Wilder, whom he later credited as his inspiration. Albee held a variety of nonwriting jobs over the next five years, living off a trust fund and finally writing his first major play in 1958, a one-act offering called *The Zoo Story.* First produced in Berlin, it initially appeared back home in an Off Broadway double bill with Samuel Beckett’s *Knapp’s Last Tape.* Albee’s association with the Theatre of the Absurd derives from this episode in his career.

From that moment on, he was hailed as an avatar of a new theatrical movement in America, a playwright capable of straddling the traditional and the avant garde. This put him in the unusual position of being regarded as both heir to American playwrights Arthur Miller, Tennessee Williams and Eugene O’Neill on the one hand, and Europeans such as Beckett and Harold Pinter on the other.

As for Albee, he gives a nod to Ring Lardner, James Thurber and Jean Genet as other important influences on his work. His principal successes traditionally have come from his original and absurdist dramas. His first three-act drama was, of course, *Who’s Afraid of Virginia Woolf?*, recipient of the Tony and New York Drama Critics Circle Awards. Albee won the Pulitzer for *A Delicate Balance* in 1966. The original plays *Box* and *Quotations From Chairman Mao Tse-Tung* followed in 1968, *All Over* in 1971 and *Seascape* in 1975, the latter earning a second Pulitzer Prize.

Renewed Vigor

Albee endured a commercially fallow period in the 1980s with his plays *The Lady From Dubuque*, *The Man Who Had Three Arms*, *Finding the Sun* and *Marriage Play*, though he taught courses at various universities. But in 1994 he rebounded with *Three Tall Women*, which earned a third Pulitzer as well as being his first commercial hit in a decade.

His most recent productions, both in 2004, were *Peter and Jerry: Act 1, Homelife* and *Act 2, The Zoo Story.*

"I get busier every year. The work seems to get more involving all the time. There's a lot more production now. *Seascape* is reopening this November. I directed it the first time, but am just supervising on this occasion. *Who's Afraid of Virginia Woolf?* is going to London in January. And I think we'll also be doing *Occupant.*"

Today, he feels his writing is a vigorous as ever. Even if the nature of the theater has changed.

"The writing changes all the time. And there's no strain keeping up. I'm in good health, going to the gym four days a week. I don't smoke or drink. I did all the bad stuff before I was 45. And the work doesn't seem to date, which is interesting. Maybe it's because no one pays any attention when I tell them how to behave.

"It's going nicely right now. But it is more difficult having an impact because of commerce. Theater has gotten just as expensive as everything else, and few want to take chances. The people paying $100 for a ticket don't want their values questioned very often, and they want what's familiar."

On February, the Overlook Press will release *The Collected Plays of Edward Albee, Vol. 3*, covering the years 1978–2003.

"When we get Volume 4 out, everything should be fairly complete. I've got about half of the last volume done. It will probably take a few more years. I also have a book of essays coming out in December, *Stretching My Mind* (Avalon), dealing with the arts and theater and politics. It starts back in 1962 and moves on to the present. I hadn't realized I had done so much stuff. I only cut one piece, because I thought I was talking very stupidly about my work."

Albee continues to direct from time to time, finding it useful as well as stimulating.

"Directing helps me in my writing career. I've directed a lot of Samuel Beckett. I learned a lot about writing plays by doing him. And you also learn a lot more about your own work. When you direct, you see very clearly why something is or isn't working on stage."

Among the most honored American playwrights past or present, Albee also values the extracurriculars of the trade. He enjoys the interchange with an audience. Usually.

"I travel sometimes to do lectures at universities. I like to share my thoughts and make a little trouble. But much depends on the situation. I'd rather have it be informal. Sometimes the people who bring me in mistakenly think I want to be (insulated) from the audience, or think I might be bothered by being questioned or approached. But that's not the case.

"I enjoy it."

October 23, 2005

Michael Cunningham's *The Hours*

Either Michael Cunningham is uncommonly accomplished at an urbanized brand of aw-shucks modesty, or he is still somewhat dazed by all the attention attending his progeny, the distinguished novel turned celebrated motion picture, *The Hours.*

Recipient of the PEN/Faulkner Award for fiction in 1999, his third novel drew on the life and work of Virginia Woolf and twined it with the lives of two contemporary women who identified with the central figure of Woolf's novel *Mrs. Dalloway* in their struggle to reconcile their inner conflicts and longings.

With the release of Stephen Daldry's cinematic adaptation Friday, following months of often exultant advance coverage, the author is caught anew in the gale of renown.

"It's a lot for a poor old novelist to take in," chuckles Cunningham. "Not in any way was I prepared for the reception the book originally received. And now this, I thought when I finished it—and my editor did, too—that this would be my little arty book that'd sell a few thousand copies, and then march with whatever dignity it could muster to the remainders table. What was so great about it all, and it is a lesson young writers should learn, is that you can't possibly know how people are going to react to a book. So you may as well go ahead and write what you really want to write."

An imposing cast featuring Nicole Kidman, Julianne Moore, Meryl Streep and Ed Harris, working from a script by British playwright David Hare, ensured that the film would command a high profile. Cunningham, naturally, was enthused from the start. Not that he expected the rapturous notices the picture has generated.

"I don't think the reception for a movie is ever a foregone conclusion, which is what makes the business so crazy," says Cunningham, who lives in New York. "I don't think that even with Daldry directing and this great cast that it would be a sure-fire hit. There's plenty of good competition right now; there are more movies I want to see this year than I have in years and years."

Born in Cincinnati in 1952 and raised in Pasadena, Calif., Cunningham earned a B.A. in English literature from Stanford University and an MFA from the University of Iowa. His first novel, *A Home at the End of the World*, was published by Farrar, Straus and Giroux in 1990 to marked acclaim. *Flesh and Blood* followed in 1995. They were successful works, together with short fiction that appeared in such periodicals as The New Yorker, Vogue, The Atlantic Monthly and the Paris Review, though none quite attained the regard of *The Hours*.

It was not in retrospect that Cunningham viewed the book as a particularly ambitious or daunting undertaking. He knew from the beginning the task he had set for himself, and the knowledge did not always rest easily.

"There was certainly a period early in the writing when I felt 'I can't do this, and certainly I can't write about Virginia Woolf!' Then I thought, 'Why would you want to attempt something you already know you can to do?' "

While there were some similarities, *The Hours* represented a major departure in texture and voice from his earlier books.

"My previous books were much more conventionally structured; I wanted them to be accessible. With *The Hours*, I took what I had learned from writing and moved on to do something that was not traditional."

Dismay is more often the reaction of an author whose work is adapted for the screen, but Cunningham says he is as pleased as any writer is likely to be at what Hare and Daltry have wrought.

"I may be the only living American novelist who is completely happy with what Hollywood has done with my book. It was clear from the very beginning to me that this movie would enjoy a body of hugely intelligent and gifted people who would try to make the best movie they could possibly make. I knew that if it failed, it would be because art is hard to do. Never for a moment was there anything cynical or hackish in (the filmmakers') approach."

No sacred text issues, then? "I don't really have that thing about the 'inviolate' text, this notion that your novel is some sort of venerated object. Any book I publish is more or less the best I can possibly do with the characters and situations at that time. Ten years later I'd probably write a completely different book. If someone I respect as much as David Hare wants to come in and see what he could do with the material, that's fine by me.

"In fact, it really seemed to me like the book needed a fresh eye. I had done everything I could with that story. Had I wound up writing the screenplay, which I was not prepared to do at the time, what I would have done is simply move it intact into another medium. And that is not necessarily what you want."

Cunningham agrees that the structural elements of the film succeed as well as those of the book, despite the inevitable distillation.

"They did, to my surprise and delight. The movie, as it has to be, is in many ways different, but in no way simplified or dumbed down. I was much more aware of the story's structure in the film than I was in my own book. That, and the interconnectedness of the characters. One reason I was so pleased with the film is that it doesn't *feel* like an adaptation, like something that came from another source. The movie stands on it own."

There were any number of things that Cunningham found compelling about Woolf. His love affair with her work began in high school.

"*Mrs. Dalloway* was the first great book I ever read, the first one that really showed me what a book could do. It knocked me out. I never imagined you could do something so vital and alive and beautiful as that with just ink and paper. It really made me into a reader—and a writer. As time passed I was struck by the fact that reading that book has been enormously important to me, that it has made a huge difference in my life. As a novelist you're expected to write about certain things, to utilize certain fodder. But I felt freed of that."

Cunningham says another reason he esteems Woolf so highly is that, while she was as well acquainted with what is dark and difficult about life as anyone could be, she nonetheless wrote "more beautifully and truly and vividly" of the pure joy of being alive that anyone he knows.

"She stood at the abyss and went over the edge, yet left behind books that more than anything else are about the miracle of the world. Hers was a kind of optimism I trust, because it survives the worst that can happen to people."

What does one do for an encore? To say Cunningham faces a considerable challenge would be to understate the case by orders of magnitude.

"It threw me at first. The book won the (Pulitzer) prize and then there was all this fuss. After feeling all bent out of shape about it for a while, I decided just to go with it and write what I wanted. The great thing for a writer about the success of a book is that it means there is a sizable body of readers out there who will stay with you as you try something new."

Cunningham refers to his current project as "the big crackpot book that everyone's going to hate," an experimental meld of genres.

"I've been interested for a long, long time in genre fiction—thrillers, mysteries, science fiction—and why people are drawn to them again and again. Some are so brilliantly written, and I want to see what I could do with a grown-up version of the fairy tales you read when you were a kid."

His new book is composed of three interconnected novellas: a Gothic horror story, a thriller, and a science fiction tale in which Walt Whitman turns out to be a major figure.

"He winds up in all three stories, as a matter of fact. But there's no working title for the book at this point. I'm waiting for it to grow its own."

January 19, 2003

Pat Conroy's *Beach Music*

You remember him, of course. Tall, a bit rotund, hair like a snowdrift (some of which has drifted away), eyes that twinkle with mischief—or look inward in turmoil.

Certainly you recall his enticingly florid prose, his mining of a mother lode of grief, and narrative gifts so disarming they provoke cascades of adulation. And let's not forget that penchant for the loaded comment, which has provoking torrents of a different sort.

Glamour magazine has dubbed him the "American Victor Hugo." "Hurricane" Hugo might be more appropriate. Yet at the moment, he finds it sufficient to be Pat Conroy, period, author of *Beach Music*, a man whose publisher (Doubleday) feels it necessary to jump-start our memories.

It's been a while, you see.

"I haven't published a book in a generation," he says. "They're trying to reintroduce me to the public."

Conroy is in a buoyant mood. Lounging in a Manhattan hotel room, he views the prospect of a three-month incarceration in interview purgatory with a mixture of glee and resignation.

After years of toil and agonizing delays, *Beach Music* soon will appear in bookstores. Although by no means a sequel to *The Prince of Tides*, Conroy's sixth novel (and first in eight years) retains many of the themes and stylistic flourishes associated with his work.

The thing is, he's not altogether sure how he feels about the book. This, despite reviewers' insistence about the total command his writing reveals.

"You know, I really don't *know* how pleased I am with it. It still seems strange to me. It didn't seem to me that I had that level of command. Not at all. But I realize now that I'll never have confidence in the writing. That will never be given to me. I can pick it up and say 'That's OK; it's not bad.' But that's about as far as I can go."

The protagonist of *Beach Music* is Jack McCall, an American living in Rome with his younger daughter, attempting to get over his wife's suicide. His mourning is interrupted by his sister-in-law's plea to return home and learn the whereabouts of a classmate who went underground as a Vietnam War protestor.

McCall's physical and spiritual journey takes him back to South Carolina, where he unearths family secrets and dark memories of the Holocaust.

The Literary Guild has bought North American rights to the book for $1.18 million and 20th Century Fox has snatched the film rights for a cool $6 million. It will make the fifth time one of Conroy's books has been adapted for the screen, following "Conrack" (based on *The Water Is Wide*), *The Great Santini*, *The Lords of Discipline* and *The Prince of Tides.*

For those who have been wintering in Tanzania, Conroy was born in Atlanta into a military family and spent his high school years in Beaufort. Apart from Josephine Humphreys, Conroy is the one contemporary writer most intimately aligned with the lowcountry. He maintains a home on Fripp Island, where his mother lived until her death, as well as in San Francisco.

For many, his love-hate relationship with Charleston in general and the Citadel (his alma mater) in particular has taken on an almost operatic quality. But it is a mistake to infer that the 49-year-old novelist is the product of a single environment, considering that by the time he was 15 his family had had 23 different addresses.

Autobiographical content has figured prominently in his work, to say the least. And not without personal cost. Unfortunately, it has led to the assumption by many—readers and critics alike—that every aside, every character quirk, every little fillip in his books in some way reveals his family's past, or his widely publicized battles with depression.

"I made the mistake early in my career of telling people that my books are autobiographical. What I should have done was write about a Chinese rickshaw driver that beat his kids and subsisted on a rice diet. I can't write a thing in a book without someone thinking it's me. I was with my father at a book signing not long ago and a woman came up to get a book autographed. She looked at Dad and said, 'It can't be you. You're dead.' She had read *The Great Santini.*"

If one agrees that Conroy's characters are, in the main, larger-than-life figures, he says this can be traced to the fact that his parents were, as he puts it, "huge characters that have led to a slightly overdone quality" in his books. Yet it took him a while to realize what rich source material his family provided.

"When I was 15 I said to a friend what a shame it was my parents weren't more interesting. I couldn't have been more wrong. When the 'Good Morning America' crew was filming Dad the other day, I watched closely. For them, it was like filming Zeus."

While even well-disposed critics have accused Conroy of skating a precarious line between the lyrical and melodramatic, sentimental and cloying, it can be argued that the border between pathos and bathos blurs in an increasingly melodramatic world.

"I'd have to say that several components of my work are irritating even to me. I never have been able to explain the lyrical thing. A former girlfriend sent me love letters I had written her, and I was struck by the overblown prose style. But it's something I can't help. It's been something I've dealt with—that, and the reaction to it—from the beginning. There is a great windiness and pomposity within me which I cannot control. And it doesn't seem to be diminishing with time.

"The thing about melodrama is this: It just means I'm telling a story. I'm telling a story in which things happen. I've read lots of books that are considered more artful where nothing happens."

The catalyst for *Beach Music* derived from the death of Conroy's mother. When he gets to the death of the mother character in his novel, there is little question whom she represents. These passages—in the novel and in real life—did not come easily. Conroy has said that is his mother's voice in which he "speaks." It is the power of her voice that compels him to write and to feel.

"Whenever I hear these stories read, I hear my mother's voice. She read to me every night when I was a child. She thought that the carefully selected tales she read to me created my love of stories. She was fierce in her desire to make me a writer.

"That two writers (his sister, Carol, is a poet) came from circumstances like ours is amazing to me. I was the first one in my mother's family to go to college. In my early writing I was speaking the stories of all the people who had not gone on to school. I was the voice to all those silent people. There's a burden in carrying the hopes of one's whole family. But it's fascinating to look at yourself in relationship to that."

The most arduous and painful period in writing the book was when Conroy, in effect, brought his mother back to life in the guise of McCall's parent.

"It was very difficult to bring her back. I had some horrible moments, but kept writing and kept writing. It was particularly hard when I had to kill her again."

There is a sardonic edge to Conroy's dark humor, not least in his continued exploration of dysfunctional families. This time his concerns extend to the broad and perilous themes of the Holocaust and the Vietnam experience.

He says he doesn't know where the mournful, plaintive tone of his writing comes from, unless it's from Charleston.

"I used to walk Charleston streets trying to memorize them, trying to absorb everything around me. I hope that I can write about that city better than anyone who's grown up there."

If only there were more time. As the eight-year interval between books implies, Conroy writes with almost glacial deliberation. But a glacier is also inexorable.

"It seems like if I can live long enough, the books eventually get out. But I wish I could write a little quicker. I don't think the way I write is going to change, though I turn 50 this year. After each and every book I tell myself I'll learn to type. But I never have. I do everything longhand."

Pad and pen next will be engaged in a novel of Charleston, or of Atlanta, Conroy says. Be warned: He is a great fan of *Midnight in the Garden of Good and Evil* by John Berendt, the same writer who profiled Conroy in this month's edition of Vanity Fair. What Berendt did for Savannah, Conroy could do for the Holy City. Something to ponder, you might say.

Oh, yes, about that American Victor Hugo business . . .

"Actually, I'd like to be 'the American Citadel graduate,'" says Conroy. "That's my favorite role. And I cannot rest until Shannon Faulkner takes the title from me."

June 25, 1995

Charles Baxter's *Shadow Play*

An appreciation for, and tolerance of, ambiguity seems the rarest of commodities in contemporary culture, which prefers simplistic solutions and easy answers.

It recalls the notion that some people go through life in polar fashion, believing everything or dismissing everything, both of which afford them the freedom not to have to think.

Not so Charles Baxter.

Ambiguity, moral and otherwise, is at the heart of this gifted novelist and short story writer's work, and is a motif most recently explored in *Shadow Play* (Norton). Here, the mercurial quality of human motivation is painstakingly conveyed.

"I think (the theme) is particularly pronounced in that novel because it is a book that is more about money and power than other books and stories I've written," says Baxter. "The stories I've written also have a certain degree of moral ambiguity. I like that territory; it interests me. I like it when a character is in a position of not knowing what to do and having no clear direction."

While much good fiction provides the opposite—stories with no Hobson's choice, in which sound courses of action are clear and bad ones avoided—Baxter says that, in general, modern literature most often deals in puzzlement, for good or ill.

"In my work it's not often so clear cut. I like it when people are baffled in my stories, but I don't like to keep them that way. Characters would rather sit in chairs, but a writer's job is to get them going, to give them jobs and fears. I think there's a quality of characters that fascinate us that is often ambiguous. The tendency to pit absolute villains and absolute heroes against each other has moved out of the kind of literature that interests me and into movies."

Baxter, a professor of English at the University of Michigan in Ann Arbor, has published two novels (the other being *First Light*) and three collections of stories over the past decade. The recipient of numerous grants and the Lila Wallace-Reader's Digest Award, his stories frequently have been selected for the yearly *Best American Short Stories* anthologies.

Critical praise often has centered on Baxter's ability to discern the extraordinary in the lives of ordinary people.

"To achieve this you must step aside from the scene you're imagining for the moment and think of what is essentially most strange about our most familiar experiences. For example, you go to a shopping mall and try to look at it through the eyes of someone who has never seen one before.

"There's nothing in American life that can't be made perplexing or fascinating with a de-familiarized glance. Giving the familiar the shock of the new. You always have to give the reader a feeling that he or she is discovering something new."

In part, *Shadow Play* concerns a Faustian pact between the protagonist, Wyatt Palmer, a young, idealistic city planner, and a former high school chum who is the owner of a chemical plant. There are no cardboard villains, no martyrs—only people, and a community in difficult straits.

More, what Baxter is getting at is the nature of the objects, people and traces of our selves that we leave behind when pivotal decisions are made.

The spiritual center of the book in this regard is embodied by the character of Aunt Ellen.

"She has a couple of conversion experiences and comes to believe that the God she has been brought up on is no longer with us, that there's another God and somebody has to write a bible about that deity. She's decided that she's the one to do it. While other people are obsessed with the literal leavings of objects, she's obsessed with the spiritual leavings."

Baxter, a Minnesota native, currently is composing a new collection of stories. He enjoys the short form because he believes a writer can say a great deal quickly, with great concentration and great freedom.

Time is not always so critical an element.

It's been said that talent, like courage, is a capital sum reduced by expenditure. Baxter, however, betrays no sense of urgency.

"I'm not a progressive. I don't think writers get better as they get older. They get different. It doesn't have to be a washcloth that you wring dry. It can be replenished. But here in America we are too fond of the metaphor of productivity. Writers are not factories; they shouldn't go into mass production. The goal is to do it well, not quickly.

"I'm more interested in the nature of modesty than that of ambition. If there's no modesty, what stands against the waves of hype?"

Having modesty as a watchword, says Baxter, also might be of benefit in conducting writers' conferences, like the one he is attending in Charleston.

"There are certain valuable things you can do for young or would-be writers. But they're somewhat limited in scope. Someone in my position can give a writer a sense of what is distinctive in his or her work. I can be a listener, and say, 'This is the direction you seem to be going in. What is the stake in your stories? What is it that your characters want or feel?'

"I don't correct stories. I make suggestions. I say 'What if?' or 'Have you thought about this?' The writers attending a conference need to find a path, and that's what I'm there for."

March 5, 1994

Joyce Carol Oates's *We Are the Mulvaneys*

Joyce Carol Oates has been called "prolific" so often she ought to incorporate the word in her name.

Unlike many writers of popular fiction, who churn out mildly diverting schlock by the truckload, Oates is devoted to the more substantive, and enduring, reaches of literature.

Not that she's stuffy about it.

The author of 25 novels as well as numerous collections of poetry, plays and, especially, short fiction, Oates is held as a gifted writer who just happens to be uncommonly productive. Noted for the edgy, sometimes horrific content of her work, she is no stranger to invention, or mischief for that matter.

Apart from referring to her as a serious artist, Oates, Roger S. Berlind Professor in the Humanities at Princeton University, defies easy categorization. Reviewers have a penchant for distilling an established writer's approach or principal concerns down to a digestible sum. But Oates does not think in terms of fixed narrative strategies.

"Each subject is different," she says from her New Jersey home. "My next novel is *We are the Mulvaneys*, about a family which is dispersed and comes back together after 17 years. The book is so close to my heart it's left me feeling kind of melancholy and emotionally exhausted. In a long novel, you're living in it as you write. You really miss those people afterward. And the novel is sort of a valentine to my own upbringing, though not specifically about my family.

"To me that novel is about change and life. How we change but are the same. It's difficult to suggest a common denominator between that and another book. I have written novels under a pseudonym that always end with the mystery explained. In my own name I don't write novels that resolve themselves so easily."

This is not to say that there is no connective tissue binding her work. For a time, Oates was criticized in some quarters for what was seen as a preoccupation with violence, as if it were somehow inappropriate for a woman to delve into such matters.

"I hear that much less now. In the past 20 years, women are writing more about the nature of violence and it's more readily accepted."

Oates brightens at the mention of her latest short story collection, *Will You Always Love Me?* (Dutton), and the unifying theme that sets it apart from earlier compilations.

"Many of the stories end with people who have discovered a real bond between each other, with a couple having come together. Several are married couples, and several others are people not yet married. There is also one involving a mother-daughter relationship. I'd never done that before with a collection. I didn't mean it to be too sentimental. Reviewers don't seem to be noticing, but just look at the title!"

The writing of the 22 stories in *Will You Always Love Me?*—Oates's first collection since *Haunted* three years ago—largely was produced during a few highly concentrated periods.

"With novels I tend to be very immersed. I might pause for a book review or essay. But I work long months at a time, long days at a time. Short stories tend to be written at another phase of my life."

Stories materialize for her with well-defined parameters already in place, as well as formative constructs.

"The stories that I characteristically write of 10 to 15 pages in length do evolve. Four- or five-page stories come in one burst of inspiration. I just write a first draft all the way through. But it takes quite a while to organize scenes for longer ones."

Currently, Oates is adapting her novel *Solstice* for a forthcoming Merchant-Ivory film to be directed by Jeanne Moreau. Originally due out in April, but recently postponed, is the release of the film "Foxfire," based on the celebrated Oates novel of four teenage girls who rebel, violently, against perceived oppressors. Where some authors would be wary of the Hollywood Treatment, Oates is enthusiastic.

"Film springs from the work of literature, but is autonomous and not analogous. Film has to be outgoing. And the screenplay for 'Foxfire' is quite different from the novel. It seems to me a different work of art, though beautifully acted and photographed and directed. The story is set in the 1990s in Portland rather than in the 1950s in upstate New York, as in my book. There's also a kind of sobriety in the movie. It's more feminist than my novel, which is about tomboys and girls in their early teens."

Oates does not participate in many conferences but applauds any opportunity for writers to gather and form a sympathetic enclave, even if for the moment.

"Writing is so solitary and intense. The writer yearns to be read seriously and meet other writers. They learn a lot. They have an audience. I have two workshops I do in fiction at Princeton. For these people to find one another and be supportive is immensely valuable."

March 17, 1996

Thomas Keneally's *Schindler's List*

With his cherubic grin, bounding energy and Outback sartorial flair, Thomas Keneally seems anything but the sedate academic his professorship would suggest.

A native of Australia, Keneally is the Booker Prize–winning author of *Schindler's List.* He also teaches in the graduate writing program of the University of California at Irvine. But he has fingers poked in numerous pies, not least the Australian film industry and a separatist movement Down Under.

Published in 1982, the novel *Schindler's List* wound a torturous route to the screen. Nominated for 12 Oscars, including adapted screenplay, Steven Spielberg's remarkable film is the favorite to walk away with the major awards.

It was Keneally, not credited screenwriter Steve Zaillian, who worked on the original motion picture treatment of his book. Keneally's early draft for the film was among a dozen screenplays the writer has penned.

"It was a great story before I even encountered it," says Keneally. "And I've discovered that inside every good screenplay is a neglected novel. The misconception is that I wrote the book for the Jewish community. The truth is, I specifically wrote it for Gentiles like me."

Keneally, who has published 25 novels, admires Zaillian's adaptation as well as the finished product, but confesses he had hoped Spielberg would have stayed with his original screenplay. That the director did not had less to do with the strength of the script than its length and emphasis.

"I wish Steven had stuck with me, but he felt I couldn't get far enough away from the book. And I can't deny that Steve Zaillian has done a great job. I was pleased to see Steven (Spielberg) get a Golden Globe because I know it meant so much to him. And I'm gratified that the Great Spielberg Film that was always in the offing has at last arrived."

Keneally was not divorced from the project. He was consulted continuously.

"The writer of the original work is like a mother-in-law on the honeymoon. But I was treated well. Working in the Australian film industry has given me an understanding of what happens to books in the process of becoming films. You have to be philosophical, though you can be sorely tested."

Keneally's latest book, *Playmaker*, also is headed for the screen. And it's "A" list all the way. Peter Weir (*Witness*), who the author says is passionate about the novel, tentatively has agreed to direct from a script by Laura Jones, who wrote "Angel at My Table" for Jane Campion. Merchant-Ivory Productions will oversee the project, which already is in work.

One of the few serious charges leveled at *Schindler's List*, the book and the film, came in retrospect. Some claimed that Keneally's depiction of Oskar Schindler, the German industrialist who saved the lives of more than 1,200 Jews, unfairly neglected the role played by his wife. The author disagrees.

"As for Schindler's widow, I had wanted to interview Emily for the book. I did consult her, but she was ill at the time. Had I been able to interview her in the flesh, there may have been a different emphasis in the book. She went to enormous pains to help, for which she is credited in the book, if not in the film.

"She deserves to have her own tree on the Avenue of the Righteous in Israel. But she couldn't have been the dominant figure (as she has claimed) because she wasn't around a great deal during the early years. The focus was inevitably Oskar; the evidence for his role is overwhelming."

March 17, 1994

Gary Smith's *Beyond the Game*

The guys who cover the guys who play don't have the jut-jawed, chiseled torsoed, piston-legged cut of the mortals who masquerade as gods.

They don't glide like Derek Jeter or swoosh like Allen Iverson or flash like Roy Jones.

They do not radiate the supreme confidence of a Tiger Woods, catapult a serve like Venus Williams or register on the Richter scale with their sacks. Their minor missteps don't rate as tectonic upheavals on talk radio.

In a jocular mood, these otherwise fortunate men and women even call themselves "wretches." Ink-stained division.

You probably wouldn't recognize them if they wore a name tag (unless they'd migrated to the tube). Though others seem to scratch insistently at memory's back door.

Meet Gary Smith.

Average name. Unassuming personality. Unremarkable features.

Very remarkable talent. Of all the sportswriters who (try to) decipher the yin-yang, double-edged nature of sport under the modern media microscope, Smith is among the most respected. And he manages to reduce the whole kaleidoscopic tableau to human scale.

A senior writer for Sports Illustrated (SI), and author of a new book with the self-explanatory title, *Beyond the Game: The Collected Sportswriting of Gary Smith* (Atlantic Monthly Press), the Charleston resident of 15 years is a man of parts, not the least of which is humility. He allows as how his probing, vibrant pieces drawn from 1986 to the present are "pretty good."

Right. And Anna Kournikova looks "nice."

Those inclined to jealousy could develop a fervent dislike for such a fellow, if he wasn't so amiably intelligent, so disarmingly soft-spoken and disgracefully decent. Even his dog Santa (as in Fe) is lovable.

Smith wins awards. Lots of them. He also wins hearts. Adopts children. Adores his wife and kids. Trots the globe taking people on their own terms. Provokes thought. Laughs at himself. Makes a mean cheese sandwich.

No Fluff Stuff

"Please," says Smith, kicking back in jeans and a T-shirt on his sun-speckled screen porch, "let's not make this a puff piece."

How about a curveball? The temptation is to approach the man obliquely, rendering a picture of a writer through his choice of subjects, and the way he has helped us discover them. But Smith, whose experimental profiles have revealed the lives of folks legendary to obscure, is intriguing in and of himself.

Such a man should be drawn and quoted.

"I'm always struck by how almost everyone is fascinating in a way. Everybody has a story, if you keep your eyes and ears open for it. You try to get into what they've lived and breathed and smelled and felt. Sports offer a fascinating laboratory that lets us see how human beings react. But that just happens to be the laboratory they're in. It wouldn't make much difference whether I was talking to politicians, construction workers or dentists. People have all these things going on in their lives and if you can get to them, that where the story is."

Gentle Incisions

As in all laboratories, the best work derives from skilled observation and painstaking research, which takes time.

The Smith family—Gary, wife Sally, and their children, Gabriela, Savi and Noah—just spent the better part of a year in Australia, a journey of discovery interrupted in July only by the need to come home and enroll their kids in school. Smith flew back to complete his assignment as one of SI's chief correspondents, training his instruments on Sydney's Olympic Games.

Twelve months of swirling journalistic vials and beakers produced a familiar compound: insight. Smith is the first to acknowledge that the truth is in the details, the deep radar, and that you don't unearth it in an hour or a day.

"Absolutely," says Smith, who returned home last month in time to celebrate his 47th birthday. "Breathing space is just critical. I want the same richness of detail that is possible in fiction. It's almost like cheating when you compare it to what newspaper reporters are faced with, writers who may want to go in a (tangential or deeper) direction but whose hands are tied. Twenty inches of space and 20 minutes of time are about all a newspaper reporter can get for a subject sometimes.

"It's only with time and space—time to think about things and the space in which to write it all in the context of what made things happen—that you can start to do it well. And I have the advantage of approaching who I choose."

Any athlete. Or anybody. But Smith, who came to SI via the Philadelphia Daily News and the late, lamented Inside Sports, followed by a short stint with the New York Daily News, takes little for granted.

"I could have become one of the regular sportswriters at SI, doing things week to week, running around the country and the world. But I think I was already starting to develop some magazine writing skills at Inside Sports, and some freedom was starting to emerge from the way I approached things.

"That pushed it for me. I did a lot of traveling, wound up living in Paris for a year, living in Bolivia for a year, and Spain for a year before Australia, taking advantage of not being in the rat race. I've had the great opportunity to really explore different places, different cultures. I'm so lucky it's amazing."

Choices, Consequences

"The choices that make or unmake a life are so small."

It's a deceptively simple line that Smith writes in "Someone to Lean On," the poignant story of a handicapped man adopted by an Anderson, S.C., high school football team, which is included in *Beyond the Game.*

The choice in question was one made by a football coach who opened his heart rather than look the other way. It made all the difference in the life of one man and in the enrichment of a community.

The choices that led Smith to his future were perhaps more prosaic. They begin with his mother.

Smith was the fourth of nine children born to Harry and Jean Smith of Lewes, Del., but the one most rabid about sports. Dad, a high school assistant principal, instilled the discipline of patience. Mom, a full-time homemaker, had a gift for encouragement—and impeccable timing.

"When I was 16 she called the editor of The Wilmington (Del.) News Journal to ask what college he would recommend to someone who had an interest in sportswriting, and he said he just happened to have an opening for a part-time clerk in the sports department. 'Send him in,' he told her.

"By the time I was a senior in high school I was working a couple of nights a week in the local news and sports departments, and it was then that I knew what I wanted to do. Later, while in college at La Salle, I started working fulltime for The Philadelphia Daily News. I'd never worked another job in my life."

Smith had been poised to do a Kurt Warner. Future Star Pays Dues Doing Supermarket Inventories. The sports editor called two days before he reported to the grocery.

"The Daily News was probably one of the five best sports sections in America. There was a great crop of about a dozen guys and I swallowed it up every day. The creativity there was such that I quickly got into that frame of mind. You tried to do something different with it each time."

John Walsh, who now runs ESPN, but at the time was steering Inside Sports, noticed Smith's work and, in 1980, offered him a job. His new editor, Jay Lovinger, sometimes would walk him around their offices in the Newsweek building to 1, 2 or 3 in the morning, talking about the possibilities of doing unconventional pieces.

"I had two very good years there. Walsh let the writers spread their wings. I worked there until Newsweek pulled the plug on the magazine. Then another door opened. Sports Illustrated already had been offering me a job to join its staff. Rather than go on to a regular staff job, I decided to sign a contract to write four long stories a year. I just wanted to travel, read, think and do a lot of fun stuff. I felt I could survive on that."

And flourish.

Set and Match

Backtrack a bit. Smith's first marriage had ended after five years. But it was his soon-to-be ex-wife, a waitress at a restaurant where Sally also worked one summer, who made the fateful introduction.

Sally was a journalism major at the University of South Carolina, and in time would distinguish herself as a writer with the Dallas Morning News and Atlanta Journal-Constitution. Then she was just hungry to learn more about the trade from the talented young man at the Philadelphia Daily News. Over the next year, they wound up learning much more about each other. And when

Smith's wife left, he began seeing more of Sally—only to leave for a six-month stint in Europe, writing a story on Russia and otherwise "just traveling and knocking around."

"I came home and it just took off from there between us. Then we moved to Paris together."

They were married on December 29, 1984, and on January 1 tipped off what was to become a continent-hopping, two-and-a-half month honeymoon, including a wilderness excursion to Mount Kenya. The fact that it was on "company" time made it all the more sweet.

"Then and now, Sally is pretty much ready to go whenever the occasion presents itself," Smith beams.

In Africa, they found adventure. In Bolivia they found a daughter.

Biding Time

"We never would have met our eldest daughter, Gabriela, had we not returned to Bolivia," says Smith. "We had visited there for a week during our honeymoon, and it was at about this time that Sally decided she wanted to go to medical school. She took a year of pre-med classes at the College of Charleston, then applied at the end of the semester to go to MUSC but was told she had to wait a year. So we returned to Bolivia so Sally could do some volunteer work."

Sally toiled in a pediatric hospital in the village of Cochabamba. The place was an eye-opener, even for a woman with experience in a burn trauma ward.

"It was a state-run hospital, a place where you never wanted to end up. I'd go in and help feed the kids and take them for walks," she recalls. "During a nurses' strike I'd already gotten to know Gabriela a little bit by then. She was 12 months old. I don't know what happened with the situation with her young parents. Though her dad, a construction worker, was trying to find someone to adopt her.

"I told Gary we had to get her out of there. It took two difficult months to get custody and get her to the U.S., where we chose to do the adoption process."

By this time Sally was pregnant with her first child. Gabriela was 2 when Savi was born, six months after the family arrived in America and in the middle of Sally's third month of medical school.

The bottom line for us is how fortunate we are," says Sally. "What a boon for our family. You can't look at life the same once you have someone (Gabriela) in the house whose heritage and appearance is different from yours. It has made our life incredibly rich."

Above and "Beyond"

Before publishers festooned their books with rapturous review blurbs, authors had to make their reputations by writing. Smith needs no blurbs, exultant or otherwise. His position was secure long before *Beyond the Game* hit the shelves. And while not every sports fiend appreciates a writer who takes his stories "out of the box," many do.

Face to face, Smith may not always summon the wittiest of anecdotes. He's not trying to. His tongue does not drip gold. But neither does he talk in sound bytes. When Smith speaks of the importance of getting the fundamental, human story, he means it. Winning a subject's trust is vital.

"He's so curious and has such great instincts about understanding people and what's driving them," says Sally, today a practicing psychiatrist and the mother of three. "He can cut to the core and then shape the story from there. It's great being his wife because he's a great listener. I read over his work and make suggestions, but I had a harder time when he was reading my stories.

"When we were in Sydney and I was taking a year away from psychiatry, I wrote a novel that's very much in the early rewrite stages. He's always asking questions, but when being interviewed himself isn't always answering."

While Smith may not like to think he's setting a standard for others, his expenditure of time and thought and need to push the envelope speaks for itself. It's no less true of his nonsports assignments, among them profiles of Dustin Hoffman for Rolling Stone and Jimmy Carter for Life magazine.

But he may be wearying of celebrity interviews.

"A celebrity is strange thing. Their very celebrity is partly what gives you the right to ask these people anything, but it can also be a barrier to getting truthful things. Yet you do get access to people. I'm completely amazed that I can just walk up to complete strangers and ask them any question I want and for the most part they answer them. But, especially nowadays, to get past the images and all the barriers that are put up by agents or handlers and PR people can be difficult.

"If I can find a story about some unknown guy with some sports hook or theme I can drape it on, that's what I'd rather do. The whole celebrity thing is just an impediment."

Still in the Game

Though a bonafide fan, Smith didn't dash to sports down the customary base path. By his mid-20s he was consuming fiction and books on philosophy. He seldom read Sports Illustrated. The breadth of his curiosity and refinement of technique shows. At his best, Smith taps a story like Ella Fitzgerald milked a lyric.

"I'm still as enthusiastic as I was as a kid. I try to approach each story differently and see what I cam learn from each one. You approach a story like a bit of an adventure and, by giving in to it, you use it as a window to learn about so much more.

"What is that person dealing with? I find out, read a lot about it, maybe reading stuff they read. You explore their lives and the things that shaped them and fascinate them, and all of a sudden you're in a whole new room. It's learning about life with and through each person, not just another story. It helps you keep a fresh feeling for the work."

At this stage of his career, Smith turns down many similar offers, the better to focus on SI and invest more time in his family. There's also the small matter of his first stab at a screenplay, being written in league with his old friend and colleague Cal Fussman from Esquire magazine. The treatment is based on the life of John Malangone, subject of *Beyond the Game's* wrenching first story, "Damned Yankee."

The Smiths' home in Charleston's historic district is as cozy, as attractive, as it is unpretentious, topped by the attic fastness of Gary's garret and punctuated by stores of books and art, the latter including Gabriela's admiring echoes of the work of family friend Dr. Richard "Duke" Hagerty, who also happens to be Smith's mock-merciless tennis foe.

But why Charleston and not, say, Montevideo or the Greek Isles?

"We had come back from France in 1985 when Sally was trying to decide what to do, continue as a sportswriter or go to med school. We had come here once previously on a four-day trip before we were married and just fell in love with the place. We thought that of all places in America, this was about as good as it gets."

More to Come

Smith has not lost his wanderlust. But, meantime, there's the spectre of Hollywood, and the changing face of Sports Illustrated. What, one asks, has become of the magazine's old elegance and erudition?

"It's a little more mainstream, a little more pop culture now. There are more boxes and blurbs—their way of dealing with short attention spans, USA Today, ESPN and not becoming 'your grandfather's magazine,' like Life. I lament the piecemealing of bits of information. Some of it should be there, and people need a few appetizers before they delve into something larger.

"But in the old days, you'd have these writers who would sort of sit back, light up a pipe and spin off an essay. A nice image. But, hey, they let me alone and give me a lot of freedom and time to do what I want to do. Who'd complain about that?"

November 11, 2000

Jill McCorkle's *Final Vinyl Days*

Jill McCorkle waited patiently as the elderly woman slowly worked her way to the front of the chapel. Her reading completed, and having met with polite applause, the author expected the usual expression of support for her first novel.

"When the old woman finally made it down the aisle to me she said, 'And you look like a *nice* girl.'"

She didn't need to add, "How could you gave written such a thing?"

It was years ago, but even now readers sometimes have a difficult time separating the Lumberton, N.C., native from her work—or from her fictional characters.

"Somehow, people can't bridge the nice, polite Southern girl with the author who creates the characters I do," says McCorkle, who spoke with The Post and Courier at the recent Southern Festival of Books in Nashville. "People sometimes ask, 'Why do you write about such a person? I wouldn't even want to have dinner with these people.' But I do feel a big connection to my characters."

In such novels as *Carolina Moon* (1996) and in short story collections like her most recent, *Final Vinyl Days* (Algonquin Books), these characters are as distinctively Southern, as recognizable—and often as amusingly grotesque—as they are contemporary. All in the aid of a kind of tragicomedy that has drawn flattering comparisons to one of McCorkle's favorite writers, Eudora Welty.

"I delight in having my work called tragicomic, actually. I think it's descriptive, and a label I would eagerly seize. It doesn't upset me when I'm billed as a comic writer because it can be read that way. What's important about labels is that they not try to limit who would read you. A word like 'regional' is dangerous in that respect, implying you're only of interest to certain readers."

Devotees insist her latest work is for anyone with a taste for the darkly humorous.

"I have found that with some of the stories I'm working on right now—there are several in motion—I feel like things *are* getting darker. But I also acknowledge that the darker they get, the funnier they get."

McCorkle made waves in 1984 by having her first two books published simultaneously. She has written five novels in all: *The Cheerleader*, *July 7*, *Tending to Virginia*, *Ferris Beach* and *Carolina Moon*. *Final Vinyl Days* is her second story collection, following *Crash Diet*.

McCorkle graduated from the University of North Carolina at Chapel Hill in 1980. She earned her Masters in writing from Hollins College a year later and has taught at Duke, Tufts University, UNC and Harvard. Currently she lives near Cambridge, Mass., and teaches at Bennington (Vt.) College.

McCorkle is a genial woman of disarming modesty, but it's hard to concur with her depiction of herself as an "apprentice" at the story form.

"I feel like I've just completed a college course after these two collections because I learned so much working on the stories. The stories that have always come the easiest to me are those first-person monologues. I really like to just slip into a body and let the voice take over. For me it's the equivalent of an adult playing dress-up."

As with her novels, the stories of which McCorkle is most proud are those that were hardest for her to compose, such as "Departures," "Crash Diet" and, from the new collection, the semi-autobiographical "Life Prerecorded." Yet there is a second kind of satisfaction McCorkle draws from her work.

"Some stories, such as 'Your Husband is Cheating on Us' or 'Dysfunction 101,' just feel like running a race, and it's fun when I'm in there doing it," says the author, who as a full-time writer, teacher and mother of two, knows something about sprinting through life.

As is the case with many writers of the short form, stories tend to come to McCorkle of a piece, well-realized if not yet fully furnished.

"It took me a long time to come to that kind of understanding, though I still have characters I think should be (the linchpin of) a story and it never fully comes into play. So I end up plugging them into a novel later. The more stories I write I think the closer I come to recognizing it sooner as a kind of whole piece.

"It's been a real evolution because I wrote novels first and had a much better understanding of that. But the short story is the form I always admired. More and more the story is closest to my heart. 'Life Prerecorded' is a story that is very close, comfortably close, to me."

McCorkle's characters *are* invented, however. At least in part, she says. And she makes full use if defining idiosyncrasies and eccentricities to limn the features of these folk. Her women seem eternally resourceful, even when they're a bit out to lunch. If there's a motif that links them, other than the act of taking command of their lives, it's that they are not the type to acquiesce to life's reverses.

"I think the women I tend to write about are survivors, and not necessarily the easiest or most ideal survival. What I think they have in common is striving for a level of acceptance of what's there. The same is true of some of the male characters that have started to make their way into my last novel and in this collection.

"I like to think there's a kind of honesty about these people that they are able to see their lives as they really are. To me that's a positive ending for them to come to, even when it's maybe not a smooth road ahead. I really do appreciate that kind of Mack truck attack on life."

Still, as one reviewer put it, at their funniest and most affecting, McCorkle's tales "plunge into her characters' souls and mine the truths about them they themselves can't admit but can't help revealing."

"That's often the case, at least early on," says McCorkle, who has begun a new novel. "But I like to think they do mine out that understanding. I think I often have characters who would not to go a therapist and analyze it and verbalize it and understand it that way, but rather would achieve understanding by way of emotional response and actions."

McCorkle savors the rather elegant notion that she surrenders to her stories in the way a dancer surrenders to music.

"I take that as a very big compliment because that means a kind of freedom takes over. For me as a writer, that's one of the most exhilarating parts of the process, that you have these characters that exhibit that same freedom."

The author does not fret that her use of period detail and pop-cultural signposts will make her work dated years hence.

"I would hope it would have the same impact 10 years later. But it doesn't bother me as a reader whether a story is still contemporary or not. It can be a wonderful time capsule. Our society is so rich with that kind of telling cultural detail, and I happen to be a fan of it. The danger, of course, is being tagged with that terrible label popularly thrown out several years ago—Kmart fiction. When that phrase is used you're being accused of not doing your work and allowing some cheap prop to do it for you. I like to think I'm using cultural detail as an accessory."

McCorkle's work soon may make it to the screen. There's a script for *July 7* currently being circulated, and *Carolina Moon* is being adapted by Susanna Styron and Bridget Terry, whose "Shadrach" just opened in major markets.

"I loved meeting Susanna. She went out of her way to find me, which was very gratifying. The way she envisioned the film was my vision. So I'm real excited that it's in her hands."

If Hollywood pans out, grand. If not, McCorkle's content.

"As corny as it sounds, I feel very lucky to be able to make a living doing something I love. It's like being a child and being told that you'll get paid just to ride your bicycle around town."

November 8, 1998

Tim O'Brien's *Tomcat in Love*

Tim O'Brien's novels and stories on the Vietnam War have furthered a worthy tradition of writers focusing on the ordinary soldier and the everyday experience of war, removed from the complex of strategy and tactics.

Few have chronicled the ground-level perspective of that war with such power as this uncommonly skilled novelist and combat veteran, author of the 1978 National Book Award-winning *Going after Cacciato* and the Pulitzer Prize finalist *The Things They Carried.*

"Certainly the books I've loved have focused on the low-level soldier: *A Farewell to Arms, All Quiet on the Western Front, The Red Badge of Courage,*" says O'Brien, whose most recent offering is *Tomcat in Love* (Broadway Books). "I look at the interior landscape. It's the things that Vonnegut did in *Slaughterhouse Five* that get at the heart of things, that find the truth of literature."

Eighteen years of writing on the war have only reinforced his conviction that, in the right hands, fiction can provide a more insightful avenue in dealing with the experience.

"I did a talk recently on exactly that subject: what it is that fiction does that you can't get at with nonfiction," says O'Brien, a Harvard University graduate and former national affairs reporter for The Washington Post. "I think it has to do with compression and selectivity. You heighten and exaggerate. You're after a different kind of truth than nonfiction, ultimately. It's those spiritual truths you seek. The world as it is is sort of irrelevant. As a culture we have an absolute notion about truth. But truth is a fluid thing."

His aims have differed from those of nonfiction writers Philip Caputo (*A Rumor of War*) and Ron Kovic (*Born on the Fourth of July*).

"They were simply interested in different things than I am," says O'Brien, now living in Austin, Texas, after 25 years in Boston. "I'm a fiction writer, first of all. Nonfiction writers are attempting to capture a sense of verisimilitude and the way it was. For me it's the interior landscape, how the war works into my psyche and into that of a whole generation of Americans. My books are not about military matters except peripherally."

Although O'Brien believes his work as a journalist and fiction writer are complementary, he says there is a point of departure for every novelist when one leaves a grounded reality and "moves into things that could have happened but didn't."

O'Brien served a 13-month tour of duty (1969–70) with the 46th Infantry, 198th Infantry Brigade, and was awarded a Purple Heart and Bronze Star. He knows that, for many, there was never a war of such apparent moral ambiguity as Vietnam, or one that provided such a corrective to the romantic mythologies of war.

"This is of fundamental importance to me, this American mythology. It's a self-congratulatory America-right-or-wrong attitude that is ingrained even in young people. I try to offer a counter to it. You can live with having killed people the rest of your life. It's important that people understand that. But I'm telling stories, not delivering lectures."

O'Brien notes that over the years his stories and books have been embraced as open-mindedly by those who protested the war as by those who fought it.

"More so, really. Because I stray so radically from the literal truth of things, combat vets will remark 'That never happened to me.' They're missing the point. But I guess they always have; war is a hell of major, life-long importance."

O'Brien continued to plumb the war in 1994's *In the Lake of the Woods.* But the author has written on a variety of subjects, especially in his widely publicized short fiction, and never worried about being "typecast" as a writer of the Vietnam War and its aftermath.

"In a way it would be like saying Toni Morrison has been typecast for writing about black people. History has a way if separating good books and bad books, and that's all there is."

A comparatively recent development that O'Brien applauds is the expansion of the literature of the war to include something that had been sorely lacking: a Vietnamese perspective.

"It's not the responsibility of Americans to do that. And it's hubris to think otherwise. There's a whole bunch of Vietnamese writers who can do it. It's not for us to appropriate. In my books, it's been a point of honor not to pretend to understand another culture's intricacies and belief systems. I'm gladdened that Vietnamese writers have this proprietary attitude about it."

He's also encouraged by the response of young people he meets during the 15 or so college speaking engagements he does each year.

"The kids seem spellbound. The Vietnam thing has stayed with us in so many ways. Books and films keep coming out about it, and I think they're curious."

As to motion pictures, actor-director Nick Cassavetes, son of the late John Cassavetes, still is working on a film treatment of *Going After Cacciato*. O'Brien will not adapt his own work, however. He prefers to "let someone else mess things up." And he gives movies on the Vietnam War a mixed review.

"Some are works of art, like 'Apocalypse Now.' They capture the feel of the war in a way 'Platoon' doesn't. The latter didn't have a sense of moral absurdity, either. It felt more like a World War II movie."

Confusion also persists in other arenas. Five years ago, O'Brien wrote a piece for The New York Times on the connections between love and war, an integral feature of *In the Lake of the Woods*. He's puzzled why some readers may not see the relevance, considering that the war impinges upon every facet of the human experience.

"Everyone who has had someone die or leave them has experienced a kind of Vietnam. The same is true of someone suffering from cancer. The world is collapsing on you and you're staring into the dark. It is something you want readers to feel and understand."

March 12, 2000

Jack Bass. Photograph by Jack Alterman

Biography, Real and Imagined

"A well-written life is almost as rare as a well-spent one."

Thomas Carlyle, *Critical and Miscellaneous Essays* (1827–1855)

Upon receiving the Whitbread book of the year prize for her two-volume life of Matisse in 2006, Hilary Spurling declared that biography was dead as a form of literature, a contention Robert Caro's magisterial, five-book *The Years of Lyndon Johnson* would tend to refute.

Death knells sounded for literature are commonplace, generally self-serving and invariably premature. But Spurling's point was well taken. A genuinely excellent biography is rare. A biographer is tasked with finding a fresh or unconventional angle of approach as well as a perspective on his or her subject that does more than simply inform and entertain. An accomplished biography is rigorous in its recitation of facts and the tissue that connects them, but also transcends mere facts to get at the core of a subject.

Sounds straightforward enough. Would that it were so. Inhabiting the heart and mind of a subject, discovering the pivotal, defining moments in a life, can be as elusive as it is exhaustive, which makes a fine biography such a precious gem. Some, having written "authorized" biographies of subjects still living, must be nimble in skirting the risks of sanitation and sanctity, that sense of the author's inquiry blunted by a compact between subject and biographer.

The writers in this section succeeded in various degrees, though all attacked their books with seriousness of purpose and an intent to enlighten. Some revealed almost as much about themselves as their subjects. The measure of their achievement is how well they illuminate, and linger in the mind.

David Quammen's *The Reluctant Mr. Darwin*

David Quammen wanted to produce a "radically concise" book on a revolutionary scientist. Not some dauntingly expansive treatise on one of history's most pivotal figures, but a compact, revealing look at a private, misunderstood man. A man whose work is almost equally misapprehended.

Charles Darwin.

After our contemporary culture wars, with its tug-of-war between champions of evolution and creationism, after ruminations on the mechanism of "natural selection," and after the melodrama of the Scopes "Monkey Trial" of the 1920s, the first thing one may associate with the British zoologist was an adventurous youth.

Quammen, author of *The Reluctant Mr. Darwin: An Intimate Portrait of Charles Darwin and the Making of His Theory of Evolution* (Norton), retrieves the man from the tradition that cocoons him. All but omitting young Darwin's storied expedition aboard the HMS *Beagle*, Quammen limns a personality who became retiring as the years passed, endured a variety of health problems and was decidedly uncomfortable about publishing his dangerous, disturbing findings. Until he had no choice.

Darwin, a field biologist for only a brief time, was nonetheless a meticulous and patient observer. After such an effort, why did he struggle so long with the prospect of making his ideas public? Their radical nature, his essential diffidence, failing health?

"It was all of those factors," says Quammen, a three-time winner of the National Magazine Award. "I don't believe any complicated human being does anything important for only one reason. The primary thing for me was to identify for the reader the handful of different factors that contributed to his delay (in publishing) and to put these different factors in perspective.

"The hardest thing about doing the book was that there is a huge amount of information from primary, secondary and tertiary sources. So the challenge was to reduce them down to a radically concise form that was still substantive, serious and accurate for ordinary readers. I hit upon a way of doing it by taking short sections of his life—short but crucial—and treating each with sort of a biographical essay. And I'm very satisfied with the result."

"Flinched and Cringed"

Quammen has satisfied his readers for years. Though his output is diverse, and includes fiction, the Bozeman, Mont., journalist and author is best known for his work on science and the natural world, both as a columnist for Outside magazine and in a battery of respected books: *The Boilerplate Rhino, The Flight of the Iguana, Natural Acts, Wild Thoughts from Wild Places, Monster of God* and *The Song of the Dodo,* among other celebrated works.

The new book, coinciding with Darwin's bicentenary, is part of W. W. Norton's Great Discoveries Series, a collection devoted to expanding our understanding of major figures in science and technology.

Quammen says at first he was reluctant to approach the subject, if for no other reason than his own imperfect understanding of Darwin's work. Many thoughtful, highly educated people do not grasp the meaning of it as well as they might.

"Originally, I flinched and cringed at such a presumptuous notion," says Quammen. "If I had not had wonderful editors paying me money to spend years reading Darwin, I would not have understood the man or his work as well, either. There is this deep, scary materialism involved in the undirectedness of the variations (of natural selection). It is disturbing to many, which was one of the principal reasons Darwin resisted making his findings public."

There also was the factor of his deeply religious wife, who would have been troubled by the implications of natural selection, and the fact that he, too, was unsettled by them.

"Then there's the fact that his scientific colleagues were mainly very pious men. Some think of Darwinism as being a science vs. religion issue, and they don't appreciate that science and the church were very closely connected in the mid-19th century."

Enduring Relevance

Quammen makes the point early on that Darwin remains relevant to education and governance, as well as to science. Still, this was by no means the most compelling reason for doing a book.

"Of all these scientists who have lived down through the centuries, he's the only one still being argued about. I think that is hugely important. It's an amazing thing, and it testifies to how significant and how durable he is, and also how durable, controversial and threatening his work is.

"But Darwin was such a wonderfully human character. I end the book in a different way from most Darwin biographies. I hope it's something that makes people feel the humanness of this revolutionary, quirky, important scientist."

The Debate

Quammen says what might have most dismayed Darwin, were he alive today, is that the discussion about evolution and Darwinism is so slipshod in the public arena and that people are arguing for or against it who don't really know what Darwin actually said.

"They attribute various sorts of things to him when he was very specific about what he proposed and what aspects of it were uncertain. I think he would say, 'Please, ladies and gentlemen, don't form your opinions, pro or con, until you've actually read *The Origin of Species.*'"

Despite years of clear, elegant science writing by people such as Quammen and the late Lewis Thomas, the larger public continues to embrace a variety of distortions and delusions on the natural world.

"Yes, but it's human nature. People love fantasy, mythology and conspiracy theories—the muscatel of the mind. Readers of our day have very great hunger for work on science. But they also continue to have an appetite for UFOs and cryptozoology. It's very human to want to think there's something bigger, murkier and scarier than what it is we see. I want people to appreciate factual writing on science, but I don't begrudge them their other fascinations."

September 10, 2006

Jack Bass's *Ol' Strom*

Like Elvis, another icon of the South, the first name suffices.

Strom.

Any American with even a passing interest in politics knows the South Carolinian who, at 95, is the nation's oldest and most enduring U.S. senator.

Strom Thurmond is considered by many to be one of the most significant political figures of the 20th century, and a new unauthorized biography by Jack Bass, *Ol' Strom* (Longstreet Press), written with Washington Post investigations editor Marilyn W. Thompson, attempts to place the man and his career firmly in context.

Thurmond's seemingly steady-state life has, in fact, been one of frequent change: from New Dealer to state judge, from progressive governor to Dixiecrat segregationist, from write-in candidate to Senate filibuster leader, from Democrat to Republican kingmaker, from civil rights antagonist to Martin Luther King Jr. holiday supporter, from an amorous eye for young wives to stories of having fathered a black daughter, Thurmond always has commanded our attention.

He still does, says Bass.

Starch and Stamina

From the alternately adored and vilified master politician of one era emerged a man venerated by some, and ridiculed by others. But none dismiss him.

"What makes Thurmond so interesting is that he's been around so long," says Bass, a Palmetto State native who, since 1987, has served as professor of journalism at the University of Mississippi. "Over time, we've seen him adapt to the times, but also adapt the times to himself. He has always had a way of interacting with events."

Bass, who covered Thurmond from 1963 to 1973 as a Columbia-based political correspondent, has developed a great deal of respect for his subject.

"The more I got into the book, the more I really understood him. Though I had been around Strom a great deal, I needed to get a lot closer to get at the core. I felt we got pretty close, eventually. Strom is a very colorful figure, enduring, and historically significant."

Bass calls Thurmond the century's most enduring U.S. political figure. In his view, what makes Thurmond so compelling is not legislative achievement, but the senator's role in redefining American political culture and his impact in changing the direction of the Supreme Court.

"It's a big legacy. And I think the argument the book makes on him altering the direction of the Supreme Court may not have been made before. He did it, and he did it very consciously. It was deliberate, the work of a master politician. He blocked Abe Fortas's appointment, and got Nixon to commit to a strict constructionist.

"And then he played a decisive role in Nixon getting the nomination in 1968. I don't think Nixon would have gotten elected without Thurmond's support. Strom was the only politician both willing and able to take on George Wallace, and make a difference. And he did make a difference in states where Wallace was ahead of Nixon early in that campaign. His message was, a vote for Wallace was a vote for Humphrey. In terms of historic impact, I think this equal to that of his changing the political culture of the South and nation."

Biographer's Delight

A D-Day veteran who helped liberate Buchenwald, Thurmond was a subject Bass had long wanted to tackle in book form. How many biographers, after all, have the opportunity to profile a man who has invested 70 years in his chosen profession?

"I'd been involved in a book proposal on Thurmond 15 years ago with Kent State University historian Jim Banks. Nobody was interested at the time, and I did other things and sort of came back to it. Actually, the book is doing double duty as a Ph.D. dissertation. I was trying to choose a subject, and I kept thinking about the Thurmond thing. It was a long period of gestation. I thought that while I was at it I'd like to do a book, and having done a biography already, it all came together."

Thurmond, however, politely refused all requests for interviews.

"What I really wanted to do was just spend a day with Strom," says Bass, whose wife, Nathalie Dupree, is host of the PBS series *Nathalie Dupree's Comfortable Entertaining.* "I called and went by his office. Being a native of South Carolina, if you insist on speaking with Thurmond, you can. I spoke with him, but he said he was getting a lot of requests for book interviews but had turned them all down and couldn't make any exceptions. I felt disappointed for about 10 minutes and thought, 'Well, I guess I have an unauthorized biography now.'"

His collaborator, Thompson, had conducted extensive interviews with Thurmond in the '80s for The Columbia Record and had drafted 20 chapters of an unpublished biography. Their new book is augmented with telling cartoons from the pen of Doug Marlette.

"Marilyn also did that long piece for The Washington Post on Strom's alleged black daughter, Essie Mae Washington, whom she located in Los Angeles. Ours was a good collaborative effort. I essentially did the writing, but she served as a very good editor. It gave a joint voice to the book."

Political Devotee

Bass, a graduate of the University of South Carolina, studied as a Neiman Fellow at Harvard. As an undergraduate, he interned for two summers at The News and Courier and, following military service, started The West Ashley Journal in 1960.

Later he worked as a reporter and editor at The State and The Columbia Record, as well as with The Charlotte Observer.

Bass invested two years as a research scholar at Duke University and 18 months as a research fellow at the Institute of Legal History at USC. Currently, he is a candidate for a doctorate in American studies at Emory University.

Bass also has written for The New York Times, Los Angeles Times, Washington Post, Atlanta Constitution and New Republic. His books include *Unlikely Heroes, The Transformation of Southern Politics, Porgy Comes Home and The Orangeburg Massacre.*

He captured the 1994 Robert Kennedy Book Award grand prize for *Taming the Storm*, a biography of Judge Frank M. Johnson Jr. of Alabama. That experience proved instrumental in the making of his Thurmond biography.

"This is a better book because of having done the earlier book on Judge Johnson. It's tighter and written with more authority."

Juicy, Too

Bass chuckles at the mention of a publisher's blurb that characterizes the book as "combining academic precision with tabloid readability."

"I don't have a problem with that. It does deal with Strom's peccadilloes to some degree. But this book is not by any means an exhaustive treatment of Strom Thurmond and his sex life."

Bass's principal concern was the political legacy of his subject, whom South Carolinians returned to the Senate for an eighth term in 1996.

"What really carried him in '96 was the failure of any prominent Democrat to run against him, combined with the reservoir of good will Strom has built up over more than 40 years of exemplary constituent service in the U.S. Senate. South Carolinians were ready to see him retire but didn't want to send him home.

"His constituent service is legendary. And he has refused to keep a political enemy. His political boldness is remarkable. He got elected as a write-in candidate, ran as the Dixiecrat candidate for president, switched to the Republican Party and campaigned against Wallace. One may say there was opportunism involved—but I didn't see anyone else doing it."

As for Thurmond's change of parties, Bass says it was not Thurmond suddenly switching from his earlier liberal political philosophy. It was like somebody gradually going out into a sloping channel, the water getting deeper and deeper, and finally he's up to his neck and starts swimming, and doesn't stop 'til he's across to the other side.

"Once he made the commitment, he was a staunch conservative."

Shifting Currents

Until Wallace, no one in the South represented resistance to civil rights legislation more than Thurmond. Bass says the eventual changes in Thurmond's point of view were genuine, not mere sniffing of the political winds.

"Certainly his views have changed on civil rights legislation and its impact. But that's part of Strom's growth and awareness. To say that Strom started changing because blacks started voting is true, but to say he changed solely because of this is overly simplistic.

"He adapts to political reality, of course, but it was more than that alone. Strom gains a lot through osmosis. He isn't particularly reflective, which is not to say he isn't intelligent. He just absorbs his information in a different sort of way. He knows what's going on."

Thurmond's career has been a matter of interacting with historic events and his own political instincts and sense of values, says Bass, whose next book may deal with the Supreme Court and how it transformed the 14th Amendment.

"Strom is an 'actor' in the sense of someone who is action-oriented and thrives in that climate. So he's much more of a tactician than a strategist as a general rule. He's also got this exceptionally keen political antenna. There are those who say that Strom is the supreme political opportunist. But he is more than that."

Son of Edgefield

Bass also sees Thurmond as someone very much shaped by the climate of his place of birth, Edgefield County, saying that if he hadn't come from Edgefield he would have been somebody quite different.

"The Edgefield legacy came into play in the move to the Dixiecrat Party. This was a county where the author of the Ordinance of Secession of the first state to secede from the Union was from there. Ten governors and two heroes of the Alamo came from Edgefield County, which has had a long history of the defense of Southern honor."

A sense of honor in more ways than one. As for the senator's alleged black daughter—now a great-grandmother—Bass says there is a strong circumstantial case for a familial relationship.

"The conclusion is that when she went to college at South Carolina State when he was governor, that forged a pact which they have kept all these years, that their relationship was a special friendship. That's the story she has stuck with ever since, publicly. There were members of her husband's family who heard her refer to her father, and it was clear who she meant. Faculty and others at the school in those years certainly believed that this was the case.

"Her mother was a teen-age domestic in the Thurmond household. People in Edgefield who knew her maintain she shared a relationship with him for quite some time. But we don't have DNA samples. You can come to various and sundry conclusions about all that. He's never acknowledged anything more than Ms. Washington has acknowledged. Neither has he made any great categorical denial."

It is one more feature of a colorful mystique surrounding Thurmond, says Bass.

"I think he savors that mystique, and feeds it."

November 1, 1998

Linda Lear's *Beatrix Potter: A Life in Nature*

The legacy of Beatrix Potter is greater than her literary renown as a writer of stories for children.

The English author, beloved for her *Tale of Peter Rabbit* (1902) and other books, was an accomplished amateur botanist and pioneering champion of preservation who, upon her death in 1943, bequeathed more than 4,000 acres of her land in England's Lake District to the National Trust to preserve its farming culture and natural landscape.

"To Americans accustomed to vast territories, this acreage may sound like a pittance, but in the Lake District, that is a lot of land," says Linda Lear, author of the comprehensive biography, *Beatrix Potter: A Life in Nature.*

"Beatrix didn't just buy up pretty vistas to protect. She bought valley heads and pristine areas that would have been forever ruined by development. Her vision was remarkable, way ahead of its time. This is what I discovered about Potter that thrills me. We need to be grateful to this woman. She was able to be such a fine artist because she loved nature so much—and found her heart within it."

Eight years in the making, the book is being published Friday by St. Martin's Press to coincide with the major-market opening of "Miss Potter," a feature film starring Renee Zellweger. But Lear's book is an exhaustively researched, stand-alone biography, by no means a simple movie tie-in.

An environmental historian and full-time biographer who divides her time between Charleston and Bethesda, Md., Lear gives the movie high marks for its preservation theme, but a mixed review of its depiction of Potter's personal life.

"The movie is wonderful, charming, in that it makes her an interesting, inventive, determined and very courageous woman. All this is accurate. But to capture a large audience it takes natural liberties. Beatrix was politically conservative. She always wanted to be married. (Potter was wed to William Heelis, a country solicitor, for 30 years.)

"She thought marriage was the crown of a woman's life. She was not in sympathy with the suffragettes or feminists. But in her life actions, she was assertive and entrepreneurial. She rejected any kind of boundaries on what a woman could or could not do."

Lear, formerly a professor of environmental history at George Washington University, currently serves as a research professor at the University of Maryland–Baltimore County. Her previous book was *Rachel Carson: Witness for Nature* (1997). Like that book, *Beatrix Potter* is most concerned with the natural world and how individuals respond to it.

While the film focuses in large measure on Potter's doomed romance with her (official) publisher, Lear's biography begins with Potter's Victorian childhood and proceeds to cover the subject's entire career as writer, illustrator, businesswoman and naturalist.

A Surprising Find

Before undertaking her research, Lear was unaware of Potter's work in fields other than children's literature. A bit of serendipity led the author to her subject.

"My husband (John Nickum) and I were on tour in London for the English edition of the Rachel Carson book when we stumbled on an exhibit of Potter's fungi paintings. I had no idea she painted these incredibly beautiful mycological (mushroom) images, or that she had any interest in that sort of history. I happen to be an amateur botanical art collector and was particularly struck by these watercolors. I thought, 'There's got to be a book about her.' But there was only one, written in 1946 by Margaret Lane, someone whom Potter did not want to do her bio. There has been a lot of writing about her children's books, but nothing that would be considered an adult biography, nothing with any substance to it."

Until now. Lear, who read the books as a child, had assumed Potter was and always had been a children's writer. It turned out she fit that mold for a comparatively brief part of her life.

"Her most prolific period was from approximately 1902–1917. After that, she became the conservationist and preservation advocate that was so important. I thought this story needed to be told, in detail."

Thanks to the botanical paintings and other evidence, Lear found that Potter had been an amateur natural scientist of the first order—the word "amateur" having a very different, more respectful meaning than it bears today—the first to discover that mushrooms reproduced by spores. Potter developed the theory that they had to reproduce in symbiosis with another organism—algae. Though she published a paper on her find, Potter was never credited with the discovery.

"Women, as a rule, could not be scientists in the 19th century," says Lear, whose book was read in five installments on BBC Radio 4's *Book of the Week* program. "But she had a very famous uncle, Henry Roscoe, who was a scientist. Potter (born in London in 1866) was long a resident of the North Country, and was of mercantile stock. Her grandfather owned the largest calico manufacturing company in all of England. And her family were Unitarians, among the foremost educators, reformers and free-thinkers of the time, very scientific in approach. I maintain that Potter got her immense interest in, and ability to conduct, science from this background."

Marketing Savvy

Potter was also a canny businesswoman and natural merchandiser.

"As soon as she created her early books, she was the first to see the merchandising potential. The ink wasn't dry on *Peter Rabbit* when she created the first Peter Rabbit doll and board game. Her next steps were wallpapers and little figurines. From there it became this incredible merchandising empire—the first time this was ever done."

Lear says she is favorably surprised not only with the performances of Zellweger, Ewan MacGregor and Emily Watson, but chiefly with how well director Chris ("Babe") Noonan's movie integrates animated and live-action sequences. More than anything, she is enthused with how the film portrays Potter as a preservationist.

"It is not so accurate on her personal life, but it is very accurate and surprisingly generous in showing how she moved to the Lake District, became a farmer and developed into one of the leading preservationists of her time. There would be no Lake District without her.

"Her children's stories endure, I think, because her animal characters were always grounded in real nature. Peter is never anything but a rabbit. They also endure because they have just the right amount of suspense and they play with language that children love. Though they are dressed up in fancy clothes, they are real animals. Potter stands alone in writing for young children, mainly because most of her best stories come out of letters to real children. But she said she wrote to please herself, that she had never grown up."

January 7, 2007

Rick Bragg's *The Prince of Frogtown*

At the end of his days, the man felt nothing but regret: over a squandered life, about the way he had treated his family. All of which came as a revelation to his son, years later, still gripped by memories of a time too brief and too wretched.

"Before, when I thought of him, I just saw a few frightening months of time from my youth," says Rick Bragg, whose late father is the linchpin of his new book *The Prince of Frogtown* (Knopf). "But I went back home and found the man before that time. When people told you these happy stories about him as a boy, it was with this incredible sadness. People admired him. I discovered a sense of humor I never knew he had. There were so many fine little stories."

Bragg, who teaches at the University of Alabama, wrote a memorable tribute to his mother in *All Over but the Shoutin'* then mined the vein of her lineage a level deeper in *Ava's Man.* Though billed as the third and final volume of an American tragedy, writing *The Prince of Frogtown*—devoting it largely to his father—was by no means a foregone conclusion.

"There were times when I knew there might have to be another book written about my daddy, but you put it off and put it off, and then you get a boy of your own—I inherited a 10-year-old, now 14—and there's hardly a day when you don't think of him. The circle needed to be closed. But it's too pat to say this book has given me that closure. It's not that easy.

"Everything I knew about my daddy was small and bad," says Bragg. "He forced my mama into years, decades of sadness. He's the reason she wasted her beauty and youth in a cotton field. It's not a cliché, not a neat Southern myth, and a book's not going to fix that any more than a book will make a plant reopen just because you've written a story about a plant closing. I had always believed that daddy didn't have regrets for what he'd done, but I found out that in the last months of his life, after committing suicide one glass at a time, he spoke of nothing but regret and how sorry he was."

The whole reason for doing the third book, says Bragg, was so that he would know more about his father than the jagged fragments of alcoholism and neglect.

"I've interviewed a lot of men in prison, and many of them are there for the worst moment they've had on Earth. Sometimes it's very much a pattern, but most of the time, they're there because of their worst moment, something they did drunk or in a rage or behind the wheel of a car. That's not all they are. In a very sad way, my family was my daddy's worst moment. And I did not want *All Over but the Shoutin'* to be the last thing I wrote about him."

What Bragg did not suspect, as the book coalesced in heart and mind, was how significant a role his stepson might play in it. The author credits the genesis of the chapters on "The Boy" to his editor at Alfred A. Knopf.

"I'd love to say it was literary genius on my part, but here's what happened: I had written in the introduction that getting this new boy had made me think more about my father. And in the epilogue, I had gone back to 'the boy' basically just to give the reader a warmer place to end because the story was so sad and tragic. My editor said, 'Well this is some of the sweetest stuff here. Do you have more?"

"I thought, yeah, I get more of it every day. He's a little boy. And he suggested I weave in and out some stories of me being a dad and give readers a place to smile and a place to breathe. As the chapters went on, it just seemed to work, and it seemed to fit somehow. Sometimes you write something and know exactly what you're doing; other times you say, 'I'm not exactly sure how that worked out, but I'm glad it did.'"

Bragg wrote oceans of articles and profiles over the years as a staffer for such newspapers as The St. Petersburg Times and The New York Times, where he won a Pulitzer Prize. There was no chance of him being dispassionate about his own family.

"I don't think you can. If you were dispassionate, it would be terrible. It would be muck. I was never dispassionate when I was writing about other people. When you're writing about people in trouble, people facing a threat or with one foot in the grave, what good are you if you don't feel something?"

What he feels most keenly today, as yesterday, is concern over the fate of the blue-collar American, not least the blue-collar Southerner. And he's not entirely sure what the mutable phrase "New South" means, what the homogenization of the South might bring or the blue-collar citizen's place in a South shorn of its identity.

"What I do know is that the modern-day South is complicated. We may not have handled them very well, but we survived the problems of the Old South. But we've taken giant steps back in a lot of ways and we have to stop doing that. We've got to rediscover the blue-collar foundation of the country and realize its value.

"It all comes down to a matter of relevance. The people that did the heavy lifting in those blue-collar jobs are not relevant in a cold economic evaluation of our region. They are not relevant in a lot of arguments taking place, in a lot of decisions being made in government and business. But they are relevant. They must be."

May 25, 2008

James I. Robertson's *Stonewall Jackson*

Libba Robertson swears she's never seen a day when her husband was bored.

Consumed, yes. Preoccupied, of course. On another planet, most certainly.

It is not simply that Dr. James I. Robertson teaches one of the largest Civil War history classes in the nation, that he appears regularly on cable TV's A&E Network and the History Channel or that he also invests one day a week in his show on local public radio.

No, this Alumni Distinguished Professor at Virginia Polytechnic Institute and State University has one overriding passion: the Army of Northern Virginia and the life and legacy of Confederate Gen. Thomas J. "Stonewall" Jackson.

But as Robertson is quick to counsel, "I am basically a social historian, not a military historian."

It is Jackson the person, not the myth, that he explores in his 950-page biography *Stonewall Jackson: The Man, the Soldier, the Legend*, released this month by Macmillan.

Robertson, who earned a Pulitzer Prize nomination for his 1988 history *Soldiers Blue and Gray*, spent eight years researching, writing and editing his new book, which many scholars and critics are calling the definitive word on Jackson.

"Probably more myth surrounds him than any other figure in American history," Robertson says. "And the dividing line between man and myth was quite muddied. What I've written is not the biography of a general, but a biography of a man who became a general—a very great difference.

"Jackson always has been viewed as an eccentric and a religious fanatic. It is true that he was totally lacking in social graces. He was raised an orphan, educated at West Point, went straight into the Mexican War, then was thrust into society very much as a fish out of water. I believe the bad initial impressions he gave people are the root of many of the oddities assigned to him."

Some of which Robertson has dismissed, such as Jackson's alleged appetite for lemons. Those who deposit lemons by his grave in homage are barking up the wrong tree. Concerned over his health, Jackson devoured fruit of all kinds, but had a particular fondness for peaches.

Apart from unprecedented research, Robertson's principal achievement is the breadth of detail he brings to the perception of Jackson as a soldier shaped by a deep sense of duty and a profound religious faith.

"The two hallmarks of my book are the consideration of his incredibly sad, traumatic and lonely childhood, which left abiding impressions, and his faith, which he found in the Presbyterian Church. Jackson was the very embodiment of the Christian soldier. Everything he did, he did for God.

"He hated to fight a battle on the Sabbath. In his official reports, he gave all the credit to God. He wanted his troops to be an army of the living God. Jackson saw himself not as a Napoleon, but as a Gideon or a David. By 20th-century standards he would be seen as religious fanatic, perhaps, but not by standards of the day."

Robertson says the most distinguishing feature of his book, what sets it apart from biographies which have come before, is that it is the product of what he terms "total research." To start, he dispatched form-letter inquiries to 280 repositories of information around the country, 80 of which responded with materials representing 370 collections of manuscripts.

"I spent three years doing nothing but looking at manuscripts. I only consulted existing biographies at the very end. My whole approach to the book was to imagine that no biography had been written of him before. I worked independently doing 'vacuum cleaner' research."

Robertson used the most reliable materials and made educated judgments on what was valid and not. He was not interested in speculation. The author says he simply set out to tell the truth.

"Over the years, biographies of Jackson have been diminishing in quality," says the Danville, Va., native, in his 30th year of teaching at Virginia Tech. "Too often people have a preconceived idea and they get just enough information to support that premise, then write a book. That's intellectually dishonest. What you do or don't do should depend on what your sources tell you."

April 6, 1997

Lisa Rogak's *Haunted Heart*

One and done.

For Lisa Rogak, the charm of life is its diversity: new mysteries to plumb, new subjects to master, new sensations to savor. No matter how engaging or rewarding an experience might be, she is not inclined to repeat it.

(Kindly overlook the fact that she has owned seven hearses).

"All you need to know about me is that I don't read a book more than once," says the recent Charleston transplant. "I don't see a movie more than once. I don't make a recipe more than once. And I certainly don't buy the same kind of car twice—well, not the same make and model, anyway. If I do something twice, it means one fewer new thing that I'm exposed to. I've always been a generalist."

And a prolific one. A revised edition of her best-selling *Barack Obama: In His Own Words* (Public Affairs) was released last month. Out this week is the bio *Haunted Heart: The Life and Times of Stephen King* (Thomas Dunne Books), to be followed by *Michelle Obama: In Her Own Words* (Public Affairs) and a paperback edition of *A Boy Named Shel* (Thomas Dunne Books), her chronicle of celebrated writer, musician, composer and cartoonist Shel Silverstein.

A writer since 1981, Rogak has 40 books to her credit. *Haunted Heart* is her fourth biography, yet Rogak does not consider herself a biographer.

"I have no desire to write any more bios because now I know how to do it. It's no longer a challenge. I'm always learning something new, which is why I still feel like an apprentice. I've changed my beat so often: travel, health and fitness, science, high-tech during the first boom. Who knows what's next? I have not been diagnosed as having ADD, but I must admit that my condition, left untended, gets worse."

In addition to her books, Rogak's work appears in a variety of national magazines. A member of the International Association of Culinary Professionals, the International Food, Wine & Travel Writers Association and the Society of Children's Book Writers & Illustrators, the New Jersey native has featured the Upper King Design District in several recent travel articles.

Eccentrics Welcome

After two decades "in the wilds of New Hampshire," Rogak decided to make one of her favorite subjects—Charleston—her home. She came to stay last April after having spent part of the previous September here on assignment.

"I wasn't looking for a new place to live. But the first morning I was in Charleston, I knew I belonged here." The city's reputation as a haven for, well, eccentrics, may have been a further inducement. "People here are much more welcoming of who I am."

Already, there is much buzz downtown concerning her latest ride, a maroon '92 Buick hearse named Ruby. How she came to be an aficionado of funereal transportation is a story in itself.

"I was writing about high-tech during the first dot-com boom and was ready for a break. I had always dabbled in garage sales in New Jersey, (a state) I left as soon as I could, and was in a junk store in New Hampshire looking for interesting things to sell on eBay. There was a little narrow suitcase with an art deco label saying 'Funeral Candles.' I put them on eBay and sold them to a funeral director in Tacoma, Wash. We completed the deal, and he asked, 'What else do you have?'

"So I went back on eBay and saw thousands of vintage funeral items: lamps, makeup kits, facial-repair kits, etc. I was off and running for the next two years. I started to contact funeral homes in New England and in Pennsylvania, which turned out to be a treasure trove for me, and seek out things in storage people didn't want. A lot came from the era of home funerals. Let me tell you, funeral directors are a scream, with a great sense of humor."

On one occasion, she bought out an entire funeral history museum.

"My first two books were a New England cemetery travel guide and one of my favorites, *Death Warmed Over*, a funeral cookbook. When I went back to writing fiction, I did a version of the book as a comic funeral novel, which I still need to revise."

Funeral directors who got wind of her curiosity asked if she was in the market for a hearse. She was. Ruby, a stately stretch, is her latest flagship.

"You can always find a parking spot because nobody will park next to a hearse," she crows. "I know of no one else who can use the words 'my hearse dealer' in a sentence. What can I say? I'm into old cars. I had 13 once in a barn in various states of functionality."

Agent of Change

Credit an agent with helping Rogak to shift gears at a critical juncture.

"I used to produce about four books a year before scaling back five years ago," says Rogak, whose other biographies, largely about writers, dealt with

Dr. Robert Atkins, creator of the Atkins Diet, and novelist Dan Brown (*The Da Vinci Code*).

"I was off in my pinball-machine world at the time. But my agent said I had to take one subject and stick with it, doing just one big book a year. What he taught me is that if you take a particular subject that is popular in other countries as well, you can sell foreign rights, too. It was a matter of making more money while working less. He had a point."

Rogak says she always has been adept at picking up on something in the news and turning it into book or article ideas. While her books aren't the sort of scholarly efforts that require years to complete, neither are they shallow "instant" books. Her biographies have been as well crafted as she could make them.

"You never think you are going to get through to a subject's inner circle. I get to the second-tier circles and do interviews as well as rely on secondary sources like newspaper transcripts and do interviews. But I am not going to turn over every stone or explore all the inner workings of someone's psychology."

Rogak, who insists she was born to write novels, says her future is in fiction.

"I have one published novel, two in work, and two more 'marinating.' Fiction feels so natural and really utilizes my talent and skill in the best way possible. It's nothing like my nonfiction writing. There are infinite worlds to explore. When I write fiction, it's like picking up a remote control. I tune in to a parallel universe, and it's like taking dictation. Where I get into trouble is when I think about the process, and then everything shuts down."

Nor is Rogak all that analytical when it comes to her taste in pastimes. A skilled musician, she plays the upright bass and accordion, but the piano is her forte.

"I was trained as a classical pianist," she says. "I was supposed to go to Juilliard and do this one thing. But again, doing just one thing goes against the grain. I only lasted one year at Walnut Hill, a performing arts high school in Boston."

Writing has provided her with a fascinating, adventurous life.

"I wake up each morning looking forward to discovering what new things I'll learn that day, which is something I think that everyone should strive for. I fling myself out there from the moment I get up."

About Lisa

Born: In Glen Rock, N.J., on the 11th day of the 11th month on the 11th minute of the 11th hour.

School: "I lasted six weeks at NYU before dropping out. I couldn't stand being in the same place five times a week, doing what other people wanted me to do. Later, in Vermont, I completed work in an adult degree program."

Children: One son, 25, in Nashville.
Favorite quote from her Mom: "Lisa, you were my biggest surprise (at birth), and you're still my biggest surprise."
Favorite baseball cap slogan: "Every day above ground is a good one."
Best advice: "Be comfortable in your own skin."
What people don't know about you: "I love to bake and I love to cook, just not the same thing twice."
What they get wrong: "I am not a flake!"
What gets you enthused: "Something I don't know about."
What are your passions: "Anything I don't have to do again and again."
What drives you batty: "People who are fakes, or who act the way society says they should act. I have a talent for getting through the outer layers. People are transparent."
Introvert or extrovert: "You need to ask?"

January 10, 2009

Donald Spoto's *High Society: The Life of Grace Kelly*

"The idea of my life as a fairy tale is itself a fairy tale."

Grace Kelly, to biographer Donald Spoto.

The Princess and the Pauper? Not at all.

Donald Spoto met Grace Kelly, the princess of Monaco, on September 22, 1975, amid the bustle of her Paris residence. With only a handful of magazine articles to his credit, the biographer was composing his first book, "The Art of Alfred Hitchcock," one of the first serious treatments of the master's oeuvre, and keen to hear Kelly's recollections of their work together.

The woman he encountered that day was unaffected, warm and as interested in his life as he was in hers. If Spoto was stunned that his request for an interview had been granted, however punctuated with the skitterings of her children about the apartment, he was astounded when Kelly later offered to write the foreword to his inaugural book.

Today, she is the subject of his 25th tome, *High Society: The Life of Grace Kelly* (Harmony Books), a book in abeyance for a quarter of a century.

"I came that day prepared to talk to her about Hitchcock and the other directors with whom she had worked in her career," says Spoto, an exemplar of the thoughtful celebrity bio. "It would have never occurred to me at that first meeting to ask questions about her private life, before or after her marriage."

The interview proved the scaffolding of a friendship that would endure until Kelly's premature death in September, 1982. Good to his word, Spoto agreed to Kelly's request that he would not pen a biography of her until 25 years after her passing. The writer and the celebrated former actress had been simpatico from the start.

"I was 34, 12 years her junior. I had not been raised in a privileged fashion, but I had good manners, and was respectful of her without being fawning. In subsequent meetings, she just felt comfortable with me, I believe. She shared many things. And she felt I would tell the truth."

Graceful Ascent

Kelly's lofty place in the Hollywood firmament was not quite the meteoric rise of popular myth. Against parental opposition, she left a life of means in Philadelphia for New York intent on a stage career, deeply influenced by her bohemian uncle, Pulitzer Prize-winning playwright George Kelly.

Paying the bills working as a model, she enjoyed her Broadway debut in 1949 in August Strindberg's *The Father* and by 1950 would be acclaimed by Theatre World as "a most promising personality of the Broadway stage."

However, her soft, lilting voice did not project well from the stage. The small screen beckoned, and soon she would make her mark in one of the most vigorous eras in American entertainment, live television, acting in 36 dramas and comedies from 1950–54.

"The TV work is absolutely staggering," says Spoto, who makes his home in Denmark. "You must realize that a goodly number of those (programs) were made before she went into films, or after she had made just two films. It was extremely difficult, fast-paced work, but she's amazingly natural in the comedies and believable in the dramas. In fact, partly due to the nature of the medium, she is better in these early TV shows than in some of her early films, in which she can seem a little ill at ease."

Feature directors such as John Ford, who directed her in her first major role in "Mogambo," and Fred Zinnemann, her director in "High Noon," could be very intimidating men, says Spoto, neither of whom could (or cared to) give direction to women. "Both were very tough on her. As was Henry Hathaway."

Hitchcock, not noted for his admiration of actors or his tact in dealing with them, was her fourth director. The difference was that with Hitch, who drew memorable performances from Kelly in "Dial M for Murder," "Rear Window" and "To Catch a Thief," she would forge mutual respect.

A Working Life

Spoto characterizes his book as "a story of a working life,' and it is certainly that. But the flame that burns twice as bright oft burns half as long.

Kelly's film career was as brief and concentrated as it was remarkable. Like the late Audrey Hepburn, another of Spoto's alluring biographical subjects, Kelly could lay claim to being the toast of the '50s, having made 11 features from 1950–56, winning a Best Actress Oscar for "The Country Girl," and exerting an extraordinary impact on the imagination of world audiences.

Her last film (notwithstanding the never-released "Rearranged") was "High Society," a tepid remake of "The Philadelphia Story" in which she and Celeste Holm came off much better than their male co-stars, Frank Sinatra and Bing Crosby. Once again, she had proven herself a gifted comedienne.

"When you see her last picture," says Spoto, "you see a woman who's our clearest exponent of high comedy."

Kelly simultaneously shocked and delighted fans by retiring from the screen at 26 to marry Prince Rainier III of Monaco, whom she had met while shooting "To Catch a Thief" in the principality.

Theirs was arguably the most captivating "storybook" wedding of the 20th century, if not precisely a storybook life. She devoted herself to being a wife, mother and philanthropist, but never lost her passion for the actor's art.

Had not the people of Monaco reacted poorly to the news, Kelly might have come out of retirement to work with Hitchcock again, as had been announced, in 1964's "Marnie."

But Spoto says we can admire Kelly as much for her unpretentious and generous nature, her undeniable talent, as for her beauty.

"Grace knew that 'the princess of Monaco' is a lovely title but that, in fact, she was the mayor's wife. She felt it was very important to keep her marriage alive and real and honest, and be loyal to her friends. She never traded her friends for fame. Her friends from her early years on the stage were her friends for life."

Nor did she believe she had conquered Hollywood, an arena she loathed, or the stage, which she much preferred, he said.

"Grace in her many conversations with me was always very clear that when she retired from films to get married, she felt she was still an apprentice, or had not yet done lasting or enduring work," Spoto recalls. "She felt that much in which she had performed might have been better had she done it when she was older, especially 'The Country Girl.'

"I think we can not only respect her for her great elegance, fidelity to friends and sense of responsibility, but also for the fact that she was a significant talent, and far more accomplished than she gave herself credit for. Just look at the 11 films she made in four and a half years, the quality and sheer variety of them. She had done just about everything that could have been done through a range of genres."

Adjusting the Record

After waiting so long, and reading what in his view were many misleading accounts of Kelly's life, Spoto was determined that his book, among other things, be a corrective to all those off-camera legends, not least Kelly's alleged affairs with her leading men.

"Grace was not well-served by writers after her death," says Spoto, whose next subject is that icon of Hollywood longevity, Joan Crawford.

"We live in mean-spirited times, and if you can't find dirt, you make mud. This happened, and without evidence Grace was turned into a nymphomaniac, a man-eater. My motto is that the biographer is obliged to tell the truth, even if it means saying something good about the subject. I will not soft-pedal a story, and Grace would have hated any whitewashing of the truth. She had been a normal, healthy young woman, with the usual desires. No more than that."

While some critics have applauded Spoto's approach, others have felt his friendship with and affection for Kelly perhaps rendered him a bit too protective, with the result that the book is too tame.

"I set out to tell the truth and I told it as I discovered it. I withheld nothing and I've set it forth that way. I do not deal in rumor. I'm writing for adults. Here was a woman who, long before we had the word 'feminist,' thought for herself, who acted strongly and independently against the constraints of the studio system (helping to hasten its demise), a woman who always had her eye on being a wife and mother and never cared to climb the ladder to success.

"She was a good and decent woman. Her life achievements and fidelity to everything that mattered are standards that anyone could emulate."

November 22, 2009

Dick Côté's *Strength and Honor: The Life of Dolley Madison*

Don't scoff. Dolley Madison's stature can be seen to rival that of husband James Madison, the fourth president of the United States.

Consider: She was the first widow and first woman of Quaker birth to become First Lady, and as First Lady was first to act as an unofficial lobbyist, to personally stop a duel of mortal combat, to publicly reproach the wife of a foreign minister, to grant a press interview, to have a ship named for her and to authorize and attend a presidential inaugural ball.

She also was the first woman to send a message by telegraph, and the first woman to be assigned a permanent seat of honor in the gallery of the House of Representatives.

Most impressively, Dolley Madison (1768–1849) was a heroine of the first rank.

One need not ask why she is significant, or worthy of biographical treatment. So says Richard N. Côté of Mount Pleasant, author of *Strength and Honor: The Life of Dolley Madison* (Corinthian Books).

"The three things for which Dolley always has been known were her heroism, demonstrated during the War of 1812; her extraordinary talents as a designer (she furnished the White House not only once but twice); and the unique social space that she created, which permitted her husband's supporters and even his most intense enemies to come together in a place where they could just be men and calmly discuss things about which they otherwise ranted.

"As vicious as the 2004 presidential campaign was, it was nowhere near as dirty as the politics of the 20-year period after the Revolution."

But Côté is quick to add that these three characteristics are well-known. What is not so obvious is that, though she was not the initial first lady, she may have been the template for her successors.

"Dolley's character and performance, taken as a whole, set the gold standard for every First Lady who followed her. She exceeded every single one of them in the nation's history in this one regard: personal heroism. Dolley volunteered to remain behind at the President's House—it wasn't called the

White House yet—during the British attack on Washington during the War of 1812."

On August 24, 1814, James Madison was in the field, trying to defend the capital with an army that consisted chiefly of volunteer militia. This, against 3,000 English regulars, the same ones who had just defeated Napoleon at Waterloo.

"She volunteered to stay behind to evacuate the nation's treasures. Not her family's wonderful things, but the nation's. She knew that the British troops were only six miles away, headed straight for the capital to attack the city, burn it and secure the subjugation of the United States government. On that fateful day, Dolley became the first and only First Lady to personally face an attacking army on her own soil."

Unprotected, one might add. There were no American troops defending her by the time the British arrived, thanks to a certain Col. Carberry.

"I don't think he's mentioned in too many family histories. Carberry and a hundred troops, with their two cannons, who had been detailed specifically to protect the President's House, evaporated when the British broke through the lines six miles distant."

Madison was born on a backwoods North Carolina farm, the child of Quakers. Few could have predicted the course her life would take.

From wife, mother and soon a grieving young widow—yellow fever took her husband, John Todd, as well as other members of her family—to the wife and partner of a future president, integrity and dedication were to characterize her entire life, earning her a reputation as one of the young nation's most acclaimed women.

Based on more than 2,000 of her letters, this portrait serves as the successor to the author's two previous biographies of 19th-century American women: *Mary's World: Love, War, and Family Ties in 19th-century Charleston* (1999) and *Theodosia Burr Alston: Portrait of a Prodigy* (2002). His is the first biography of Dolley Madison published since 1972.

Recipient of the Bobby Gilmer Moss Award in History from the Daughters of the American Revolution, Côté is a native of Connecticut. He studied political science and journalism at Butler University. After serving on the staff of the South Carolina Historical Society for several years, he invested the 1980s and 1990s in researching and writing about Southern plantation life, social history, architecture and local "microcultures."

Access to the 2,000 letters was, of course, pivotal.

"When a biographer decides he or she would like to write about a subject, there's often a basic challenge. There are loads of desirable subjects for which adequate source material is not available. Enough for a 1,500-word article, perhaps, but not enough for a 400-page book. Finding the proper subject is first, and I'm pretty well-specialized now in strong Southern women of extraordinary character.

"I was 'led' to Dolley via a personal introduction from the late Mrs. Joseph Alston, Theodosia. And I'd been introduced to Theodosia courtesy of the late Mrs. William Pringle. So you research one story and then you run into something else, and so forth. You can always ask lots of questions, but whether or not you can answer them depends on adequacy of the source material.

"In the case of Mary Pringle, I had 167 letters to work with. With Theodosia, it was 110 letters. In the case of Dolley Madison, I had over 2,000. The reason is simple: Dolley was extremely fortunate in that when she married Madison, her papers were considered to be an equal part of the papers of the president. This is the first time ever that a First Lady's papers have been given the same scholarly treatment, care and collection, with the same diligence, that the papers of her husband were. James Madison's papers first became available at the University of Virginia, and from day one, the staff there sought out Dolley's letters with the same zeal and enthusiasm. This did not happen for Martha Washington or for Abigail Adams. And Jefferson's wife died before he took office."

What this meant, says Côté, is that a scholar can find either the original or copies of every piece of paper that's got her name on it—coming or going—in one place.

"I had already read about 1,000 of her letters, which have always been available from various sources, but last fall, the entire collection at UVA became readily available as the university was preparing a digital edition."

Côté says he brings different tools to bear, depending on the subject. But his basic approach is first to choose a subject who has enduring qualities, "not just pop-culture history," and after taking that fundamental step, to dig in.

"Dolley was particularly intriguing. I was fascinated by the conundrum she inherited when she married Madison, for he was a major slave owner, and John Payne, Dolley's Quaker father, had, as a matter of moral imperative, emancipated his slaves a decade earlier. That noble act of emancipation cost him the largest part of his net worth, and John Payne soon went bankrupt. I got the sense that Dolley may have resented her father for having sold his slaves, the act that sent his family spiraling into financial instability and ultimately ruin."

Côté also was amused that Aaron Burr, a notorious womanizer, should have played Cupid to the Madisons. Burr, Madison's old college chum, made the introduction. At the time, Dolley was a young widow helping her mother with a boarding house in Philadelphia.

"She lost her first husband and another son in the 1793 yellow fever epidemic in Philadelphia. Because of his many courtesies to Dolley and her mother (in Philadelphia, Burr was living in Mary Payne's boarding house), and to assure her son a good education in case she died, Burr became his guardian."

Dolley Madison would, however, end her days in financial straits. She was not divorced from the upper reaches of Washington society, but neither was she aided when she had critical needs. Small reward for a life well spent.

November 21, 2004

Jack Hitt. Photograph by Wade Spees

The Traveler's Muse

"Travel is fatal to prejudice, bigotry and narrow-mindedness. . . .
Charitable views of men and things can not be acquired by
vegetating in one little corner of the earth all one's life."

Mark Twain, *The Innocents Abroad*

The siren song of travel, real travel, is the prospect of the unexpected, of unanticipated pleasures (or challenges) that can be transformative.

The possibility of reinvention is no illusion. It is real. Unnerving, perhaps, but for many irresistible. As Paul Theroux has said, the longer the time away from home, the greater the chances you will return a different person.

"I am not the same," wrote a Japanese poet, "now that I have seen the sun set on the other side of the world."

This power has fascinated travelers and writers on travel for ages because they have discovered that the vastness of the world and its cultures does not make one feel small and insignificant. The way travel works its alchemy is quite the opposite: one feels humbled, yes, yet enlarged, granted passage to a broader and keener perception.

It is particularly true when one travels alone, open and receptive. The seasoned traveler ventures to other places and other lands by first leaving his or her preconceptions and cultural biases out of the suitcase, preferably along with laptops, smartphones and tablets—gadgets that insulate you from experience and keep you at arm's length from the people around you.

Carson McCullers once wrote that we are torn between "a nostalgia for the familiar" and the urge to discover the strange, but "as often as not, we are most homesick for the places we have never known."

That's the crux of it. To be sure, some are indifferent to travel. And others can discover a universe in their own backyards. But to deprive oneself of seeing the planet on which we live in all its great diversity of landscape and society seems antithetical to living.

It's unfortunate when a fine aphorism becomes a cliché through overuse. Such a fate has befallen St. Augustine's pithy remark that life is a book, and those who do not travel read only a page. But it remains altogether true. Listen to the writers below. They know the book of travel is inexhaustible.

Paul Theroux's *The Tao of Travel*

Socrates, a notable stick-in-the-mud, dismissed the glories of travel with a shrug. See one mountain, one sea, one river, he opined, and you have seen them all.

He might have benefited from a conversation with the contrastingly philosophical Paul Theroux, widely regarded as the finest travel writer at work today. But even Theroux acknowledges the genuine, if less expansive, pleasures of staying put.

His latest book, *The Tao of Travel: Enlightenment From Lives on the Road* (Houghton Mifflin Harcourt), devotes an entire chapter to "Staying Home."

"It's a whole section about going nowhere," says Theroux, also a distinguished novelist. "Emily Dickinson never went anywhere, but was a wonderful (if housebound) writer. There are virtues to staying in your hometown, and I tried to demonstrate that. (Henry David) Thoreau is an interesting case because he was so militant about the uselessness of foreign travel."

Theroux is more than willing to discuss the less savory side of the travel impulse, and to include accounts of many a disappointing destination, yet *The Tao of Travel* is chiefly a celebration, assembling the most engaging and perceptive writing on travel that shaped him as author and adventurer.

Among the literary lights featured are Henry Fielding, Samuel Johnson, Mark Twain, Robert Louis Stevenson, Freya Stark, Paul Bowles, Jan Morris and Evelyn Waugh.

In addition to the author's introduction, a mini-memoir, the book also is liberally spiced with quotes from Theroux's own books, such as *The Great Railway Bazaar*, *The Kingdom by the Sea* and *Dark Star Safari*.

In much the same way Theroux retraced his steps from an earlier journey for *Ghost Train to the Eastern Star*, this new compendium reflects his having revisited and reconsidered (in detail) the work of those who captivated him.

"This is absolutely the case," he says. "A revisiting of books I read when I was a child, a student, a young adult, a Peace Corps teacher in Africa, a traveler. And as with all revisiting, I saw new things in the books, details I had missed. Some were improved by my re-reading, others did not stand up to a new reading. But the great ones endured, as powerfully as ever, and these were the ones I used in my book."

Theroux, who is completing a new novel set in Africa, also canvassed traveling and writing friends for their suggestions, while haunting libraries.

"I was continually reminded of the richness and wisdom in libraries, and the inaccuracy and questionable sources of much that passes for information on the Internet," he adds, noting that the project of distilling so much memorable writing was more than he bargained on.

"If someone regards this book as a friend, and keeps this book by their bedside, or on a table next to their favorite chair, and dips into it now and then to be amused or enlightened, I will have achieved what I'd hoped. It's the perfect present for anyone who is curious about the world and loves felicitous prose."

The strengths of the book, says Theroux, are the strengths of the marvelous writers within: "The bold, the brave, the great stylists, men and women alike, who set off to see the world, and reported back each in their own way."

If *The Tao of Travel* has a definable theme, it's that there is no such thing as a typical travel book.

"There are so many: ordeals, quests, love stories, residences in far-off places, dangerous feats and a lot of invention, the fictionalizing of a trip. Steinbeck invented a lot of *Travels with Charley*, (Bruce) Chatwin did the same in his travels. This is why I introduced and described so much of the book, because these quotations and excerpts need context."

That travel harbors the magical possibility of reinvention is an idea Theroux has embraced for 50 years of sojourning to the furthest reaches of the world. It lures him still, albeit tempered by a discerning eye and distaste for superficial perceptions.

There are plenty of places he hasn't been, and many hold little appeal for him as traveler or observer. Yet he is drawn back to lands such as India and Africa, to "ancient places where people are talkative and approachable, and preserve their traditional culture: language, music, dance, storytelling."

And typically, he goes alone.

"In the best travel books," Theroux once wrote, "the word 'alone' is implied on every exciting page, as subtle and ineradicable as a watermark. The whole point of traveling is to arrive alone, like a spectre, in a strange country by nightfall, not in the brightly lit capital but by the back door. . . . Arriving in the hinterlands with only the vaguest plans is a liberating event."

May 29, 2011

Gregory Jaynes's *Come Hell on High Water*

A draught of hemlock might have been simpler.

Gregory Jaynes had enjoyed a career that would be the envy of any journalist. He had cut his reportorial teeth with The Memphis Commercial Appeal, The Atlanta Journal-Constitution and The Miami Herald, been a foreign correspondent and featured columnist for The New York Times, written a column for Time magazine and excelled as a contributing editor to Esquire.

Yet here he was in his mid-40s, exhausted, despondent, his marriage imperiled, casting about for answers to a malaise he could not name.

What else to do but get away from it all?

Unfortunately, he landed on the deck of the *M. V. Tiksi*, a converted Russian icebreaker whose owners had the bad taste to turn into a passenger ship—headed for the South Seas, no less, out of Liverpool.

The agonies of that journey, comic and otherwise, are vividly rendered in *Come Hell on High Water* (Farrar, Straus and Giroux), a memoir in the form of diary entries.

The Problem

"My 40s have just been an awful period for me. I can't wait to turn 50 next July and get out of them," says the Alabama native, who was visiting Edisto Island this past week in the company of his wife, Madeline. "I was just neither here nor there, fish nor fowl, and didn't know what to do. All I knew was that I was unhappy. It seemed I'd tried everything to snap out of it except a cocktail waitress named Brandy and a new red Ferrari. I tried drinking too much. I tried drinking not at all.

"I started splitting time writing for Esquire and Time, freelance. But it had just lost its punch for me and I couldn't pick it up again. After a year and a half of going to the world's hot spots, here and abroad, I knew I was in some kind of psychological trouble."

The Fantasy

In the time-dishonored tradition of many a middle-aged man, Jaynes wondered if he had peaked too early. Clearly he was adrift. He fantasized about just sailing away.

"My notion was that if I could carve out that much space and isolation for myself, I would come up with an idea of what to do with the rest of my life. It seemed to make sense to me to get myself on a ship going 'round the world and work things out. The bottom line would be that if nothing else, I'd write a story for a travel magazine and get my investment back."

Jaynes called a travel agent who dealt with that recently fashionable alternative to cruise ships, the converted freighter. Amenities were few, but the tab worked out to only $100 a day, room and board.

Its chief selling point: Kathie Lee Gifford was not on the passenger list.

The Pitch (and Yaw)

The refitted Tiksi was hardly the stuff of a James Michener adventure. A plodding, double-hulled work ship of less-than-graceful lines, it never had seen service outside the Arctic Ocean. Now it set course for where the waters boiled.

"Soon enough I found I had booked passage with people a lot older than me. It was OK, but old people can be very set in their ways and not flexible at all. Suddenly these factions formed. Great hostilities formed between the passengers and also between the Russian crew and the ship's British officers.

"The food was absolutely abominable. The Russian cook could do soups and breads wonderfully, but the Brits were trying to turn him into a three-star chef with nothing more than a Better Homes and Gardens cookbook. Here he's trying to make Beef Wellington and trying to make everything look like the pictures in Better Homes and Gardens. And he wants it to be pretty. So he turns out French toast with a sprinkling of paprika. He uses oranges for a tomato sauce. It was awful. And here's this middle-aged American, me, in the midst of this trying to work out of his inner turmoil."

Trapped in a "maritime community penal colony of 40 dull souls," Jaynes began wondering: Where's a U-boat when you need one? It's one thing to be in a remote village someplace where you can just wander off and scream, Jaynes realized. Quite another to be marooned on a ship. To make matters worse, Jaynes slept fitfully at best. This had something to do with the positioning of his cabin—directly above the Tiksi's constantly vibrating diesel engines, which made a 24-hour vibra-bed of his bunk.

His own personal voyage of the damned was scheduled to last 120 days. But with the prospect of another 30 days aboard without landfall, Jaynes jumped ship in Singapore and flew back to the States, diary in hand. But not before suffering an emotional collapse.

The Breakdown

"I think it probably diminishes a genuine nervous breakdown to call what I had that. But out of nowhere I suffered some emotional collapse in Papua New Guinea a month before I jumped ship. One day I went into the captain's quarters and began crying uncontrollably. It was a sudden, frightening release. After two more crying jags that day I felt emotionally better, but fragile. I describe this graphically in the book."

Contact with his wife was sporadic during the ill-fated sojourn, largely by design.

"This is dealt with candidly in the book as well," he says. "About 10 years ago I started feeling that marriage wasn't for me. I loved this woman but not what I saw as the ways it confined me. She understood my argument about having trouble with being married but didn't agree with me. So getting on the ship was also about sorting that out. I guess I considered it a separation, and she did as well."

The Breakthrough

Back home in Savannah, where he and his family had moved in 1988, Jaynes resumed work. Besides the magazine piece, he thought he might develop a more ambitious idea, perhaps for a novel. Instead, he engaged in the cathartic experience of a nonfiction memoir.

"I imagined all this material would all get used but not necessarily as a memoir. I'm grateful for it, but it's come at some cost. In revising the manuscript, I threw away a third of it. I refused to bore myself, and I think that's why this book is out there and being generally well-received."

On reflection, Jaynes sees his voyage not simply as some misguided romantic notion, but as a crucible.

"This was not whimsical. It was not a conventional escape. Not once do you read the phrase 'midlife crisis' in the book, although a favorable Village Voice review alludes to that. That's irksome. Everybody would like to be suffering from something exotic or be very special, but it may be that this is what was happening.

"It cost me $11,000, plus. And as I told someone the other night, you'd be better off giving your wife the $11,000 and asking her to shoot you. It'd be less painful and chances are you'd recover quicker. So I have to say to those two or three men who contemplate such things: Forget it! I'm sorry to destroy this fantasy, but even if you don't draw a Russian icebreaker, it ain't for you. It really takes some sort of special energy to do it. Yet, in a weird way, it worked out. But first I had to hit bottom."

The Epilogue

Jaynes has begun work on a task at least as daunting as his oceanic odyssey. He is writing a comprehensive history of the New York Police Department, also for Farrar, Straus. His editors expect the book by 2001, a date Jaynes says is roaring down on him like a freight train—no nautical metaphors, please.

"It's a 1,000-page book that's basically the evolutionary history of New York, starting in 1625 and ending in 1999—not an evanescent piece of journalism. Now I'm putting all my skills together in a grown man's way. It complements my mental state at this stage."

No passport required.

October 12, 1997

R. W. Apple's *Apple's America*

A genuine gourmet, the maxim holds, can ascertain from the flavor whether a woodcock's leg is the one on which the bird was accustomed to roost; from the wine's "nose," not merely from what region of the country it was derived, but from what slope in which vineyard.

It is not too great an exercise in hyperbole to append such skills to R. W. "Johnny" Apple Jr., roving associate editor of The New York Times and the author of *Apple's America: The Discriminating Traveler's Guide to 40 Great Cities in the United States and Canada* (North Point Press).

He may, however, disavow such talents. At least for print. Apple, whose wife Betsey has lowcountry roots sunk deep as the name Pinckney, was in Charleston last week to shoot a "CBS Sunday Morning" segment on the city with network correspondent Martha Teichner, a part-time resident.

Apple held forth beforehand from his room at the Princeton Club in New York. An amusing perch, given that he had twice been asked to leave Princeton University while a student.

"It's about me and my book," says Apple, 70, betraying little hint of the allegedly robust ego for which he is famed. "I have a great fondness for

Charleston and go there a lot. The book came about after I'd written several (travel) articles for the Times. They liked them enough to keep asking me to continue.

"I had gotten too old, regrettably, to be a war correspondent. I thought maybe I could put these pieces together, rewritten and rethought, fill some holes, correct some mistakes and update them. It's been in the works for about four years."

Possessed, perhaps, of more sobriquets than any reporter in the history of the Times—Three Lunch Apple among them—the 42-year veteran of America's paper of record is an engagingly Falstaffian figure attuned to the rich patchwork of culture, not cuisine alone. He also bears the reputation of a reporter of acuity and refinement.

Reading Calvin Trillin's lengthy 2003 profile of Apple in The New Yorker, one cannot help but be reminded of such classic pieces on dining as A. J. Liebling's "A Good Appetite," Russell Baker's satire ("Francs and Beans") of the $4,000 feast for two in Paris enjoyed by Craig Claiborne, of Isak Dinesen's *Babette's Feast*, or of Robert Morley's publisher-gourmand in the film "Who Is Killing the Great Chefs of Europe?"

How is it that a newspaperman has enjoyed such high sailing on gustatory seas? A legendary Times expense account may have proved the passport, but Apple still had to discern what borders to cross, and how.

"It's not all high sailing," he insists. "It is one of my favorite restaurants in Charleston, but I would not describe Hominy Grill, for example, as a grand place. It is unpretentious, and quite good. But I have been interested in eating, always."

"Like Trillin, I'm a native Midwesterner whose family was in the grocery business. When you've moved around a lot like I have, eating is a hobby you can take along with you. Almost every place has restaurants, if not a museum or orchestral music. But I must give the boss his due: The Times has been very supportive of my eating."

Even as a political and war correspondent, Apple reasoned, like Einstein, that an empty stomach did not lend itself to shrewd assaying of the affairs of the day. When he assumed the post of London bureau chief (1977–85), it heralded the beginning of a grand adventure at the table as well as in journalism. The Apples entertained regularly, and with a characteristic flourish.

Writing increasingly of food and travel, these years set him squarely on the path he now pursues, as always, with unabashed relish.

"Absolutely it did," says Apple, who, when not motoring the country with Betsey, his driver (she refers to him as Mr. Daisy), resides in Washington, D.C. "I lived well in London. I was able to range very widely both geographically and in terms of subject matter. I worked all over Europe and the Middle East. I covered everything from elections to the attempted assassination of the pope to doing an interview with John Gielgud on his 70th birthday. I even did a little bit of sports.

"When I went into the business, the ideal was to try to be a generalist, to have a little to say about all subjects. London was great for that. The New York Times had a voracious appetite for things British."

Before departing for England, Apple had worked in the Times bureau in Washington, D.C., in the early 1970s. It was in the nation's capital that the culinary lore surrounding him—and his discriminating tastes—swelled to prodigious proportions. (It has been suggested that his expense accounts be enshrined in the Smithsonian.) Apple would return there as bureau chief from 1992–97.

D.C., naturally, plays a featured role in Apple's new book, a core curriculum on intriguing cities of North America reflecting a fascination with history, museums, galleries, gardens, watering holes (wineries, when applicable), sporting events and, of course, restaurants.

Though just as opinionated, happily, it was approached quite differently than his earlier work, "Apple's Europe."

"In that book, there was no particular focus on cities. This one is tightly focused on them. I think there's something over the rainbow almost everywhere. Detroit is an example. There is a lot that is interesting in Detroit, but people dismiss it as unattractive and dangerous. That's a little narrow."

What then, are his chief criteria for a city's greatness?

"I think it's very important for a city to have a distinct character. I'm not interested in going to a place where I cannot identify it a few minutes after arriving. I like places with some history behind them, cities with an interesting ethnic aspect. For instance, I've always been very interested in the Huguenots in Charleston and their influence upon the place. My wife and I were in South Africa a few months ago and explored the history of the Huguenots there, too.

"I'm also attracted to places where the cityscape is good for walking." His favorite: Boston.

What is most important for a writer visiting them, he says, is an insatiable curiosity.

"I think my two best attributes, and those I looked for most when hiring other reporters, are an intense curiosity about almost everything, and stamina. You can never get bored."

Apple's enthusiasm is palpable, and contagious, but he seldom pulls his punches even with cities he loves. Even friends say the mature, mellowed

Apple still can be formidable. Not surprisingly, he has a few critiques of Charleston, such as front-desk hotel phones that go unanswered. That, and absentee ownership of peninsular homes, with the resulting risk that the Historic District one day might become a Williamsburg. Which is to say a facade, an uninhabited model.

Now in his fifth decade with the Times, most recently as chief correspondent, and with stints at the Newport News (Va.) Daily Press, the Wall Street Journal and NBC behind him, the Akron, Ohio, native has made contributions so wide-ranging that one wonders if anything is missing from his resume.

"I've been very lucky in that I got to cover most of the great events of my day," he says. "But I'd like to go to Antarctica and write a story there. I'm too old to go to Iraq; we have a lot of good youngsters reporting there. Besides, the wife would break my neck. It occurs to me that I have been to every continent except Antarctica. Yes, I think that would be the place."

Splendid idea. But it comes with a quandary: What wine marries well with grilled filet of seal?

March 27, 2005

Sue Monk Kidd and Ann Kidd Taylor's *Traveling with Pomegranates*

Sue Monk Kidd, the novelist, had yet to emerge. Ann Kidd Taylor, the writer, remained nestled in her chrysalis.

Together, mother and daughter stood before a relief in an archaeological museum in Greece, reflecting on the images of Demeter and Persephone, figures of myth and the embodiment of a universal passage from estrangement to reunion.

Keenly aware of passages confronting them in their own lives, Kidd and Taylor, real-world parent and grown child, discovered that the Greek myth suggested a path toward a new equilibrium.

"The story of Demeter and Persephone is one of the oldest and most enduring, and there's a reason for that," says Kidd, recalling the epiphany. "It has this powerful message about mothers and daughters. It is about loss, search and return. We realized that our mother-and-daughter journeys were happening at these incredibly transitional moments in our lives. Ann was kind of lost and didn't know what to do with her life, fighting depression, grappling with finding her place in the world as a young woman. Her sense of self was shifting all around, as was mine.

"There are these partitions that come up, and it seemed we were trying to find a portal through which we could connect in a completely new way, not as a mother and her little girl, but as two independent women with a deep and intimate friendship. The passage through these thresholds, we realized, was the story we wanted to tell."

Their travels in Greece and France between the years 1998 and 2000 yielded not only a new bond, but almost a decade later, a new book. To be released Tuesday, *Traveling with Pomegranates* (Viking) is a heartfelt dual memoir: part travel chronicle, part spiritual quest and rumination.

At the time, Kidd was unsettled by the prospect of turning 50. Taylor, having graduated from college and looking forward to graduate school, was thrown by a detour from her carefully drawn roadmap to adulthood.

"We went to Greece not with the idea that we were on a mother-daughter trip, or on a journey to explore our relationship," says Kidd, renowned today for the novels *The Secret Life of Bees* and *The Mermaid Chair.* "We were doing it to celebrate some milestones in our lives. Then we got over there, and within the first 24 hours it became apparent to me that this journey was about something else.

"Ann had left home and had established her own life, and I could feel this distance and silence that had grown between us. We were becoming a little lost to one another, and I really missed her."

For Taylor, the divide was a subtle one.

"Things were nice enough between us; they were warm. But I found myself in that place where I wasn't a child anymore," she says. "While there were some things I shared with my mother, there were some things, perhaps too personal, that I did not share. It was finally talking about it that became the very thing that allowed us to find each other again, and find a new way of being in a relationship. Standing in front of that relief of Demeter and Persephone is what started our exploration."

The ventures abroad became more of a pilgrimage than either had anticipated. Both were drawn to art and imagery, particularly such iconic images as the Black Madonna, which would have such resonance for Kidd in the novels to come.

"It was on this trip that I first stumbled upon these icons. I felt a strong connection to them, to their power to help us change, to grow and be inspired," Kidd says.

Although the trips were not taken for the express purpose of producing a book, Taylor, who had not even made the decision to become a writer until

2000, was the first to envision a travel memoir based on her experiences. Meanwhile, Kidd was focused on her first foray into fiction.

It was Taylor's revelation, in the midst of writing her book, that only half the story was being told. Convinced that her mother should be contemplating her own metamorphosis as well, she approached Kidd in 2003 with the idea of collaborating.

"But that only became apparent long after our last trip to Greece together in 2000," Taylor recalls. "Eventually, I started to see that there was more to this story and these travels. It was not only what I was doing and experiencing. I realized that if it was a transformation for me it must also be a transformation for my mother. There were three stories that could not be told separately."

But Kidd was imbued with the nascent novel *The Mermaid Chair*, gearing up to write, and Taylor was pregnant. The moment was not opportune. It would be three more years before they undertook writing together.

"Ann already had been working on a book for so long, and when she handed me her first chapter, I could not believe how accomplished it was," says Kidd. "It was our agreement that we were going to be brutally honest with each other, and believe me, we were. Ann was able to say things to me about my work that I was grateful to hear."

Not to say it wasn't a bit daunting for Taylor to work with her mom, also an experienced writer of nonfiction.

"That came later," says Taylor, who approached the project as an apprentice and, like her mother, kept a detailed journal of their travels. "I was so excited and passionate about writing the book that the fact I was doing it with (a famous author) didn't quite hit me until the rewrites. But it also made me go deeper. I think having that experience only helped me. Seeing this book today, I'm incredibly encouraged as a writer."

For Kidd, who is incubating an idea for a third novel, it was the hardest book she has ever written. Also the most satisfying. The hardest not simply because she had never written a book with anyone, nor because the collaborators had these wildly different visions (they didn't), but because of structure.

"It was hard to bring these stories together in a fluid way," says Kidd. "It was her story of moving into young womanhood, my story of moving into older womanhood, and then the story of us. It was challenging; it took longer. But in the end we were very compatible. There were struggles in the writing of this book, but they were not interpersonal ones, though I imagine Ann may have been frustrated from time to time with my perfectionism. But this was a very deepening experience for our relationship."

During the three years it took to finish the book, Kidd marveled as her daughter's literary voice marshaled authenticity and strength.

"I think what Ann has done is a beautiful debut. Our editors felt the same. What we offer in this book is a story, not advice. But hopefully, readers may see their own stories in ours, find words to articulate them, and see answers that work in their lives."

September 13, 2009

Robert Olen Butler's *Had a Good Time*

MEMPHIS, TENN.—There's something inherently poignant about the messages written on the backs of postcards. The best ones can be masterpieces of brevity, harboring fragments of keen observation or expressions of comradeship, affection and wit.

When they are from people long since gone, the effect is only amplified.

Novelist and short-story writer Robert Olen Butler has crystallized that effect in *Had a Good Time: Stories from American Postcards* (Grove), his third collection of stories.

Appearing recently at the Southern Festival of Books here, Butler, who teaches creative writing at Florida State University in Tallahassee, again embarks on an exploration of America. This time by mining the artful in a place no less fascinating for being "mundane."

Butler has collected picture postcards from the early 20th century for years, less for the images on the front than for delineations of the personal (and personal travel experience) on the back. He calls these messages "captured souls." That they should have inspired fiction comes as no surprise.

"I became very intrigued initially in collecting postcards with that very thing in mind, the notion that these little objects not only held images from the past, but also held this fleeting moment of feeling or thought in a person who's long since passed from this Earth," says Butler.

"That moment has been forever preserved here, although in a kind of lost way because when I came upon the cards, first of all, the card was saved till the (recipient's) dying day, then passed into the hands of the descendants of that person and now that thread has been broken. Because for me to have them, they were dumped into the public sphere."

Butler suddenly found himself the caretaker of this moment in time and feeling.

"That's how I thought of it for the first four years in my collecting. But then the mandate seemed greater. Not only was I the caretaker, now I had in my creative unconscious the fuller life which I could articulate from those fragments."

The 15 stories in the book had an interesting gestation period, but it wasn't a matter of his collection reaching a sort of critical mass. When Butler decided to write a book, he had between 200 and 300 postcards.

"The critical mass that was most important was the critical mass in my imagination. The great British writer Graham Greene said all good novelists have bad memories. What you remember comes out of journalism, what you forget goes into the compost of the imagination. So I had to collect the cards and have them for enough years that they just got out of my vivid, immediate, literal memory and dissolved themselves into the compost heap of my imagination."

Butler has published 10 books since 1981, including eight novels and two earlier volumes of short fiction, *Tabloid Dreams* and *A Good Scent from a Strange Mountain*, the latter of which won the 1993 Pulitzer Prize for Fiction. He is a recipient of a Guggenheim Fellowship in fiction and a National Endowment for the Arts grant, and has had stories published in The New Yorker and Esquire. Since 1995 he has written numerous feature-length screenplays and two teleplays for HBO.

The St. Louis native, a one-time editor in chief of a business newspaper in Manhattan, is a versatile and questing writer. He produces books that evince widely different voices, a seeming reinvention of the self each time out.

"By the time one of these books is ready to write, all the voices are already jabbering away in my unconscious. It's just a matter of deciding on who I'm listening to this week and opening up to them. Do they take pleasure in surprising me? They do indeed. The only thing I get a fix on is what the character is yearning for at the deepest level. My feeling is that fiction is the art form of human yearning. All plot and narrative flow are built around the dynamics of desire, people wanting things and having them blocked or thwarted or challenged."

Had a Good Time heeds the same reinvention impulse, though drawing on an enduring personal interest.

"The world is divided into two kinds of people. There are collectors and there are noncollectors. In fact, my last novel, *Fair Warning*, was built around the upscale auction world, using collecting as a metaphor for human relations. Postcard-collecting probably had its origins in my single-digit childhood when I collected baseball cards. As an adult, being around postcards in antique malls and paper ephemera shows really got me interested."

Not only was the decline of artful correspondence a deciding factor in the time period Butler selected, so was the invention of the telephone.

"It became clear pretty quickly that if I was interested in messages, those first two decades were going to be the most fruitful, because in the first two decades phones had not yet become common and there were two or three mail deliveries a day. So when people had those passing thoughts and feelings, instead of picking up the phone and those messages passing into the ether, they got recorded. After phones became common, the interesting messages were fewer and farther between."

Butler views these travelers's cards as revealing capsule commentaries on a hopeful, still young America at the dawn of a new century.

"The larger shape of this book is really a portrait of America. I chose these 15 cards particularly to get the cross-section of America regionally, to split it by gender, and also to suggest thematically the issues of the early 20th century. The major issues that stood before us were similar to the issues of the 21st century: war, the rich vs. the poor, race, gender, epidemic illness, the advance of new technologies and their influence."

Butler insists that there is a gestalt to all his books.

"It's true of every one of my three books of stories. Even the order in which the stories appear is carefully chosen. This new book draws on newspaper items of the time as well, and they have been chosen to resonate into, or out of, or contrast with the stories around them."

The author says that if he were not a writer, he would be reading literary fiction voluminously. But he doesn't care to risk having other voices impinge on those of his own creation.

"In between projects I read a lot more fiction. And when my students are ready to find their own voices . . . I advise them to significantly throttle back on their reading. Because every aspiring artist is faced with the very daunting task of negotiating a way into her unconscious, which is a scary place. And there are a lot of distractions and defense mechanisms that a young writer has not to go there."

The danger lies in becoming a voyeur to experience.

"Akira Kurosawa said to be an artist means never averting your eyes. Instead of coming to terms with what one knows about the world, the easy out for a writer is to go read another good book."

October 24, 2004

Jack Hitt's *Off the Road*

Jack Hitt was a self-described "35-year-old ex-Episcopalian skidding his way into a midlife crisis" when, in 1991, he undertook to brave the ancient, grueling, 500-mile pilgrim's route to Santiago de Compostela in Northern Spain.

The Charleston-born journalist quit a cushy job as an editor at Harper's magazine, sublet his New York apartment, and bid adieu to the creature comforts of modern life.

A contemporary Quixote? Not precisely. More a man yearning to hit the road in pursuit of fresh air and a fresh perspective—at a rapturous remove from CNN Headline News.

Hitt, son of the late Robert M. Hitt Jr., former editor of The Evening Post, chronicles his exacting trek from France across the Pyrenees to Santiago in the whimsical, irreverent, fascinating *Off the Road* (Simon and Schuster), a narrative of the 1990s with more than a passing resemblance to Chaucer's 1380s (and the road to Canterbury).

"The pilgrim reduces everything to a human scale just by the very act of walking," says Hitt, in Charleston for the holidays. "When I first went on the road, I really expected to have this sort of clichéd 'experience' where I'd be alone on the face of the earth and just walking from day to day, month after month.

"At some point, having emptied myself of all the cultural baggage of being a modern American, I'd be away from everything that plagues us day in, day out. Having submitted to this rigorous journey across Spain, all of that would disappear and these great ideas would descend and my life would be changed immeasurably. And of course, none of that happened. What happened was that all sorts of other things and other purposes kept interrupting my clichés, like getting caught up in the Chaucerian absurdity of it."

During the Middle Ages, a million people a year made the pilgrimage to Santiago. For centuries, what drove pilgrims was the belief that the bones of St. James the Apostle, the brother of John, were buried there. Hitt says no one, not even the pope, believes it now. But this very fact is what lends the journey such gravity.

"What's interesting is that the reason for walking to Santiago has been eliminated. What makes walking it today (meaningful) is that your very motive for going there becomes part of the search for why you're going. What my book turns on, to some degree, is what various of those involved felt was the proper motive for going to Santiago."

Apart from arduous though "purifying" physical demands and its historical significance—the pilgrimage came into being in 814 A.D., chiefly as a means to draw enough men and goods into Spain to oust the Moors—Hitt was drawn to the pilgrimage for what turned out to be a complex of reasons.

"In the Middle Ages there were three great pilgrimages: one to Jerusalem, one to Rome, and one to Santiago. They constituted a belt of traffic around what was considered Western civilization. Trips to Rome were often more or less political junkets. So anyone who went on it probably had secondary motives. Jerusalem was also very much a merchant's route.

"But the road to Santiago had basically nothing going for it other than the fact that you got to Santiago. That was it. There was no magic involved, no miracles involved, no gifts or benefits. You got nothing but the satisfaction of having completed the walk. So there was something about the purity of the whole effort that attracted me to it."

The first few days of the pilgrimage might best be described as "Ode to a Spanish Blister," or "How I Overcame Several False Starts and Finally Hit My Stride."

Soon, Hitt was able to cover as many as 42 kilometers in a single day.

"And I almost perished from the effort. Blister care becomes a major preoccupation until you get past the first week. You build up calluses, but that first week is unbelievably painful. Once your feet have turned into nice solid blocks of wood, you're fine."

A layer of callus also was required to endure a gradual accretion of less-than-engaging fellow travelers, who dogged his heels like the throngs accompanying Forrest Gump. Yet, friendships evolved over time, ones not due exclusively to shared discomforts.

"You're thrown together with these other pilgrims and are forced to work out whatever accommodations you can. You forge what we would now recognize as a community. One of the things I found fascinating and revealing was how messy and cumbersome real community is. It ain't Norman Rockwell church picnics and potluck dinners.

"Some of the people were disastrously drunk all the time, and some were holier than thou and pious. All the classic weirdos and uptight people and airheads are all there. They're on hand for my delectation, and I'm there to some extent for theirs. Maybe they saw me as a glorious eccentric. But you never knew anybody's name; names were meaningless on the road. Our identities changed: we became pilgrims. This is what the book tries to capture."

Close to Santiago there were huge crowds of pilgrims on the road. Hitt and his companions posed nothing less than a municipal problem, with everyone trying to reach Santiago by July 25, the feast day of St. James.

"By the time I neared Santiago I could not look anywhere and not see pilgrims—a long, long, slow conga line of sweaty, dirty, ugly people exhibiting gathering awe as we neared where we'd been heading."

Upon his arrival, Hitt was interviewed by a priest who asked his motive for making the journey.

"I said, 'To discover my motive.' And he got a little annoyed at that. This was not an acceptable reason to the Church."

Blisters long ago healed, if not forgotten, Hitt has returned to Harper's as a contributing editor. Residing with his wife and newborn daughter in New Haven, Conn., he also contributes frequently to Esquire and The New York Times Sunday Magazine, as well as editing the periodical Lingua Franca.

But his recollections remain vivid.

"You start off with all the big ideas and great, preconceived notions of what a pilgrimage is supposed to be, and then what happens is that the road beats that out of you. They're gone within the first couple of weeks. Most of your time is spent wondering where the next drink of water is coming from. And there's something to be learned from that."

His publisher wasn't entirely sure how to market *Off the Road.* Was it a travel book? An adventure book? A religion book? An historical book? Hitt says it's really all of those things, albeit without practical travel advice or any logical progression to his movement.

He set out to write something altogether different, and succeeded. But not at first.

"I wrote it all once in 1991 and threw almost all of it out. My then girlfriend, now wife, was very candid about its shortcomings, specifically the fact that I was hiding my personal experiences behind history. I wanted to have history in there but whether I liked it or not, the walk was a very personal and revealing experience, and I was going to have to write about that. The personal and spiritual, if you will, were very difficult for me to exhume and amplify in the book."

Part of the fun, Hitt says, was finding out how useless and irrelevant the basic outline he drew up ahead of time became. Ditto for the meticulous journal he kept.

"Not a word from that journal shows up in the book. And very few impressions I'd written. It's amazing that when you're in it you're thinking 'Here's what's important.' When the trip's over and you've reflected on it at length—what Wordsworth called spontaneous emotions recollected in tranquility—

you realize that all these events and encounters you thought were so important weren't nearly so significant as the ones that started to resurface in my mind. You make a *story* out of it.

"The real development of the story didn't begin until we (the pilgrims) returned, garbed ourselves in new clothes, ate rich food, and sat down to tell tales, packing up our experiences like baggage after a trip. It's when I began to recognize that the diary was little more than a day-to-day account which, like most diaries, was boring."

Well, perhaps it was not boring the day he almost froze in the lee of a mudslide in the Pyrenees, following a fruitless, circular trek through the mountains.

Off the Road undergoes various shifts in tone, from profound observation to playful self mockery. And there are numerous side trips along the way.

"There are a lot of digressions in the book, whether it's referring to my own cloudy motives or a historical side trip or an account of what happened one day on the road with fellow pilgrims. A lot of what the book is about is bringing tradition into the present. And being a Charlestonian you're pretty much born with that instinct or impulse."

January 8, 1995

Roy Blount Jr.'s *Not Exactly What I Had in Mind*

Roy Blount Jr. has been on the road for a month. And it shows. His usually pointed wit is blunted, his irreverent mien a bit shopworn from too many hotels, too many interviews, too many banal questions.

Roy? Hello? You OK, boy?

"Uh, yeah. Sure. Say, did you know that the average person's skin weighs nine pounds? No? Well, mine feels like 90."

It's been *that* kind of afternoon.

His walking tour of Charleston, just completed, was pleasant enough. But a pall has been cast on the day, a sort of threshold-of-awareness ennui that has insinuated itself into his bosom and curls there, drowsing.

Perhaps it has something to do with being a displaced Southerner returned to the old element, a child of homilies, if not grits, turned urbane and maybe a touch blasé.

He sits, or rather, sags, in the lobby of the Lodge Alley Inn. There is a prominent wound on his left cheek, the legacy of a late-night brush with a wall. It throbs.

Our subject, ostensibly, is his latest book, *Not Exactly What I Had in Mind.*

Neither, it appears, is this interview.

Blount sighs, resigned, and tries to make a go of it.

"You know, I can tell I'm gaining weight because the grease spots on my shirt are getting lower and lower."

A feeble round from this man's arsenal, but still droll *a la* Blount.

That's the spirit.

Well distanced now from Sports Illustrated, if not from his kinship with Dan Jenkins and Paul Hemphill, Blount is enjoying a felicitous existence, or at least what passes for it among free-lance writers.

There are a wife and kids, a run of successful books, and money in the bank. This day's doldrums notwithstanding, he wears the years like a feather in a hatband, accepting the world with indulgent grace, exhibiting an engagingly self-effacing style.

His writing may evince a down-to-earth (if conspiratorial) tone. But this, one suspects, is a pose. Blount is exceedingly well read. Who would expect, in the middle of a satirical essay on cat books, to find obscure asides from French literary criticism?

Folksy, he ain't.

Rather, Blount's disclaimers about the South are echoes of an exchange between two men—one Southern, one Northern—in Faulkner's "Absalom, Absalom." Again and again, the former insists, unconvincingly, "I do not hate the South. I do not!"

"All my best friends who came north say the same thing, over and over. My turn now. 'I don't hate the South.' I feel enthralled and oppressed by the South. I was thinking about that the other day while sitting at the lunch counter at Woolworth's, realizing I couldn't eat potatoes and gravy anymore. That's depressing in a way."

His fifth book is anything but. Blount melds that rarest of all capacities, the power of accurate observation, with the good sense to laugh at what he finds. With an instinct for the absurdities and discordances of life and a gift for pillorying them, he is funny in the way only such an observer can be.

"Not long ago, I climbed up into the Statue of Liberty's head," he writes. "It felt good in there, and I thought rousing thoughts. What a woman! A blend of Einstein, Garbo, and Jelly Roll Morton. *And* Jesse Helms. When her cornerstone was laid, *Huckleberry Finn* was at the printers. Not being Jesse

Helms, I didn't presume to speak for her. But I have a hard time believing that America today is exactly what she had in mind."

Blount says he never had it in mind to begin his career as a sportswriter. But one doesn't argue with a free lunch. Born and raised in North Georgia, Blount attended Vanderbilt University on a Grantland Rice Memorial Sportswriting Scholarship. He received his Masters in English from Harvard, also on scholarship.

Following two years in the army, he worked as a reporter and op-ed columnist for The Atlanta Journal. Blount went to Sports Illustrated as a staff writer, interviewing most of the notables of the day, and later was elevated to associate editor.

In time, he left the lofty SI pantheon, trading the currency of security for the fool's gold of freelancing. But Blount has made it work, selling a few film scripts (none of which has been produced, as yet) to augment his books.

"In 1975 I moved to Mill River, Mass., which kind of reminds me of North Georgia, except for the fact that it's cold there 14 months of the year. I thought the pastoral setting would provide a much better environment for writing than did New York. And it has. The trouble is, when you're working for yourself, you're constantly trying to tell yourself that you've got to this and you've got to do that. But then I ask, 'Why should I listen to me?'"

Given enough financial pressure, that inner voice becomes more insistent.

"Hunger is a sure cure for writer's block, too," says Blount. "Typically, I find myself doing a lot of things at once, which tends to blow a lot of my circuits. I put things off until I get a burst of adrenalin inspired by desperation. Frankly, I don't like the writing to come too easy, too regular or too steady."

While most critics applaud his breezy approach, some occasionally fault Blount for injecting too much of himself into his writing.

Rubbish, he says.

"I miss it when writers leave themselves out of their work. It depletes it. And I don't trust the story unless I know who's telling it, and why. On the other hand, I understand the criticism and vow, here and now, that I will be more circumspect in the future.

"At the moment, I'm writing a book about hair. Actually, I'm doing the text for a book of photographs on hair. And I promise not to put too much of my hair into it."

In the meantime, Blount will continue to rip and snort his way across the landscape, with frequent layovers in Lake Wobegone, where he commiserates on the air with fellow humorist Garrison Keillor.

He will continue to take the glitterati to task for its arrogance, skewer our pretensions, and ponder the survival of humankind in a world of digital timepieces. All the while, he will be honing his skills as an organic gardener, and wondering why writers of his stripe are not taken seriously.

"People tend to think of a humorist as a lower form of writer. Admittedly, the title doesn't sound nearly as compelling as 'novelist.' But the value of humor depends on what you do with it.

"Anyone can be funny. I want to make sense."

December 15, 1985

Edward Ball. Photograph by Brad Nettles

The Late Unpleasantness, in Fact and Fiction

"It is well that war is so terrible lest we should grow too fond of it."

Robert E. Lee, quoted in Edward Porter Alexander's *Military Memoirs of a Confederate*

Growing up in western North Carolina in the 1950s and '60s, the words "civil war" usually referred to sibling rivalries at the neighbor's next door. Outside of a high school classroom, the phrase was seldom uttered. "Yankees"? That was the baseball team in New York.

Very occasionally, my grandmother would correct those who spoke of the War Between the States by any other name. But generally speaking, it was something that had happened in the remote recesses of American history, whereas World War II and Korea were comparatively recent events, the scars still visible.

At least, this is my recollection. So it came as something of a cultural shock when at age 32, I moved to South Carolina in 1980 and found the war was still being "waged." I had lived in Virginia for five years, and though Richmond may have been the seat of the Confederacy, Virginians of the 1970s seemed more consumed by the history of the Revolution. I discovered that South Carolinians' fervor for "their" war far exceeded that of their colleagues to the north.

By the time I became book review editor of The Post and Courier in 1982, I was accustomed to the deluge of novels and nonfiction works on the Late Unpleasantness, and knew it would be my responsibility to see that the best of these received suitable treatment in the paper. The fact that I did not share this passion, that my chief historical interest was in antiquity and the origins of civilization, was irrelevant.

I benefited immensely from the counsel of such Civil War devotees, amateur and professional, as Richard Hatcher, the historian at Fort Sumter National Monument and for more than 20 years one of our most valued book reviewers. The authors themselves were fonts of information and perspective, of course, and gradually I began to set aside my initial distaste for what I saw as a romanticizing of the war. While I would never feel as captivated by the struggle as a native, I garnered an appreciation for the times, for the people who endured the war and its aftermath.

The writers in this section bring a powerful attachment and impressive expertise to the subject, whether it be the battlefield or the home front. It is history that resonates, well beyond the boundaries of place.

Charles Frazier's *Cold Mountain*

Some men regard fame warily, as a crop of misunderstandings they prefer not to take root. The only renown they look for in life is to have lived it quietly.

Meet Charles Frazier, the soul of privacy. Genuine article.

So soft-spoken he's occasionally inaudible, the Raleigh, N.C., resident doesn't know quite what to make of his sudden celebrity. With some of the most rapturous reviews this side of *A Farewell to Arms* bestowed upon his best-selling first novel, *Cold Mountain* (Grove/Atlantic), Frazier has emerged as an "overnight" literary phenomenon. Emphasis on literary.

"It is an adjustment to go from quietly working at home for six years on this book to going out and doing a book tour," says Frazier, 46. "But it's fun to hear people's reactions. I'm just grateful that readers are reacting the way they are, that there is something about the book that is appealing to people."

So private and unassuming is Frazier that his wife of 21 years, Katherine, had to smuggle 100 pages of the unfinished manuscript to a mutual friend, North Carolina novelist Kaye Gibbons. Gibbons helped Frazier acquire an agent, and the book—still unfinished—was snapped up for six figures.

The commercial success of *Cold Mountain* initially was due to word-of-mouth advertising.

"I have to give a whole lot of credit to booksellers and readers who helped this book find an audience the old-fashioned way, without the kind of modern book-selling apparatus we've come to know," says Frazier.

Now everyone seems to be scaling Frazier's mountain, including Hollywood. MGM/UA recently bought the film rights to the novel, with Anthony Minghella ("The English Patient") set as director and screenwriter. Sydney Pollack will produce the adaptation.

Frazier earned his undergraduate degree at the University of North Carolina at Chapel Hill and a Ph.D. in literature at the University of South Carolina. He was living a modest existence as a part-time teacher at North Carolina State University until fame snatched him up.

A romantic saga with keen observations of the natural world, *Cold Mountain* is being called the finest novel of the Civil War since *The Killer Angels.*

But Frazier says the war serves chiefly as backdrop to the story of Inman, a wounded, emotionally hollowed-out Confederate soldier who leaves an army hospital in the dead of night to begin an odyssey home to the Southern Appalachians of North Carolina. And that of his love, Ada Monroe, a Charleston-bred woman struggling to adjust to rural life.

"The war is background; Inman's story begins when he *leaves* the war."

Inman's memories of Ada and his prewar life are his only sustenance on the difficult journey home from the hospital in Raleigh, a trek compounded by the prowling Home Guard, teams of vicious men who hunt down deserters.

As Inman's path brings him closer to a reunion with Ada, the reader discovers the characters have grown in new directions.

"They're different people from the last time they saw each other. Quite different. And they don't know each other well enough to determine if they still want each other. They're in a process of learning who they are and who this other person is."

The genesis of the novel is threefold. Frazier, who grew up in the foothills of the Southern Appalachians, always had wanted write a book set in the region.

Then he discovered a family history his father was writing. It contained a single paragraph on Frazier's great-great uncle, W. P. Inman, a Confederate soldier who walked away from the Civil War. There also were those stories passed down by Frazier's great-great-grandfather.

"My dad had heard these stories from childhood, but as soon as he told them to me I started writing in a matter of days. My great-great uncle is the basis for the Inman character in the book. Maybe I used a little bit of my great-great grandfather to develop the character, too.

"The stories gave me a kind of very sketchy outline for a novel and also gave me the freedom to fill it in. I'm glad I didn't have a great deal of information about him and what his journey was really like. All I had was that he made this journey and he made it home."

Long an avid hiker and backpacker, Frazier had been keeping notebooks on fragments of cultural and natural history of Western North Carolina for some time. He walked and biked the Cold Mountain area trying to place his character's route.

"When I heard the story, I realized that here was the thing that would make all these diverse bits of information hang together in the narrative. On my walks, I'd just explore an area that I thought might be a place I wanted to take Inman. Just seeing the lay of the land might suggest to me what I wanted to happen to him."

Inman's meditations on nature are integral to the story. Frazier says he wanted the mountains to be like one of the main characters of the novel, partly because it's the landscape he loves most.

"I wanted to be clear on what Inman was going home to. And for Ada, who's trying to learn to live there, I wanted to make sure I understood the environment she was learning to deal with."

Ada likewise experiences a journey, a growing awareness of her connection to the natural world around her farm. She is an educated woman coming into her own—another way in which this novel of the 1860s speaks to contemporary times.

To capture her "voice," Frazier accessed library sources for actual diaries written by Civil War-era women.

"One of the things that really interested me was finding so many letters and journals from women that were about these themes. They were well aware of what it meant to be educated and in that culture. As much as anything, these materials reassured me that I was getting the character right and not plugging a contemporary character into another period."

Reviewers have characterized the principal themes of *Cold Mountain* as humanity's place in nature and love transformed by the war. Frazier says these are not necessarily themes.

"The things I was thinking of most when I wrote it were 'What do these people want out of life? How do they learn to live in the world that they've got instead of yearning for a world that doesn't exist? What are the qualities of war in addition to violence, dislocation and disruption? What are the qualities of home—peace, quiet and centeredness—that affect these characters?'

"As far as the book speaking to our day and age, I think what people fear and want, and how they learn to live with both of those things, doesn't change a lot over time. It's kind of like *The Odyssey*. What Odysseus wants and what he's struggling toward is much the same for all of us."

When his book tour ends in the fall, the stay-at-home parent may turn his attention to another idea that's in the percolating stage.

"I'm interested in those elegant mountain resorts that appeared around the turn of the century, and just as interested in the cotton mill towns that produced the wealth that let people go up there for three months and beat the heat."

Frazier, however, won't be able to avoid the heat of the spotlight any time soon. When you've succeeded at capturing the spirit of a bygone age through characters as vivid and real as the folks next door, you have to face the consequences. Quietly, of course.

August 17, 1997

Edward Ball's *Slaves in the Family*

In the hermetic quiet of a library in the South Carolina Historical Society, Edward Ball gingerly turns a yellowed page of an account begun by his family in 1720. It itemizes not grain or vegetables, but people.

Tattered yet intact, the page lists the first, and only, names of slaves who toiled for Ball's forebears at Comingtee, first among the 25 rice plantations owned by this prominent South Carolina family at the apex of its wealth.

One hundred years later, the record would number not 20 or 30 slaves, but thousands. Between 1800 and 1865 alone, some 3,000 babies were born into slavery on the Ball family's simple but extensive properties.

If Ball sounds dispassionate as he reads off the names, be assured he is not. The three years invested in researching and writing *Slaves in the Family*, just released by Farrar, Straus & Giroux, and the contacts he made with descendants of these slaves were as personal and as difficult as anything the former Village Voice columnist has undertaken.

"I wrote this book because we are facing a racial crisis in this country, a deep wound. This is one individual's attempt to apply medicine to that wound."

Not to Judge

A few days removed from an emotional, national television appearance on "Oprah," a telecast taped some weeks earlier, Ball reiterates that he didn't set out to judge those of his ancestors who were slave holders.

"I set out to tell a story and to uncover evidence of what actually happened on these plantations. If you read the book you'll see I don't have an agenda, except to put a human face on what is often an anonymous and badly sketched Southern legend.

"I feel good about what I've done. It's never been my desire to embarrass the family. On the contrary, I believe that what I've done in the long run might bring honor to this family."

Born in Savannah, Ball spent 12 years of his youth on Sullivan's Island, where an estimated 40 percent of slaves entering America first arrived. He moved back to Charleston from New York in September 1994 to begin work on the book. And it is here that he will open a 25-city national tour on February 19.

Troubling Truths

Looking at the family legacy from a fresh perspective was no easier for Ball than for family members, not all of whom were enthusiastic about the project—to say the least.

"The Balls, among themselves, have talked about slavery quite a bit. It's part of the lore of our family. I have broken a certain kind of silence in writing about it and talking about it publicly. This might not have been done 25 years ago, but I don't think I've broken any kind of taboo because we've all known since childhood about . . . the family business, shall we say.

"What I've done that's different from the family is to study it a little more carefully and talk about it in detail, honestly and publicly."

"Red Cap" Arrives

The family's history in the Americas begins in 1670, when English settler John Coming set foot on New World soil at Charles Towne Landing. In 1698, his half-nephew and countryman, Elias "Red Cap" Ball, arrived in South Carolina to take control of his inheritance of 740 acres at Comingtee plantation in Berkeley County. The bequest included 25 slaves.

In the ensuing 165 years, the Ball clan accumulated more than two dozen plantations, most situated along the Cooper River, and, by 1863, as many as 4,000 slaves.

Counted among Edward Ball's ancestors was the leading slave importer in Colonial America, Charleston aristocrat Henry Laurens, who helped negotiate peace with the British at the end of the Revolutionary War.

The family stories Ball absorbed while growing up told of a genteel plantation life and humane treatment of slaves, when they were mentioned at all. On those occasions when he did hear his ancestors' benevolence questioned, it generally came from his father, the Reverend Porter Ball, a Charlestonian who fulfilled a succession of Episcopal parish assignments in the South.

In the Archives

For the better part of a year between 1994 and 1995, Ball walked from his spartan room in the then-empty Branford-Horry mansion at Meeting and Tradd streets to the S.C. Historical Society, where he immersed himself in family records.

Like most of his relatives, Ball had little concept of the scale of the plantations, among them Hyde Park, Limerick, Middleburg, Mepkin and Quenby.

"We knew there were a certain number of Ball plantations, and that a lot of people worked in the rice fields. But once I started looking at the records—the slave lists—and counted the numbers to tally up the plantations, the scale of the thing was a surprise.

"The Balls were in the plantation business from 1698 until 1865, and after 1865 they did sharecropping for another 40 years. During the period of slavery, the slaves on the plantation numbered 4,000 people—my best estimate. The descendants of the Ball family slaves number between 75,000 and 100,000 people around the country."

In the Field

Next, the author began to locate and approach some of the African-American families whose stories interlaced with those of the Balls. Rather than undertake many different encounters with black families, which he felt would be superficial, Ball chose to approach seven or eight families and attempt to establish relationships with individuals in each.

To do this, he traveled down many a lowcountry back road, frequently unannounced, sometimes encountering anger, sometimes developing friendships. He even ventured to West Africa to meet descendants of traders who sold slaves to the Balls.

Mistrust of his motives was initially a difficult chasm to bridge. Also, some black writers and academics who learned of the project were vehemently opposed to what they saw as Ball's appropriation of their history, just as his ancestors had exiled slaves from their culture.

Others found his discoveries, in company with plantation records, indispensable in charting their own African-American genealogies.

Though each family exemplified "a certain experience" of what happened after emancipation, Ball says that at least half the African-Americans he met, including many with whom he forged bonds, knew little about their ancestors' lives and where they lived. A small minority had some details, and a tiny number possessed lore from the slave period that survives generations of forgetting.

"It is my feeling that after emancipation there was a purposeful period of forgetting on the part of both the white and the black side. Over and over again I heard that generations who were freed did not often talk with their children about what had happened.

"When I came along in 1994 these processes were a century old, and it was as though I was looking across at an abyss. Merely to make contact with a black family was like an electrical charge. It was very cathartic in most cases, both for me and for the black families. But it was hard at first to reach across the color line."

Parallel Stories

The meticulously detailed family records, combined with the oral histories he obtained, offered Ball a unique opportunity to, as he puts it, "bring the stories of the obscure side by side with the powerful, as they had been in life," and to unearth their fates.

"I have had marginal success. In the case of the Ball family, I've written about the descendants of just a handful of those who were in slavery. But I believe the mingling of the white and black stories is one of the unprecedented things about this project. We often get the white story, and in the last 20 years we've gotten the black story. Both are partial histories. What we need to do is try to find a shared history, and that's what I tried to achieve."

At the same time, Ball has assayed the broader issue of slavery's legacy, how the lives of later generations of blacks and whites—as well as our national identity—have been shaped.

"I think the country is now in the process of re-examining the tragic parts of its history. Americans are making themselves familiar with the unpleasant aspects of our past. During the Cold War, our national attention was so focused on an imagined external enemy that the national memory, I believe, suffered and was compromised and narrowed.

"Since the end of the Cold War, we've begun to focus our energies more on ourselves and have tried to understand who we are as a people. Part of that is the re-examination of our tragedies: the decimation of Native Americans and slavery, which was part of our communal life for 250 years. I think my book and my work is part of that larger project."

No Less an Imprint

Girding his resolve during the long months of work was Ball's conviction that his life has been shaped by the history of slavery just as much as the lives of blacks have been shaped.

"It is important for whites to acknowledge this. Not just the descendants of slave owners like myself and like thousands of Charlestonians and millions of Southerners, but all white Americans.

"Black people in America were in slavery for twice as long as they've been free. And we have to talk about this. We can't point the finger at some other nationality or generation. I am not personally responsible for the cruel things the Ball family did. However, I believe that I am accountable for what we did. To insist that it doesn't involve you is, I think, dishonest."

For three years, Ball wrote an architectural column for the Village Voice. Before that, he did free-lance art and film criticism. Ball had studied semiotics at Brown University as an undergraduate, and cinema at the University of Iowa as a graduate student.

None of this prepared him for the enormity of this first book.

Neither was his family prepared.

"When I started the book there were more members of the family who were wary of it, but no one tried to stop me from writing the book. As time has passed and people have seen the seriousness with which I've worked on this, there's been less nervousness about it. It even may be fair to say that in the family there is general support for what I've done."

Not to say there haven't been differences of opinion.

"Some in the family would rather I didn't try to open the lid on the Ball plantations. But it's my feeling that the Ball story is no longer a private family story. Perhaps it never was. Neither are the plantation stories of other South Carolina families. The Ball story contains the stories of the tens of thousands of people alive today. And it is no longer our private property."

Galvanized

"White Like Who?," the meditative piece Ball wrote for the Voice in 1993, was not the genesis of the book. That came in the form of a Ball family reunion in the summer of that same year.

"I had been living in New York for many years and had not looked back. When I got the invitation it was as if a door had opened. I had been thinking about my childhood and about the South. The plantation stories were resurfacing. I decided to go back to the event and use it as a way of beginning to remember. I began writing the book a year later."

It may be argued that the repercussions of slavery in the lives of the black families Ball met supersede the story of his own.

The "Oprah" telecast, during which he asked forgiveness of Charlotte Dunn and her mother Katie Roper, Charlestonians and descendants of Ball family slaves, was not his first public apology. Ball tendered one four years ago on a PBS radio program. Shortly thereafter, he came to see the apology as "arrogant and inappropriate," saying it was a mistake he would not repeat.

Obviously, he changed his mind.

"I think that an apology is an important gesture," says Ball, who has decided to remain in Charleston. "I had gotten to know the Roper family pretty well. We had been through a lot, and they had shared the family lore about the slave period. It felt genuine. An apology without a real emotional bond would be artificial. It felt right at this time, and they were very moved by it. I think it has made a difference in their lives. It certainly has made a difference in mine."

February 1, 1998

Tony Horwitz's *Confederates in the Attic*

NASHVILLE—Only a few days have passed since Tony Horwitz finalized his move from The Wall Street Journal, for whom he won a Pulitzer Prize in 1995, to the tonier tableau of The New Yorker.

He's pleased, to be sure. But so offhandedly modest about it you'd think he had just accepted a job with The Podunk Gazette doing rewrites.

"We've been negotiating for the past couple of months and finally got it all straightened out. I haven't started yet, so I'm in that delicious between-jobs state. I'm not getting a paycheck, but there's no one breathing down my neck for copy."

Not yet.

Horwitz, author of *Confederates in the Attic* (Pantheon), released earlier this year to unqualified praise, is perfectly delighted to be attending the Southern Festival of Books here. Just because he no longer covers the American South for the Journal doesn't mean the Washington, D.C., native, who lives in Virginia with his wife and son, finds the subject any less compelling.

Within moments, the discussion dips below the Mason-Dixon.

"I think I've remained fascinated for the same reason it's been an enduring fascination for millions of other Americans. The drama of the event has almost got a classical symmetry to it. I was introduced to the war as a child through the photographs. And I think that helps explain why we're so obsessed with the Civil War and not, say, the Revolutionary War. That's as far back as we can reach and bring back images that are strikingly modern yet also connect us to this time long ago.

"Also, in a real way, the issues are still unresolved. In South Carolina, the political issues are still hot. States' rights, the Rebel flag, etc. There are all kinds of ways in which the Civil War is still with us."

Horwitz is a graduate of Brown University and Columbia University's Graduate School of Journalism, Prior to capturing the Pulitzer for national reporting at the Journal, the 39-year-old reporter spent 10 years as a foreign correspondent in the Middle East, Australia, Africa and Europe. He won the 1992 Overseas Press Club Award for his coverage of the Gulf War.

Horwitz's other books include *Baghdad Without a Map and Other Misadventures in Arabia* and *One for the Road: Hitchhiking Through the Australian Outback.*

A genial, easy-to-like fellow, Horwitz invested two years, on and off, discovering those places where the legacy of the Civil War remains an integral part of life. Occasionally, an obsessive part.

"The most abiding interest in the war tends to break down along rural-urban lines. Charleston is a little unusual. It has so much history and is so in love with its history. But generally speaking I would say that in the Nashvilles, and the Atlantas and the Charlottes you would not find it as keen as you do in the smaller towns and in the countryside, although there are exceptions. I certainly found the fervor stronger when I got out of the major cities.

"In any case, there were certainly no family ties to the war. No one in my family fought in it. I grew up in suburban Maryland, so I don't really have a regional tie to the North or South."

Horwitz encountered the innocent, the intriguing and the spooky in his travels, not least in the lowcountry. He explored not only the museums and shrines that encompass the war, such as the Museum of the United Daughters of the Confederacy in Charleston, but the people who resurrect it. Namely, the battle re-enactors.

Horwitz also participated in a re-enactment with elements of the "hardcore" Southern Guard. Total immersion and a period rush, as he characterizes it.

"I think mainstream re-enacting is mostly innocent, though a lot of people look at it from the outside and think these are militia types or people who want the South to rise again. That sort of sentiment. By and large I found that for most of the people who are really interested in the history of the war, or interested just in the costumes, it's almost like a theme camping trip.

"A lot of women are involved. The re-enactors bring along their families. There's almost a hippie strain to it—people enjoying dressing up and inhabiting another role for a weekend, living communally. At heart, it's a very trusting kind of escapism."

Horwitz notes that the persistence of the past is now of interest to more than historians and cultural historians, and people's involvement in such activities as re-enactments sends multiple messages.

"That's why I find re-enacting, which I initially viewed as just very strange, as actually a very fascinating and revealing activity in terms of what it says about the culture. It's not just cultists doing this. There's a kind of low-grade discontent with modern life, and people want to recapture some of the drama of that era.

"It reflects a popular strain: people want to do their own history today. They're not waiting for some historian to pronounce from on high what they should think about the topic. They're saying, 'I'm going to go into the archives, I'm going to do my own history, I'm going to put on a uniform and experience what it is to be a soldier."

Horwitz says this suggests, in part, a reaction to the failure of professional historians to speak to the average reader.

"But it also reflects what's going on in the culture generally. People want to go beyond the books. Genealogy also has had a lot to do with it. The emphasis has shifted from leaders to the common soldier."

While the author found that the various shrines and museums he plumbed varied widely—some offering a rather old-fashioned presentation of information; together they were very revealing of another history—the history of the remembrance of the war.

"There are really two histories. One is how it happened. The other is how it's remembered. To me, how it's remembered, which is what the book's really about, is just as fascinating."

Throughout the South, Horwitz sensed a feeling on the part of some that the region and its people have been put down and kicked around for 130 years, largely because of what happened in the Civil War.

"They're right to a certain extent. And the South still is being kicked around, particularly by Hollywood. I've become more sensitized to the sanctimony and the hypocrisy of the way many Northerners still look at the South, and the last thing I wanted to do in the book was reinforce any of the stereotypes.

"But I'm sometimes saddened by the extremes this put-upon attitude can lead to, this feeling of being under siege and refusing to give another inch."

Horwitz had unsettling experiences, as well. He says one has to be very careful to distinguish between the different kinds of remembrance. He regards groups like Aryan Nation, the League of the South and Sons of the Confederate Veterans, though treated fairly in the book, as reflecting an insecure and often xenophobic sentiment—though it's certainly not confined to the South.

"Generally, it was the upland South where I found feelings that were raw and the views the harshest, not in the lowcountry or black belt Alabama and Mississippi."

Which prompts some interesting questions, says Horwitz.

"Is this because the Civil Rights movement didn't happen to a great degree in these more isolated areas while the Deep South had to go through that period of change and searching and self-reflection? Or is it an economic thing, the competition between poor blacks and poor whites—the traditional view—while in the lowcountry you had a tradition of *noblesse oblige*?"

November 22, 1998

Winston Groom's *Shrouds of Glory*

"Life is like a rubber band; the harder you go forward, the harder you snap back. So do not make slip-ups."

Had he known him, this sage advice from none other than Forrest Gump might have saved Confederate Gen. John Bell Hood a whole lot of trouble.

But Gump's counsel came 130 years too late. Too late to divert the pell-mell charges of the impetuous young Rebel soldier, whose strategic acumen did not quite equal his strengths as a tactician.

Hood's flamboyant role in the Civil War's dramatic Western Campaign, and that campaign in general, are the subjects of *Shrouds of Glory: From Atlanta to Nashville*, an informal history by Winston Groom due out this month from Grove/Atlantic.

Groom, whose renown as the author of *Forrest Gump* now approaches global proportions, spoke to The Post and Courier by phone from his home in Point Clear, Ala.

Utilizing eye-witness accounts, military communiques, journal entries and newspaper articles, Groom delves into the hearts and minds of all the principal players: Jackson, Lee, and Nathan Bedford Forrest, as well as Union generals Sherman, Grant, and McClellan.

Hood, a Kentuckian tagged with the sobriquet "Old Woodenhead," is the linchpin of the book. An unlikely choice to succeed Gen. Joseph E. Johnston as leader of the South's last great offensive, Hood's singular, distinguishing feature, says Groom, was that he was a fighter.

"He was one of those generals—and there were several in the Confederacy—who always would carry the battle to the enemy, if given the choice. He was fearless, but young and impulsive. While he probably should not have been placed in command of any army, or perhaps not even a corps, very few could have stood up to him as a division commander.

"But Jefferson Davis placed him in the position of formulating strategy. Hood understood his task to be to fight."

Shrouds of Glory suggests that Hood was prematurely thrust into command. And although he rose to the challenge in many respects, devising a cat-and-mouse stratagem to baffle numerically superior Northern forces, his recklessness led to the heroic but disastrous charge at Franklin, Tenn., where six generals perished and the Confederate Army of the West effectively was brought to ruin.

"You have to understand, first, that he was youngest (33) commander in the army, and second, that the entire Confederacy was on its last legs and grasping at straws. When Hood was placed in command, there was a slim possibility that the Confederacy could have won at the negotiating table what it couldn't win in the field.

"My own theory was that Hood had been very much weakened by losing a leg and most of an arm during four years of war, and hampered by a lack of experience in command. Hood was a tactician who tried to model himself after his old commander, Stonewall Jackson. But, you know, it's hard for someone to know when to quit."

Groom, happily, hasn't tried. He completed *Gump and Co.*, the sequel to *Forrest Gump*, last Sunday. "It's a chore I relished doing, but you hang yourself out there with it." The book will be released by Pocket Books next fall.

Upcoming is a history of pirate-turned-patriot Jean Lafitte, which Groom jocularly characterizes as "a great excuse to go to New Orleans, drink some good whiskey and eat some good food."

Groom, who defines himself as a novelist, says writing history is something of a relief.

"I can only write a couple of hours a day on novels. It just drains you. Every once in a while I like to take on a history, which I can work at seven or eight hours a day. I'm not a professional historian. But I try not to be an amateur; I want to be more conscientious than that. History writing is a lot of hard work, but the beginning and the end already is there, which appeals to the newsman in me."

Formerly a reporter (1969–1976) with the late, lamented Washington Star, Groom was born in the nation's capital, raised in Alabama and was graduated from the University of Alabama in 1965. Commissioned a second lieutenant in the Army, he served a tour of duty in Vietnam before returning to the States to embark on a career in journalism.

That lasted eight years, at which time Groom determined to become a full-time author. Apart from *Gump*, his novels include *Better Times Than These*, *As Summers Die*, *Gone the Sun* and *Only*. He also has been a regular contributor to periodicals ranging from The New York Times Magazine to Southern Living.

The Battle of Nashville always had been an absorbing interest of Groom's. Writing about it, however, was not something he had anticipated.

"I was in between books about three or four years ago, and asked myself what I really might enjoy doing," says Groom, who currently is building a house in the Carolinas. "Exploring some aspect of the Civil War period was intriguing. Quite frankly, I was thinking that for 25 years I had read great bodies of work on the war and all of a sudden thought 'Hey, I could turn a buck on this and enjoy writing it in the process.

"I already had an enormous interest. It occurred to me that the story I might tell in *Shrouds* had been told, but no one did it quite the way I planned. The idea was to construct the book in such a way that the average reader could be persuaded to investigate further into this amazing episode in American history. I tried to couch the plight of the Confederacy and Union during the last months of the war in terms of political, economic and military effects."

It may be argued, however, that the effects of his sudden celebrity have sealed Groom's fate. He is more likely to be recognized as the creator of *Forrest Gump* than for any other accomplishment, at least by the general public.

So why did it take the various Oscar recipients forever to praise his contribution to the film when *Gump* dominated last month's Academy Awards?

"I was there, sitting with Mykelti Williamson and his mama. But it didn't bother me. This wasn't a Pulitzer Prize ceremony; it was the Oscars, and these people's turn to shine. Still, there was a bit of a flap over it back east, all these people writing about the fact that I wasn't given as much credit as some columnists thought I might have.

"But the night before the thing, I was at a party with the whole crowd. At the end someone brought in champagne and everyone was toasting each other. I felt like the bastard at the family reunion. But then (Tom) Hanks toasted me and gave me a big hug. That was more gratifying than having my name mentioned on a TV show. Actually, I had been mentioned slightly. But that kind of thing doesn't bother me a bit."

Like everyone associated with the film, Groom had no notion it would become a phenomenon.

"Nobody expected anything like this. I'm sometimes at a loss to explain it, and probably shouldn't try. I'm not saying it's a fluke, though. All I can say is that it was a story about dignity, and that you don't have to be rich and famous or brilliant to be dignified. It touched people. Of course, the great performances had much to do with it. The whole thing is fascinating."

April 16, 1995

Shelby Foote's *The Civil War: A Narrative*

Even God can not alter the past, noted the great English satirist Samuel Butler. But historians can.

And they do, voluminously. But it is not entirely a matter of intellectual fashion or ideology.

Like the self-corrective nature of science, re-evaluation of accepted histories serves a useful function, says Shelby Foote, author of *The Civil War: A Narrative*, a three-volume historical chronicle. Foote entered the national spotlight in 1990 during PBS's telecast of Ken Burns's "Civil War" documentary series.

"Some of it (revision) is quite human and some of it is quite healthy," says Foote, a Memphis resident who enjoyed his first visit to Fort Sumter this week. "I've thought a good deal about that in connection with the writing of history of all kinds. Some reviewers, in their enthusiasm, said (after reading his series) that this subject need never be handled again.

"That couldn't be further from the truth. Each generation needs to look at important historical events, especially in their own nation's history, from its point of view. Gibbon's *Decline and Fall of the Roman Empire* really could not have been written any time except in the late 18th century. History is always influenced by the time in which it is written. And therefore it's a good idea to examine it. Now, the revisionists do go sort of crazy every now and then."

The most glaring error contemporary revisionists make, says Foote, is to equate facts with truth.

"They think that if they can get all the facts together, they've told the true history. History is not just facts. It's facts interrelating with each other and interpreted by the people who were living it. It's a great error to think that history does not need a narrative to tie it together. It does need that.

"In the minds of many people, including the academics, to make a narrative of history is to romanticize and cheapen it. I deny that vehemently, although I certainly agree that it's open to that kind of thing."

Everyone from Ambrose Bierce to Frances Fitzgerald has made sport of the art of the historian. But Henry Ford was the most succinct: "History is bunk," he said. And Foote is in qualified agreement.

"I think it's profoundly true. All art is an attempt to do something that can't be done. History can never tell you what happened and how. But it can approximate it, and some of the approximations are beautiful. It is the bunk; in other words, it's not going to be a perfect picture, not by a long shot. It's going to be full of mistakes and misapprehensions and forgeries and God knows what all. It's an imperfect thing. But this imperfection has nothing to do with the attempt to do it."

Foote knows something of attempting the impossible. Between 1946 and 1954 he published six novels, including the Civil War–era fictional work, *Shiloh.* The late Bennett Cerf, then editor of Random House, thought Foote the ideal writer to do a brief history of the Civil War, and approached him with the proposal.

The project metamorphosed—rather than evolved—into his massive trilogy, which avoided a "capsule" history's potential for reductiveness and distortion.

"As soon as I settled down to doing it, it seemed to me a short summary of the war, no matter how one touched on the highlights, was a highly unsatisfactory way to spend your time either writing or reading. I suppose there's a use for such a thing, but it would be more like an encyclopedia article than a book."

By no means did Foote anticipate how the assignment would expand . . . from an estimate of one to two years to complete a short history to the reality of two decades for *The Civil War: A Narrative.*

"I misunderstood the writing of history. When I began, it was going to be about a 200,000-word thing. And my output over the years is generally about 100,000 words a year, working very hard. In any case, I thought I'd do these 200,000 words of history in one year. Since most of it was already written for me, all I had to do was put it into marvelous prose.

"I thought it would be easy. It was not. It was exactly the same. And I turned out about 100,000 words a year."

Surprisingly, he says writing an historical narrative felt no different from writing fiction.

"In writing history you get your facts out of documents, and from a wide source of reading and picking up this, that, and the other. In a novel you get your 'facts' out of memory or imagination. But once you've got them, I didn't find any difference in my treatment of them, whether a fact came out of a document or it came out of my memory or imagination. They were both very real facts to me."

Foote insists that the Civil War is an experience central to the lives of Americans, Southerners in particular. It is in many respects our *Iliad.* And like that timeless work, its chief value rests in defining who we are as a nation.

"I think that anybody who really wants to understand modern America has to understand those things that in mid-19th century America led to the fight, the fight itself, and the things that led away from it. How can Americans know who they are unless they find out where they came from? I deplore disinterest in American history in anybody. To me, American history is one of the most dramatic of any national history I know of.

"We are unique in being this really patchwork creation of all kinds of races. It's what gives us our identity. And not to understand how that came about and the various tribulations that resulted from it is to me to miss a great experience, with truly remarkable people you meet along the way."

As for writing about that grand, amorphous, somewhat theatrical realm we call the South, Foote says the principal task is dealing with all the paradoxes it presents.

"It's a challenge because Southern history is so full of all kinds of contradictions, more here than anywhere in the country. You run into all kinds of strange things."

Foote, who moved to Tennessee from his native Mississippi in 1953, attended the University of North Carolina. But the closest he ever got to the Holy City was forays to Myrtle Beach as a student. The Delta, it appears, is simply too compelling to leave.

Even in fiction. In the works is *Two Gates to the City,* which Foote describes as "a big long Delta novel I intend to finish if I can ever stop all this hoo-rah and get back to it. All six of my novels really have been about the Delta."

June 18, 1995

Howard Bahr's *The Year of Jubilo*

June 1865. War's end finds a young Confederate soldier on the road to his Mississippi home. It is a year of jubilation and contrasting turmoil.

Gawain Harper, a former English teacher, is about to discover the passions stirred by the Civil War haven't yet been expended.

The inspiration for Howard Bahr's second historical novel, *The Year of Jubilo* (Henry Holt), arrived in the image of a boy, late of Confederate service, standing in a road on a summer morning, transfixed by the sounds of a sawmill.

"There are two important symbols in that image," says Bahr, 53, a one-time railway worker whose first book was the widely praised *The Black Flower* (1997). "The boy coming back from that terrible experience, carrying with him ruin and chaos and death, is returning to a world turned upside down. On the other hand, he hears this sawmill, a symbol of rebuilding and regeneration.

"The world is already beginning to rebuild itself just as he comes out of the darkness. And he's going to be a part of that."

Bahr has rendered a book superficially similar to Charles Frazier's *Cold Mountain* in that it taps into that most primal of human stories: the voyage home after a far-flung and perilous "adventure."

Harper is no epic hero, however. He enlisted in the army only to mollify the father of Morgan Rhea, who made marrying his daughter contingent on Harper volunteering for service. She is waiting for him, he hopes, but also in wait are the forces of anarchy, prelude to the coming nightmare of Reconstruction.

The Year of Jubilo, a title drawn from the bitterly comic song by abolitionist Henry Clay Work, is an exploration of the Civil War's aftermath through the eyes of soldiers and civilians.

"Work's song, like most comedy, turns on bitterness. It's an expression of black resentment against the white masters. It corresponds to the story in that what I wanted to show in all these people is that they are all trying to get free of that dreadful war. When they finally did, it was the year of jubilo for all of them."

As with most wars, the interim of jubilation succumbs to the stark reality of the consequences. Harper's hometown of Cumberland, Miss., is occupied by Yankee troops, and there are marauding bands of ex-Confederate soldiers who prey on them as well as on Southerners deemed not to have contributed to the conduct of "the Cause" as fervently as they might.

Harper wants to resume his life and renew his relationship with Rhea, only to be drawn into an exercise in revenge by her father, whose other daughter and son-in-law were murdered by the renegade rebels.

"This chaos is a significant part of the story and something I'm quite interested in," says the Meridian, Miss., native, curator from 1982 to 1993 of Rowan Oak, the William Faulkner homestead and museum in Oxford. "Harper confronts a total loss of order and structure in society. What order there was could only be maintained by the people themselves—and the Yankee army. In Mississippi, they were lucky in a way that the late-arriving Federals were there."

Bahr, a professor of English at Motlow State Community College in Tullahoma, Tenn., deflects the notion that his own experiences in coming home from the Vietnam War—to find a nation changed and still contentious—were fodder for the novel.

"I was a sailor, and I had no problems coming back. But the idea of war and its effect on the human spirit always has interested me."

Like Faulkner, Bahr is principally concerned with the human heart. He says a novelist of the Civil War has advantages not at the disposal of an historian.

"Mr. Faulkner said that truth and the facts are not always the same. I think that if you read a book of history about the Battle of Chancellorsville, you get the historical facts. But you don't read the truth—the things of the human heart—until you've read *The Red Badge of Courage.* Along with that comes a responsibility for the novelist to tell the story as truly as possible, and without having an agenda."

Rather than a new literary groundswell, Bahr believes work of the caliber of *Cold Mountain* and his own books, which reviewers have praised for their lyricism, represents points on a continuum of worthy Civil War fiction.

"Civil War fiction will get better as times goes on, as we move further away from having an agenda and as we grow more able to present the experience authentically and realistically. I have the advantage of having been a re-enactor, which people look at with a jaundiced eye from time to time. There's a large extremist fringe, to be sure. But re-enactors also have uncovered an extensive body of knowledge that was lost on the minutiae of the soldier's daily life. Re-enactors brought this back, not professional historians."

Most gratifying for Bahr is knowing that readers are falling in love with his characters as readily as he did.

"It's a joy to me. And it underscores that the most important things are the story and the characters, not me. Creative talent is something one is a steward of. One of the mistakes people make is to take themselves too seriously. Take the gift seriously, the art and the craft, but not yourself."

Bahr wrote for years before getting his first book published by the Nautical and Aviation Publishing Co., which moved its offices from Baltimore to Charleston two years ago. And he credits N&A publisher Jan Snouck-Hurgronje with steering him toward a larger publishing house.

"That small press took a big chance on me and gave me my start," says Bahr. "I suppose nothing happens until it's supposed to. I wrote for a long time. It just took me longer to get there.

"And yes, I do feel some pressure to live up to a certain standard. It's the second novel syndrome. I'd hoped there wasn't a third-novel syndrome, but there is. I'm halfway through my third book, which is set in the 1930s, but for practical as well as moral reasons, I'll never accept an advance of royalties until I have a completed and approved manuscript on the editor's desk."

June 4, 2000

James M. McPherson's *Writing the Civil War*

James M. McPherson, Pulitzer Prize-winning author of *Battle Cry of Freedom* (1989), may be the preeminent Civil War scholar in America today. He is most certainly among those in greatest demand as a consultant and speaker.

A professor of American history at Princeton University, McPherson gained heightened renown as a source and on-air contributor for Ken Burns's PBS series "The Civil War."

McPherson will be in Charleston on Friday as moderator of a round-table discussion, "Writing the Civil War: The Quest to Understand." Featuring a panel of 13 of the country's most distinguished scholars, "Writing the Civil War" opens its two-day, two-city run on Thursday at the Capstone Conference Center on the campus of the University of South Carolina in Columbia.

"I would say that discussions such as this help to stimulate intelligent interest in inquiries into a whole range of issues associated with the war," says McPherson. "There is a huge reservoir of interest in the subject, and there are many ways to manifest that interest. The real contribution of round tables and lectures, where there is a question period following (the address) is that there's direct communication involved. It's the best way to learn, in my opinion."

McPherson will be joined at both sites by fellow moderator William J. Cooper Jr., professor of history at Louisiana State University, with whom he edited the 1998 book *Writing the Civil War* (USC Press), on which the conference is based. Apart from McPherson and Cooper, the panel is composed of noted historians Gary W. Gallagher and Michael F. Holt (the University of Virginia), Reid Mitchell (the University of Maryland–Baltimore County), Emory M. Thomas (the University of Georgia), Michael Les Benedict (Ohio State), Peter Kolchin (University of Delaware), James L. Roark (Emory University), Phillip Shaw Paludan (University of Kansas), Joseph T. Glatthaar (University of Houston), Drew Gilpin Faust (University of Pennsylvania) and George C. Rable (University of Alabama). Each participant contributed essays to the book, which not only underscored the scope and diversity of Civil War scholarship, but also suggested new directions for inquiry.

"One area that I think is fairly new but very promising—and I know a lot of studies that are going on right now about it—is the study of the impact of the war on communities, not only communities in the South, where it is most obvious, but also in the North: in Boston, Chicago and New York, for example.

"Even in the South, a book on the impact of the war on Gettysburg never had been done, but a colleague of mine is doing it now. We want to learn what kind of effect it has on a society or community. The focus of so much Civil War history has been on the military and political dimensions of it. This differing perspective is a belated consequence of what's been happening in the field of American history in the past 30 years, which is a much greater emphasis on social history, a recognition of the importance of this question."

All told, McPherson has written nine books on the war, most recently *For Cause and Comrades: Why Men Fought in the Civil War*, which garnered the 1998 Lincoln Prize.

In researching the book over a period of years, he read nearly 25,000 letters penned by about 800 soldiers, as well as the diary entries of some 250 other combatants. Together, they helped afford a feel for what the average soldier was really fighting for.

"Every now and then you strike a nugget," McPherson says. "Gradually the picture starts to form and gets rich over time. Even the routine helps us build a picture."

The last time a concerted look at this subject was taken was almost 40 years ago in Bell I. Wiley's two-volume study, *The Life of Johnny Reb* and *The Life of Billy Yank*.

"Wiley certainly pioneered this kind of inquiry. After his second book came out, a long time went by before another generation of historians started looking into it. There were several books on soldiers that looked at this question in part in the late '80s and in the '90s, but none that probed to this extent."

Unlike many, McPherson's enduring fascination with the war has its roots not in youth, but in graduate school. "I was at Johns Hopkins University in the early 1960s, at a time when the early civil rights movement was gaining momentum in a major way. It made a huge impression on me. At the time I was studying Southern history and was struck by the parallels between the times and events in which I lived and what had happened years before.

"I was drawn to the Civil War as a way of trying to make more sense of my own time."

February 21, 1999

William C. Davis's *Look Away!*

From Cannae to Chickamauga, the romantic sweep of generals and their campaigns, their great battles and blunders, has had a stranglehold on the popular imagination.

A preoccupation with the trumpets and pincer movements, charismatic figures and brigands, has been the Achilles' heel of many an historian. What has often been lost is the broader social context and the political machinations transpiring behind the scenes.

Among the foremost writers on the Civil War, William C. Davis takes us inside the hearts and minds of the Confederacy's founding fathers in *Look Away! A History of the Confederate States of America* (The Free Press), with an emphasis on the career of ardent secessionist Robert Barnwell Rhett.

"This is not a pro or anti-Confederate book," says Davis, director of programs at the Virginia Center for Civil War Studies at Virginia Tech. "While I don't believe in this business of celebrating the past, it doesn't mean the people I've written about don't deserve respect and understanding. They deserve to be taken at face value, on their own terms, and not have what they did or failed to do recast into a mold that fits some contemporary ideology."

Twice nominated for the Pulitzer Prize, the Independence, Mo., native is the author or editor of more than 40 books on the Civil War and Southern history, and remains the only three-time winner of the Jefferson Davis Prize for Confederate History.

In offering a more comprehensive history of the Confederacy, *Look Away!* also presents an alternative view of the thrust of the Confederate "rebellion," scrutinizing the accepted portrait of the Confederacy and recasting it as not so much a revolutionary movement as a reformist one.

Davis maintains the individuals involved saw themselves quite differently from what has emerged as the conventional image of militant secessionists who fomented war rather than alter their way of life and submit to the North. Rather, their self-image was that of defenders of the democratic principle who sought to address flaws in the U.S. Constitution by developing one of their own.

In their view, this "noble experiment" was not a drive to establish a wholly new system of governance. They thought the right of secession needed to be recognized. They instituted the first civil service reform in the U.S. with their constitution, and abolished pork barrel legislation—ironic, since their descendants would become masters of it. They also gave Jefferson Davis a line-item veto as well. These were genuine reforms. They thought they could create a system without political parties or partisanship, which of course was naïve.

"The Confederacy tried to institutionalize a form of democracy that suited their needs and their times. Confederate democracy was the last gasp of 18th-century Tory conservatism. Most of the Confederate states were essentially run by oligarchies—20 families ran South Carolina, for example, and perhaps still do. They all observed the forms and rhetoric of democracy—freedom and individual rights—but they resisted spreading the vote and extending education."

It is universal human instinct to preserve what you have and protect the world you know, Davis reminds us.

"There was tremendous fear over the abolition of slavery and over losing control of their world. Along with that, the motive forces behind secession were the issues surrounding slavery itself. States rights is an argument that comes out of a Lost Cause myth. The issue of the spread of slavery to the new territories was just as important."

Davis insists this is not a controversial approach.

"I don't find much controversy in this at all. I really try to reflect what the people themselves were doing and saying at the time. Robert Barnwell Rhett said unequivocally, and I quote: 'The occasion of secession was slavery.' And since he was for years a leading exponent of secession, I think he knew why he thought he was doing what he was doing. The founding fathers of the Confederacy were unapologetic about it. They said throughout 1860–61 that it was about slavery."

Davis says his overriding interest in researching and composing the book was in trying to break down persistent stereotypes and clichés about the Confederacy, "all of which are still heavily in use today by social groups on the right and left."

"A more complex and much more interesting story is that of the political movement. The Confederate founding fathers were reactionaries, to be sure, but also reformers, ideologues but also idealists—a very contradictory position. By knowing more of the nuances of the Confederate story there is a better chance of finding out why this episode of the past is so much with us today, and why we misunderstand it."

One of the chief misconceptions was that there was uniformity of opinion within the Confederacy. In fact, political contentiousness was pronounced. And Rhett was one of the most impassioned and contrary figures, a man who led a group of disgruntled extremists in forming what was, in essence, an opposition party within the Confederacy.

"I think it's remarkable the Confederacy survived as long as it did when you consider what it had to go through," says Davis, who intends to branch out into earlier periods of Southern history. "Rhett, for example, was the complete ideologue. He was referred to in his own time as a one-idea politician, and that idea was secession. A perversely fascinating man, bigoted and hypocritical, with a fanatical dedication to this one idea. His family, as well as his personal and political fortunes, suffered for it. Although he and his defenders characterized it as having the courage of his convictions, it's an example of the kind of extremism that brings on revolutions like this. The same thing happened in France.

"Rhett was immediately sidelined after secession came to pass. He was too impractical. He'd kill a new nation on principle as quickly as he'd kill the existing one. He spent the rest of the war attacking the new Confederacy, creating a second party in what was to have become a one-party system."

With four books out in the past 13 months, Davis took a different tack with *Look Away!* by employing the voices and letters of the common people to a much greater degree.

"I try not to pass judgment, pro or con, but to report what happened and why. But I certainly hope a sense of empathy is there for those people caught 'in the gale of the world.' They should not be judged by the ethics or sensibilities of today—slavery was legal then, remember. They should be seen in the context of their time."

April 7, 2002

Lee Smith's *On Agate Hill*

One should excuse Lee Smith for feeling a bit like Inman in *Cold Mountain*, hobbling through the countryside on his way to sanctuary.

For Smith, whose novel, *On Agate Hill*, introduces us to another Odysseus of the Civil War era, sanctuary is the company of kindred spirits—avid readers—her audience at the annual Post and Courier Fall Book and Author Luncheon.

She will move gingerly to the podium, nursing a broken ankle suffered not in heroic flight, but while ambling in the woods with her dog, Betty.

"I have a broken ankle and a big cast," says the Hillsborough, N.C., author," but I'll be there."

On Agate Hill, her 12th novel, is Smith's first true period piece. And she had a tough act to follow in 2002's Southern Book Critics Circle award-winning novel, *The Last Girls.*

"I was very lucky with *Last Girls* and amazed that it did so well," says Smith, recipient of an Academy Award in Fiction from the American Academy of Arts and Letters in 1999. "It was the first time I ever had a book on the best-seller list.

"The new book presented a very different writing experience. The reception to it has been surprising to me, too, because this one is almost so private to me. With *Last Girls*, I knew I was tapping into a big demographic—my age group of women—but with *On Agate Hill* it was literally a personal outpouring."

Chance Encounter

"When my husband and I moved into this very old (1838) house in Hillsborough, suddenly a neighbor appeared, an old man, with a long story about the house. There was this whole legend of obsessive love. One thing led to another. It was like falling down the rabbit hole into another century and another world. It was a wonderful experience for me."

But not one without a measure of pain.

The new book is a departure for Smith in several respects, not simply its period setting, but its extended use of letters to further the narrative, a somewhat more muted description than is customary in her writing, the panoramic scope of the story and the framing device that uses a modern-day student writing a letter.

The novel's protagonist, though hardly the lone distinctive character, is Molly Petree. We meet her at age 13 in 1872, a precocious, post-Civil War Southern orphan, and a "spitfire," says Smith.

"She tells us this from the start: 'I do not care. This is the way I am and this is the way it was. And I'm going to write the story of my life on this Earth.' I admire that: her grit and her determination, too."

Yet early on, Petree is a girl adrift. We see her first in a ruined North Carolina plantation called Agate Hill, the home of her dying uncle, Junius. She is making her first diary entry: "I am like a ghost girl wafting through this ghost house seen by none."

"She goes from that uncertainty to being fully a woman and claiming it all: responsibility, and every other thing she can get. The book is kind of dialectic between hanging back and going for it."

Mass Movement

In addition to letters and journal entries from varied characters, Smith employs poems, recipes, songs and court records in her narrative.

"I've always been so interested in all kinds of documents and artifacts and the way they can combine to tell a story. I've done a lot of oral history work and have always been fascinated by the arbitrary nature of history. It all depends on who finds the box of letters and journals. One person can conceive of a particular sort of story, and another can produce something quite different from the same material.

"One aspect of the Civil War I had never considered began to seem really apparent to me as I became more addicted to reading old letters and diaries, learning what life was like in North Carolina during the war and Reconstruction. It had not hit me the degree to which there were so many refugees. There were all kinds of people of every cast and station, leaving where they were and fleeing north. Everyone was uprooted and on the move. I became interested in the whole refugee movement. Molly is a refugee girl, one of many girls and children and orphans who ended up in our part of Piedmont North Carolina."

Smith had no inkling of just how intensely personal the experience of writing the book would become.

"The devastation of Hurricane Katrina was going on as I was writing, and seeing those real refugees tugged at my heart. Then my son, Josh, died (at 34), and we were unmoored. Suddenly, Molly's plight became real to me—when I was able to write again. I felt displaced and a pilgrim, myself. The book references her emotional urgency, and the story turned darker. It became a book about loss, the loss of all kinds of things."

Flexing New Sinew

Smith also exercised literary muscles she had not used before.

"It was *all* very new for me. I was writing in different voices. I was engaging the reader a lot more than I had in the past. Different narratives and different kinds of storytellers are used, and the reader really has to help me figure out the story and understand it. I'm really accustomed to planning a novel all the way through, but with this one, the writing experience was so intense that the story just took off and I let it go where it was going. I threw my outline away. Near the end, a kind of grace arrived, and this figure comes into the book that represents my son."

Smith strove to balance a melancholy tone with a sense of what is true, making the familiar touchstones of the time work for her.

"You don't want to become melodramatic or self-pitying or sentimental. The deeper and truer the emotion, the more you want it to be deep and true in the writing; I don't want to tidy it up or prettify. Also, the big problem for anybody who wants to write about the Old South is the fact that so many of the elements of Southern literature have become so hackneyed and clichéd. But you can't change the actual details. What you have to do is find an original voice and hope the authenticity of that voice will overcome the familiarity of the details.

"In the end, this novel was a real gift to me. I can't exercise any sort of purchase on it at all. It was such an experience that now I'm just coming up for air. I think I want to write some short stories for a while."

November 5, 2006

Robert Rosen's *Jewish Confederates*

Robert Rosen knows the tentacles of political correctness extend not merely into the present, but into the past. Revisionist history is one thing, vacant history another.

In *Jewish Confederates*, which will be released Monday by the University of South Carolina Press, the Charleston lawyer and author says one of the principal factors in the invisibility of Southern Jews who supported and fought for the Confederacy is the reluctance of Jewish historians to recognize them.

"First of all, the Jewish community in the South was very small and, after the war, they were as devastated as everyone else. So there were fewer Southern histories written than Northern ones.

"But another reason, I believe, is that people in the Jewish history profession don't like the fact that there were Jews fighting for the Confederacy."

Among the more astounding things Rosen discovered during the 10 years he invested in researching and writing the book was that the first practicing Jew in the Senate, Benjamin Franklin Jonas of Louisiana, who had been a Confederate soldier, was never written about.

"If you asked a thousand educated Jews who was first, they'd probably say it was FDR's right arm, Herbert Lehman of New York."

Why is it, Rosen asks, that scholarly journals see fit to include the most inconsequential material about the most marginal people, but utterly ignore a man like Jonas?

"It's political correctness. No one is actively suppressing the information. It's just that the academic world is not interested in it."

Rosen counters by introducing readers to Southern Jews of the 1860s. Apart from the prominent figure of Judah P. Benjamin, who served in Jefferson Davis's Cabinet, the legacy of Jewish Confederates has been largely unknown.

Rosen chronicles the extent of Southern Jewry's participation in the war and the strength of Jewish commitment. He uncovers a wealth of information—enlivened by biographical sketches—on the experiences of officers, enlisted men, businessmen, politicians, nurses, rabbis and physicians.

Rosen suspects his third book, successor to *A Short History of Charleston* and *Confederate Charleston*, will be somewhat controversial in Jewish circles, owing to his conviction that Southern Jews were doing something laudable in fighting for the Confederacy.

Quite apart from the issue of slavery, he says, "They were living up to what they saw as their patriotic duty."

In his commentary on the book, noted historian William C. Davis states that "perhaps no identifiable group of Southerners represented a greater paradox than the Jewish community . . . Rosen opens a window on the unlikely story of a people apart, with their own religion and cultural customs, functioning within a Southern community that regarded itself as separate and distinct from other Americans."

But tolerance, at least in this one regard, was the order of the day.

"One of the principal myths was that the South was unfriendly to Jewish people," says Rosen. "This is the exact opposite of the truth, which, like the stereotype of Jews being uniformly liberal in attitude, really refers only to certain points in time. People are thinking of a later period.

"There was much less anti-Semitism in the South than in the North in the Civil War era. Jefferson Davis and Robert E. Lee were very close to many Jews. The history of the antebellum South in general and the Confederacy in particular speaks very well for the South in terms of equal treatment of Jewish citizens. But this is nothing I discovered. Any book of Jewish history confirms this much."

A second misconception, equally as persistent, deals with the motivation of Jewish citizens who fought for the Confederacy, Rosen says.

"First of all, Jews were more equal and more accepted in the South. They, in turn, accepted Southern beliefs about honor and race. They weren't opposed to slavery; some even owned slaves. They felt they had to prove they were loyal citizens. Just like African-American troops who fought for the Union, Jews who volunteered for war service felt they had to prove themselves as patriots and as men."

The majority of Jewish Confederates were recent immigrants who represented a cross section of all economic and social strata. Rosen, mindful of the hazards of superimposing modern sensibilities on earlier periods, may not agree with their positions on a given issue, but he applauds their commitment.

"I'm very clear on that. The Jewish community in the South has to wrestle with the fact that, as has been said, they fought on the wrong side of history. But they paved the way for the acceptance of Jewish people. Their mission was to do their duty as they saw it. You must remember they had left Germany and Poland where they couldn't vote and were given a great gift here in the South."

To those who object, believing that defense of the Confederacy is in opposition to the tenets of Jewish faith, Rosen responds that it is as much an oversimplification as the belief that the war was entirely about the issue of slavery.

"People always want their ancestors to have behaved in an admirable fashion—but by *their* contemporary standards. The reality is that it was not against the tenets of Judaism as practiced then, but as practiced today. That's the big point on the question of morality. Jews were supposed to support the state when it was the law of the land. They were very comfortable as Southerners and as Confederates."

While there may not have been generals or legendary war heroes, many of the people Rosen profiles (and often recovers from obscurity) served with distinction.

"Benjamin was the most successful politically as secretary of state, while (Prussian immigrant) Maj. Adolph Proskauer of the Alabama 12th was the most effective commander. Another was Alexander Hart of the 5th Louisiana. Naturally, there were those who were ineffective as well."

Some dealt with distinct disadvantages, such as Col. Abraham C. Myers, whose task as quartermaster general of the Confederacy was complicated by the South's shallow pockets and pivotal lack of industry.

As with all historians, Rosen's research also yielded its share of frustration: material that could not be unearthed, some tantalizing piece of information that could not be confirmed.

"There are some of those. There is one fellow named Eschelman, commander of the Washington Artillery, a Louisiana unit, who has a Jewish name. But I never could prove it. Most Jewish immigrants were German, and I could have claimed him, but I didn't. There were several people like that, plus a lot of high-ranking officers who many Jewish historians would like to claim.

"You can imagine how rare photos of Jewish Confederates are, and I've collected as many as I could. But it's hard to document conclusively that they were Jewish. Of course, this is true of any history; you've got to let go of certain things.

"It's frustrating to end the book feeling like I didn't cover certain communities in the South. My ambition was to write a book about the Jewish South, and I've done the best job I can."

Striking a balance between academic rigor and general-audience accessibility can be challenging. Rosen employed a highly readable approach girded by 50 pages of footnotes and a substantial bibliography.

"I tried my best to write a book that is a scholarly and popular history at the same time. But this *is* a book of primary research. I traveled extensively and pored over some 10,000 pages of documents.

"I'm very proud of *A Short History of Charleston*, which is a kind of love poem to the city, but this was a much greater task. I think I held myself to a higher standard on this book. In the past I relied on other historians for their interpretations, at least those with whom I agreed."

Rosen says that another of his motivations in writing the book derives from family history.

"My grandfather came here and was accepted by the community 40 years after the war. One reason he was so readily accepted is that people remembered that Jews did their part during the war. I wanted to reveal their stories. These people deserve to be remembered."

October 15, 2000

Douglas Bostick's *Charleston Under Siege*

It is the task of historians, popular or academic, to put flesh on the bones of history, to verify and interpret events and attitudes based on the sensibilities of the age in question.

It is a lesson in which Douglas Bostick is well-versed.

"And it is one of the more challenging things to do when attempting to write history through 21st-century eyes," says the James Island native, author of *Charleston Under Siege: The Impregnable City.*

"For any historian, no matter how well-intentioned, it is your responsibility to go back to the original materials for your research," Bostick says. "It is important to try to immerse yourself in what was happening at the time, and you can't do that through secondary stories or a superficial understanding of events. All of us bring some degree of bias to the work, but those of us who succeed do so because we try to put our bias to rest as much as possible.

"These are not political statements, but descriptions of what actually transpired."

Bostick's book, his 15th, is the latest entry in the Civil War Sesquicentennial Series being published locally by The History Press, and a chronicle of Charleston that seeks to tell a more complete story.

A broader depiction of the Siege of Charleston often is overshadowed by the drama of single events, says Bostick: the "first shot" on Fort Sumter that precipitated the war, the story of the Confederate submarine Hunley or the July 18, 1863, attack on Battery Wagner that inspired the 1989 film "Glory."

"I've been noodling around with it (the book) for a number of years. Mainly, it was with the idea of bringing these often forgotten stories to the forefront again, so that as the sesquicentennial observance unfolds over the next four years, people will have an opportunity not only to understand these stories but to search for themselves. There are so many stories to be told about the horrific nature of the war here and the accomplishments on both sides."

Bostick, an eighth-generation South Carolinian, earned degrees from the College of Charleston and the University of South Carolina.

He is a former staff and faculty member of the University of South Carolina and the University of Maryland. His previous book in the Sesquicentennial Series was *The Union Is Dissolved! Charleston and Fort Sumter in the Civil War* (2009).

Charleston was the glittering brass ring, the prize that the Union Army and Navy coveted. And not necessarily to merely occupy.

As Gen. Henry Wager Halleck wrote to Gen. William T. Sherman, "Should you capture Charleston, I hope that by some accident the place may be destroyed."

Despite 567 days of constant attack by infantry, gun batteries and the Union fleet, Charleston was bloodied but not shattered. It would not be until the evacuation of Confederate forces to reinforce Gen. Joe Johnston in North Carolina that the federal government finally gained control of the city.

"In effect, Charleston never fell to an invading army," Bostick says. "It was the strategic choice of the Confederacy to remove its troops. But if Sherman had come, he would have taken the city with no trouble. There are all sorts of theories as to why he didn't."

How did the city withstand such an unrelenting assault?

"Truthfully," says Bostick, "some of it was due to what in some ways were inept Union commanders. On the other hand, one of the most interesting aspects of the story is how forward-thinking some commanders were. Of all the generals in both armies, Gen. (P.G.T.) Beauregard on the Confederate side and Gen. (Quincy) Gillmore on the Union side were as fascinated with the new technologies of the age as anyone. Both chose to employ them here in their own strategies. In the 1860s, this was very cutting edge, and it was all happening right here."

Bostick cites the example of Gillmore's use of a system of hydrogen gaslights during the Union defense of Fort Sumter, both to confuse Confederate forces and to provide his men with the ability to fire with effect.

"Then, on the Confederate side, there was the development of new mines and torpedoes deployed in the defense of Charleston, so much so that when (Fort) Sumter was reduced to nothing more than an infantry outpost, the Union Navy was still too intimidated to loop around Sumter and get into the inner harbor. Beauregard's other accomplishments involved the use of semi-submersible steamers called Davids."

Bostick is a member of the First Shot Commemorative Committee, which, in coordination with S.C. Department of Natural Resources and the town of James Island, is holding an event April 12 to commemorate the first shot fired on that date in 1861. "We've located a mortar which is an exact match of one of the two batteries that were there," he says, "and it is being shipped here from Wisconsin by the owners. A commemorative shot will be fired during a one-hour ceremony which honors all South Carolinians, white and black, who perished during the war."

December 26, 2010

James Hutchisson. Photograph by Brad Nettles

The Southern Renaissance

"The man who writes about himself and his own time is the only man who writes about all people and about all time."

George Bernard Shaw, *The Sanity of Art* (1907)

I confess. As a fellow sometimes given to cynical pronouncements, I have counted among my heroes such worthies as Oscar Wilde, George Bernard Shaw, Ambrose Bierce, Dorothy Parker and H. L. Mencken.

Known as the "Sage of Baltimore," it was Mencken (1880–1956) who ignited southern ire with scathing essays on the region, notably "The Sahara of the Bozart" (1920), in which he dismissed the South as an intellectual wasteland. There was something deeper behind these caustic satires, namely a distrust of populist democracy and the "ignorant" hayseed, that was not confined to his Southern whipping boy.

But at least one period in early 20th-century Southern history belied Mencken's summary wave of the hand.

The post–World War I phenomenon known as the Southern Renaissance dispensed with romantic glorifications of the Lost Cause in favor of three sober, complex themes: the yoke of history; individual identity in a region dominated by community, religion and family; and race. These themes—and a vital critique of the South from within—were accompanied by the new techniques of modernism, and over the years their exemplars have secured a niche in the pantheon of American letters (though in some cases their reputations had to be recovered and revived). Often, the same themes were embodied in the fine art of the era.

The roots of this cultural rebirth usually are attributed to The Fugitives, an assembly of poets and critics at Vanderbilt University that included Robert Penn Warren, John Crowe Ransom, Allen Tate and Donald Donaldson.

But Charleston and South Carolina also contributed a significant share of "revolutionaries" to this admirable movement.

Here, in brief, are contemporary takes on their enduring value, as artists whose lives and work inspired some of the greatest writers of the following generations and as unique individuals.

James Hutchisson's *DuBose Heyward*

James Hutchisson's face breaks into a sheepish grin as he recounts the genesis of his biography of Charleston literary lion DuBose Heyward.

After publishing *The Rise of Sinclair Lewis* in 1995, the Citadel English professor was casting about for a new project when a friend suggested an appropriate, and stimulating, subject might be Heyward, who shot to fame with the novel *Porgy*, but saw his star eclipsed after collaborating with George and Ira Gershwin on the opera "Porgy and Bess."

"I thought DuBose Heyward was black."

Learning otherwise was the biggest surprise in all his research on a figure pivotal to both the Charleston and Southern literary reawakenings of the '20s and '30s.

The result, *DuBose Heyward: A Charleston Gentleman and the World of Porgy and Bess*, has just been released by the University of Mississippi Press.

"Once I'd read 'Porgy' carefully, I realized that the voice of the novel was very much the voice of a sort of white aristocrat, though not at all a condescending one," says Hutchisson. "The more digging I did, the more I discovered that there was a great story waiting to be told here—this white Southerner who develops an interest in Gullah culture and not only goes on to immortalize a people but to broaden his own social conscience as he matured as a writer."

Heyward's transformation from social conservative to ardent progressive was both an evolutionary process and the result of an epiphany.

"It was evolutionary in that everyone's sensibilities change and grow, but I think it was when he got to New York in 1926 and 1927, after *Porgy* made him an overnight sensation and the play was going to be staged there. In New York, he began to see African-Americans in an entirely different context. This was the beginning of the Harlem Renaissance, and Heyward consorted with many of the now famous black writers. I think that was the epiphany."

A private, modest man who as a youth had been immersed in Gullah culture, Heyward moved from relative obscurity in 1924 to overnight celebrity one year later with the publication of *Porgy.* It also meant ostracism from the more traditional elements of Charleston society, something exacerbated by his later book, *Mamba's Daughters.*

Hutchisson says that although people link Heyward with "Porgy and Bess," first produced in 1935, this came well after the apex of his fame in the '20s.

"He was a versatile figure. He was a poet. He was a charismatic lecturer on poetry and art. The newspapers dubbed him the Missionary Poet, after he traveled around preaching the coming of the ascendancy of Southern poetry. It was then that he peaked. 'Porgy and Bess' was something that he had been working toward. He and George Gershwin had talked about doing it, off and on, for 10 years. It was a very long wait for him before it came to pass.

"I don't want to say it was the end of his career, but in some ways it was. The few things he did after that were not nearly as potent and vital as the work he did in the '20s."

Hutchisson, whose next book, *The Conjugal Muse*, will deal with famous writers who were married to each other, sought to amplify what we know of Heyward's involvement in most phases of the production of the opera, a larger role for which he has rarely received credit. Heyward wrote the libretto and nearly half the arias singlehandedly or in collaboration with Ira Gershwin.

"To this day, he has been overshadowed by the Gershwins. By all rights, on some of the arias Heyward's name should have gone on them as single lyricist. Ira tried to convince him to do this, but Heyward didn't want to take the credit. And I really think this is one of the reasons that his reputation has gone into eclipse.

"He was so self-effacing, someone who did not want to be in the spotlight. He was a reticent Southerner. All the writers and artists during the Charleston Renaissance were very private. I think they were as intimate a group as the Bloomsbury people, and so on, but they didn't have that modernist sensibility where they would record all their subjective thoughts about themselves in letters and journals. A lot of the letters they sent out they told people to burn them up after reading."

After the Charleston gentry recoiled from *Porgy*, Heyward, who already had begun to distance himself from the city by the mid-1920s, was living either in and out of New York or in the home he had built in Hendersonville, N.C. Though wounded by the snub, he remained devoted to his art.

"Heyward was willing to sacrifice what he had to in order to achieve his aims. He realized he couldn't survive as an artist in Charleston. He needed to have that distance. Ultimately, the Carolina Art Association provided a salve for his wounds. The city not only invited him back but embraced him. Times had changed somewhat, but not that much."

The Dock Street Theatre was where Heyward came to lick his wounds following the initial financial failure of "Porgy and Bess" in 1935. Fleeing New York, he bought his South Battery home in 1937.

"It's a wonderful example of the way you can go home again, and find a very receptive audience," Hutchisson says. "Few recall today that 'Porgy and Bess' was a relative failure. The Gershwin brothers and Heyward lost the $5,000 each had invested in the show, so it was a financial failure.

"And then the critics carped at it because they couldn't decide whether it was a legitimate opera or a Broadway show. Rouben Mamoulian, who was the director of the play version and the opera (and later an innovative film director), had a wonderful line about that. He said, 'You give people something delicious to eat, and then they complain because they have no word for it.' Which is true. And to some degree today that question persists. What exactly is it? A hybrid form?"

Hutchisson views the question in a positive light.

"I really think that Gershwin, with Heyward's input, did succeed in bringing about a new form of art. The fact that it was a form of art that enfranchised African-Americans in the theater made it all the more significant."

It also has staying power, having metamorphosed over time, which Hutchisson believes all great works of art should do.

"'Porgy and Bess' was something entirely different in 1935 than it was in the 1950s and '60s during the civil rights era, and it's something entirely different today in the festivals in Europe where you see it performed. It has become this transcendent human document. Like 'Hamlet,' it's taken on archetypal significance. To me, that's the greatness of the opera."

Hutchisson writes that although Heyward has been slighted for his role in furthering the Southern Literary Renaissance, it was not so much Heyward who embodies the neglected factor as Charleston itself.

"That is, the group of writers that composed what we now loosely call the Charleston Renaissance group. He was certainly its spokesperson and the most visible, but collectively all of those people were on the leading edge of what would later emerge as the Southern literary movement."

In assaying Heyward's versatility as a writer of verse, short fiction, plays, novels and screenplays, Hutchisson had two principal goals: to recover Heyward from the "detritus of literary history" and to chart the development of a social critic who broke free of the trap of lofty social position.

"It may be stretching things a bit to refer to 'Porgy' as the first major Southern novel to portray blacks sympathetically, without condescension, but it was certainly among the most famous, and in terms of stirring up the literary establishment's self-consciousness of what it was writing about, the book was a wake-up call about a rich body of material that had been neglected or treated shabbily."

March 19, 2000

Susan Millar Williams's *A Devil and a Good Woman, Too*

Prominent among the handful of Southern writers championed by H. L. Mencken as a new breed of literary "anarchists," South Carolinian Julia Peterkin was the most unlikely of revolutionaries.

In the early 1920s, when the celebrated but caustic social critic of The Baltimore Sun was dismissing the South as an artistic and intellectual wasteland, Peterkin was one of the first to subvert what Mencken ridiculed as the mawkishly sentimental and tradition-mired world of Southern letters.

She was the first white writer to pen realistic novels and stories through the eyes of black plantation workers, telling her own story through the lives of the people around her—and creating a firestorm of protest. This enigmatic and almost forgotten figure—the first South Carolina native to win a Pulitzer Prize—defied convention and wrote precisely what she pleased. Until an unaccountable change of direction in the 1930s, Peterkin could be counted among Hemingway, Fitzgerald, Cather and O'Neill as writers who helped mold America's sexual and racial attitudes between the two world wars.

She is the subject of *A Devil and a Good Woman, Too: The Lives of Julia Peterkin* (University of Georgia Press), a comprehensive biography by McClellanville resident Dr. Susan Millar Williams, a professor of English at Trident Technical College.

Due out in October, the book was 10 years in the making.

"Julia Peterkin is one of the great characters in American literature," says Williams, who had unprecedented access to letters and other original materials in researching her first book. "The project forced me to become a generalist and learn to tell a story. A great storyteller deserves that her story be well told."

Peterkin (1880–1961) was the author of three novels, a short-story collection and, with photographer Doris Ulmann, a collection of essays titled *Roll,*

Jordan, Roll (1933) which, in a bizarre reversal, effectively repudiated many of her most ardently progressive opinions.

In 1903, Julia Mood married W. G. Peterkin and moved to Lang Syne Plantation near Columbia. For 15 years, she was tutored on the logistics of managing a large estate, which at that time embraced a community of 500 blacks and five whites. By 1920, Peterkin was a dutiful plantation mistress, an active member of the Daughters of the American Revolution and the United Daughters of the Confederacy.

Then came her story collection, *Green Thursday*, published by Knopf in 1924. It did not fare well commercially but did manage to stir a flurry of outrage from Southern whites. Peterkin's first novel, *Black April*, was released by Bobbs-Merrill in 1927, followed by *Scarlet Sister Mary*. The latter, in portraying the largely unfettered life of a vibrant black woman, was to some extent a reflection of the woman Peterkin wished to be: sexually liberated, independent and outspoken, Williams says.

"Most of all, Peterkin wished she could live as a man of that era, free to speak out, to be judged by her work, to make love to whomever she wished."

Peterkin's third and last novel, *Bright Skin*, now considered a brilliant dissection of social upheaval, appeared in 1932. Though she and Mencken had a falling out after her first book, he remained an admirer, as was Carl Sandburg.

"Peterkin was a breakthrough figure in the Southern Renaissance and also in the development of African-American fiction. Part of her gift was not to be attached to the prevailing ideologies or propaganda of her day. Yet no one ever seemed to talk about her. I made the commitment to doing this biography almost instantly after discovering her work.

"I had never encountered anything like these books before, and I absolutely fell in love with them. Before 1920, no writer had ever crossed the boundary between black and white in such a way."

Basic accounts of Peterkin's public life provided a starting point for Williams's research, but there was a dearth of material on the private Peterkin. Much of her life story was obscured by the writer herself.

"She resisted the idea of biography. She burned letters, covered her tracks. I think she's an amazingly contemporary figure, and the people in her day certainly would not have accepted her very well."

The first boon came when Williams put an ad in The New York Times Book Review and learned of 90 folders of love letters stored at Syracuse University—an unexpected trove of new material.

"I was also able to talk to members of her family and to the families of the people she wrote about. This was a second breakthrough for me. A door would seem open at exactly the right moment."

To devote her full energies to the book, Williams, who had just had a baby, quit all her jobs, only to be slowed by the visitation of Hurricane Hugo. But she slugged away, in part motivated by the University of Georgia Press's promise to reprint Peterkin's novels.

Peterkin's influence is a matter of opinion among modern writers and academics, black and white. Some see her as the progenitor of Zora Neale Hurston. Others do not. She may not have made a conscious attempt to produce a chronicle of the collapse of plantation agriculture on South Carolina's Gullah coast, but her skillful reportage of the scene nonetheless achieved it.

"She was terrified over the prospects of collapse, but she was also very good at reporting what was going on around her—very clear-eyed and realistic—without filtering it through the usual stereotypes and self-defensive strategies of the period. Peterkin was able to react simply as a human being and react to those human beings who were not being treated as such."

Peterkin was 40 when, in 1921, she began writing. And she remained a plantation mistress until the day she died, attended, somewhat paradoxically, by black servants.

Williams lauds her "Chekhovian detachment, her gift for capturing character in a few words of dialogue, her deadpan humor, her spare, lyrical prose." But subject always was paramount.

"No one else wrote about the plantation in this way, before or since. She seemed to view it as a settlement of black people and not as anything defined by white boundaries or purposes. She was also a great scene writer. And she found a way to render Gullah in literary form, not as an unintelligible joke dialect as some whites used it. No small achievement."

Apart from the nobler motivations, Williams suggests Peterkin also used her writing as a kind of revenge on the men in her life, who had always tried to silence her. She had a pronounced love-hate relationship with her father, in particular.

What were the forces or influences that drove the self-taught writer to explore the lives of plain black farming people? Peterkin seemed to envy what she perceived as their freedom, particularly that enjoyed by black women—a freedom of behavior and expression not permitted to "proper" white ladies.

"In a very large degree she was telling her own story," says Williams. "What I've tried to do in the book is trace how that worked. She had no gift for writing about white people. She couldn't get enough distance on herself; her ego would get in the way.

"Her writing about black characters—based on real people she knew well—was almost photographically accurate. Some felt that in some way she had stolen these stories. But I think some people she wrote about were collaborating with her in a way. They wanted their stories told. When Peterkin is at her most powerful, it's on subjects such as jealousy, death and disease."

Peterkin is a complex and sometimes mystifying subject, one of the reasons it took Williams so long to complete her biography. But Williams thinks she understands why Peterkin abruptly stopped writing only 12 years after having begun, and why she has not been reclaimed until now by literary historians.

"There are a whole bunch of reasons why she stopped," says Williams, who taught at The College of Charleston from 1986–88. "The simple version is that she sort of wrote herself out. She had begun not to be popular in the literary sense. Her swing back to the conservative values of her childhood didn't sit well with those accustomed to her as a revolutionary.

"One of the reasons she was not reclaimed in the '60s or '70s was this division in her. You can't pigeonhole her as a heroine. I encountered one elderly woman who knew Peterkin who said she was not the great emancipator. She did not contemplate changing society. And she became a segregationist in her old age—a little troubling for someone trying to turn her into a saint."

In some ways, Peterkin faced a no-win situation in being a part of the plantation universe on the one hand, while trying to survive in the New York literary world on the other.

"But her work," says Williams, "is transcendent. And there is definitely no shortage of plot in her story. It was a gift to have been given so interesting a figure to pursue all these years."

September 6, 1997

Martha Severens's *The Charleston Renaissance*

Martha Severens has considerable affection for the Holy City and respect for its legacy. Still, there are times the author of *The Charleston Renaissance* feels it might benefit from embracing its more recent history.

"Time marches on, but Charleston has been wrapped up in its distant past. It has been important for me in the last 20 years to look at, and to get others to look at, the more recent past and how it has shaped our present."

Specifically, the years 1915–1940, and the pivotal artistic and literary ferment of the day.

Severens, curator of the Greenville County Museum of Art and former curator of collections for the (then) Gibbes Art Gallery from 1976–87, invested almost three years in researching and writing *The Charleston Renaissance* (Saraland Press). This large-format, 232-page volume describes the cultural revival that unfolded in Charleston, the scope and influence of which is underscored by numerous color and black-and-white reproductions.

Severens focuses not only on the local artists and writers who became the vanguard of this renewal—among them DuBose Heyward, Elizabeth O'Neill Verner, Alice Ravenel Huger Smith and Alfred Hutty—but also on the gifted artists drawn to the city. Their number included Childe Hassam, Edward Hopper, Birge Harrison and Lilla Cabot Perry.

"In terms of the writers, DuBose Heyward and John Bennett were the most important, but the topic of my book is the artists. Three ladies, all natives, were in the forefront: Smith, Verner and Anna Heyward Taylor. The fourth major artist, a Midwesterner by birth, was Hutty, who divided his time between here and the Woodstock colony in New York."

Severens's previous books centered on Smith and Andrew Wyeth. In researching *The Charleston Renaissance*, is says she was astounded at the number of people making art and writing poems here during the period.

"I tried not to look just at the artists in Charleston, but also at artists who came to Charleston. To my knowledge, this hasn't been done to the extent this book takes it. Many were nationally known, like Hopper and Hassam. Norman Rockwell was stationed in Charleston in 1918. Wyeth was on the coast in the late 1930s as well."

"So part of what I've been trying to do is to discover those outsiders and try to figure out why some of them came. In some cases I was able to interview some senior figures. Palmer Schotte, who at the time (1934) was a student in New York, is a visual artist who wound up in California, where he is much better known. He told me that one very cold and rainy winter he and a friend just decided to come south. They found Charleston and fell in love with it. Others were attracted by what I'd call the aura of *Porgy*, the novel that became the play that became the opera."

The milestones that marked the cultural rebirth exerted an influence very much still felt in the Charleston area.

"One milestone was the book *The Dwelling Houses of Charleston* (1917), a collaboration of Alice Smith and her father, D. E. H. Smith. Her wonderfully evocative drawings of Charleston houses and street scenes, and the book's somewhat antiquarian text, began to lay some of the seeds for what would become the preservation movement, as well as a recognition of Charleston's architectural heritage."

By no means was this the only move afoot, Severens says. There was considerable ferment at the time. In the late teens and 1920s, Susan Pringle Frost was beginning her own drive to buy, restore and resell houses, largely along East Bay and Tradd streets. Earlier, this advocate of suffrage had opened eyes in Charleston by becoming a real estate agent (1909). Nine years later, she was the first woman to have an office on Broad Street.

"The predecessor to what we now call the Preservation Society was founded in 1920 and named the Society for the Preservation of Old Dwellings. During the early '20s there were several such entities, among them the Cultural Society, the Society for the Preservation of Spirituals and the Charleston Etchers Club. It became almost a cultural collaborative.

"Because of all this activity, it was the beginning of the tourist movement as well as that of the preservation movement."

From faded grandeur to revitalization, it was a passage that turned Charleston into a coveted tourist destination.

"I try not to take sides, but I say in the book that it is because of what happened in this area that, in many respects, we are what we are today."

The book's publisher, Robert M. Hicklin Jr., of Spartanburg, is owner of what is believed to be the nation's only gallery exclusively handling fine art of the American South. Hicklin plans to open a second location here in January, the Charleston Renaissance Gallery, which will be located at 103 Church St. at St. Michael's Alley.

"He's very pleased with the final product, though I'm not sure the book was what he expected," says Severens. "I made it clear from the beginning I didn't want to do a chapter on each individual. I wanted weave certain threads. For one, the whole idea of the selling of Charleston and the making of images, vernacular and high-style images.

"I also wanted to look at how African-Americans were handled as subjects. There's a chapter on landscape, dealt with not just on the subject of painting but touching on the creation of Brookgreen Gardens and how they differed from the Middleton Plantation and Magnolia Gardens experience."

Another chapter in which Severens takes particular pride deals with conservative tastes and the reaction to Modernism, not least the exhibition of Solomon Guggenheim's nonobjective painting collection at the Gibbes in 1936.

Severens, curator of the Greenville Museum since 1992, sought to amplify existing scholarship on the one hand and expand it on the other.

"I think the amplification may have to do with pulling these things together. But I also did a fair amount of research into the local press at the time. I looked at how Charleston was promoting itself, how the city was being planted in people's consciousness."

December 6, 1998

Barbara Bellows's *A Talent for Living*

What matters is the story.

As it was for Charleston writer Josephine Pinckney (1895–1957), so it is for her biographer, Barbara L. Bellows.

The story's the thing. And it begins with the wellspring of ideas.

"On one of the surviving pages from her notebooks, dating about 1953, Pinckney instructed herself, 'Believe in things. My own life. My autobiography would be interesting to write not because I am remarkable, but because it would be the stuff of which other people are made. My failures, my successes would echo theirs. The human heart is the stuff of literature. Write a candid autobiography (including stuff from my diaries) and lay it aside as clay to make poems and novels of.'

"With Pinckney," says Bellows, "it was always about the story."

In *A Talent for Living: Josephine Pinckney and the Charleston Literary Tradition* (LSU Press), Bellows, a Charleston native, has produced the first fully furnished biography of her subject, a pivotal figure in lowcountry letters.

Billed as "one of the last Carolina aristocrats and the first of the Southern modernists," Pinckney was a best-selling author whose work frequently was compared to that of Edith Wharton, Jane Austen and Isak Dinesen. Perceptive social commentary amplified her gifts for storytelling. Apart from stories, essays and reviews, Pinckney also wrote poetry. Of her five novels, *Three O'Clock Dinner* was the most successful.

Pinckney often used Charleston as her setting, "blending social realism with irony, tragedy and humor in chronicling the foibles of the South's declining upper class." Bellows regards her life story as being the history of a place and time, as well, not to mention a conduit for Bellows's own return to the place of her birth.

"There's some thought that maybe she picked me (as a biographer), rather than me selecting her as a subject," says Bellows, who splits time between here and Pound Ridge, N.Y. "The University of South Carolina Press has a Southern Classics series, bringing back memorable books that have gone out of print. In 1997, they asked me to write an introduction to the reprint of Pinckney's most famous book, *Three O'Clock Dinner,* and I got interested in her in the process of doing this.

"It seemed nothing had been written, and there are several reasons why. She was an intensely private person. Going through her papers, you really had to tease out information. She left instructions that her most personal papers and journals be burned. People (potential biographers) gave up when they heard that. But she left tracks, left clues, for the inquiring mind. She would leave things that a curious person would want to know about."

A Homecoming

Bellows is the author of *Benevolence Among Slaveholders: Caring for the Poor in Charleston, 1760–1860* and co-author of God and *General Longstreet: Essays on the Lost Cause and the Southern Mind.* Initially, she imagined it taking no great amount of time to plumb Pinckney's life and times.

Pinckney had left voluminous papers to the South Carolina Historical Society. Even so, Bellows thought it would take a couple of years to wade through the material and produce a book.

"It took five. She lived in Charleston, but she also traveled greatly. I went up and down the East Coast doing interviews. In the course of writing the book, I came back to Charleston in 2000 and bought a house here.

"The book was part of my own journey back to Charleston, which is why I enjoyed it so much," says Bellows, who taught at Middlebury (Vt.) College for 17 years. "It reconnected me with a lot of things I had left behind. I had a network of Charleston friends and was able to talk to people who actually knew her. To some people, she was enormously warm. To others she could be quite abrupt and cold. (What set her off) was self-righteousness."

Bellows says Pinckney is overlooked today partly due to the fact that her papers are not easily available, yet chiefly because she does not fit into the conventional Southern author mode.

"She was not a moonlight-and-magnolias writer. She was a modern writer, but haunted by the past.

"One of the most interesting things about her writing and her life was the influence of the Gullah culture, which she studied. This comes out more in her poetry. She described Charleston's physical image beautifully, but her whole interest was in writing about what she calls 'The Same Old Adam,' people being the same everywhere with their foibles and good points.

"She was also more humorous than people give her credit for. There was a very strong satirical line in her narrative. But if it was satire, it was a loving and sympathetic satire. She was not out to denigrate, but to point out the failure of the South after the Civil War: the upper class lost in a poverty of mind and spirit who did not uphold their responsibility. She blamed the old aristocratic class for its own decline."

A Clear Vision

Bellows is quick to note what made the cosmopolitan Pinckney, who cofounded the Poetry Society of South Carolina in 1920 with DuBose Heyward, Hervey Allen and John Bennett, so distinctive.

"People say she had this very elegant simplicity about her, and an authenticity. I agree. It was her most powerful characteristic. She wrote from a deep understanding of a people, a place and a time. It is important to know she became one of the most influential interpreters of the South and the South Carolina lowcountry to readers of the Northeast. She was also instrumental in helping some of the most interesting Charlestonians meet some of the most interesting people from around the country."

Today, in assessing Pinckney's legacy, Bellows says one should not forget the sheer pleasure of reading her prose.

"If you think of her in a larger, symbolic way, it is as an acute observer. She belonged to a generation that lived through the transformation of the South from an Old South, lost-cause mentality to the modern mind-set."

June 4, 2006

Louise Allen's *A Bluestocking in Charleston*

Laura Bragg had neither the temperament nor inclination to be a suitable Southern lady. Nor the time, for that matter.

Demure was not her style. Getting things done was.

Born in Massachusetts, in 1881, and the daughter of an educator, Bragg arrived in Charleston in 1909 at the behest of Charleston Museum director Paul Rea. By 1920 she would become the first woman in America to lead a publicly supported museum. A year later she made the unprecedented move of opening its doors to blacks.

Bragg mentored two generations of local literary figures, bringing missionary zeal to the task of reinvigorating a cultural "backwater" and reaching an uneducated populace.

Charleston author Dr. Louise Allen assays Bragg's achievements and enduring influence in *A Bluestocking in Charleston: The Life and Career of Laura Bragg* (University of South Carolina Press), with an emphasis on her museum work through 1939.

An early feminist and motive force of the Progressive Era, Bragg may have been obscured by time, but her legacy has not, says Allen.

"She had a tremendous intellect and was a tremendous person. Her legacy is almost a thing apart from her achievements in museums. Her real legacy consists of all the men and women she mentored, helping them to develop intellectually. And she continued to touch lives."

Deaf by the age of 6, but no less a communicator for it, Bragg developed into a woman of forward-thinking sensibilities and a keen aesthetic eye, not a customary feature of early 20th-century Southern culture.

"Her deafness was not a part of who she was," says Allen, assistant professor of education and graduate coordinator of the Educational Leadership Doctoral Program at the University of North Carolina–Charlotte. "She didn't let it define her, any more than she let being a woman define her, or being a Yankee in the South."

Allen, who divides her time between residences in Charlotte and Charleston, notes that the two childhood years Bragg spent in Mississippi, where she saw first hand the conditions of being black and uneducated, exerted an enormous influence.

Her act of opening the museum to black adults and instituting educational programs such as traveling exhibits helped to transfigure Charleston culture. Bragg, owning a degree in library science from Simmons College, was a founder of the Charleston Free Library, taught at Columbia University, conducted a survey of Southern museums for the American Association of Museums in 1924, and also directed the reorganization of museums in Richmond, Va., and in Pittsfield, Mass., where as director of the Berkshire Museum in the 1930s, her stature grew significantly.

"At the Berkshire Museum, what she did for modern art and unknown modern artists was incredible, especially for someone who for the 22 years she lived in Charleston had very little exposure to modern art. She got that in summers back in the North.

"From the beginning, she was very different from other women in the South. More women like her had gone to college and started to embrace careers in the North. Her power base also didn't come from who her family was, but from political connections she made."

Ultimately, Bragg secured the chief goal of early feminists: economic, social and political equality on her own terms.

She died in 1978.

Hers is a career much admired by Allen, though she initially undertook the biography with a certain reluctance.

A University of South Carolina graduate and former teacher and school administrator here, Allen was the first postdoctoral fellow at the Avery Research Center for African-American History and Culture at the College of Charleston.

"Initially I was perplexed that I didn't know that much about her early life and couldn't find anyone who knew her prior to 1939. Those in Charleston primarily knew her after she returned here that year and retired. But as I read the letters to her father, I found she had written some things about her early life, and together with interviews, I was able to fill some things in.

"The most stunning piece of information about her early life was that after her father tried to find a cure for her deafness in Boston, where she learned to lip read, he resigned and took the family to Mississippi, where he was a math professor for two years at a freedman's college. These were pivotal years in her decision to be a social missionary in the South, just as her father had done."

Allen says that the writing of a biography is in some respects also an autobiographical process.

"I think you have to know who you are or be willing to discover who you are in order to write a biography. You can't put yourself on one side of the table and your subject on the other without discovering both of you. Many women who are looking into others' lives are exploring how their own experiences and lives have been affected. It's autobiographical in terms of what you discover about yourself as well as what you come to understand about the other person."

April 15, 2001

Mickey Spillane. Photograph by Alan Hawes

Crime and Punishment

"You can get much further with a kind word and a gun than you can with a kind word alone."

Al Capone, as quoted in *Peter's Quotations: Ideas for Our Times*

Why do we find crime so reprehensible in reality but so entertaining in fiction? What's so "cozy" about a murder? From Arthur Conan Doyle and Dashiell Hammett to Raymond Chandler and Agatha Christie, high crime has had a high profile in the novels and short stories of almost every language.

Each generation of writers ushers in a "New Wave" of *auteurs* for whom crime and its consequences take center stage.

The hard-boiled private eye is a staple of American crime fiction, tried and true. So are police procedurals, gentleman detectives and the so-called cozy mysteries that remain popular today. But novelists such as the late John D. MacDonald helped introduce biting social commentary to the mix, influencing many a writer, not least such contemporaries as Carl Hiaasen and Sue Grafton, widely respected authors whose work is represented in this section.

In fiction, if so rarely in the real world, we have the gratification of seeing the bad guys get theirs, in spades. The corrupt fat cats, too; it's Cardinal Richelieu's dictum come to pass: "Nothing so upholds the law as the punishment of persons whose rank is as great as their crime." And perhaps this kind of karmic retribution is one of the reasons we are drawn to crime as reliable fodder for fiction. Not to say some malefactors don't get off scot-free (from the Scandinavian word for tax, "*Skat*," as in getting away with not paying one's taxes).

Justice achieved, or thwarted, the vicarious thrills of danger and the chase win out.

Carl Hiaasen's *Stormy Weather*

Disgusted with suburban sprawl, the late historian and social critic Lewis Mumford once said our national flower should be the concrete cloverleaf, a sterile freeway interchange leading nowhere.

Carl Hiaasen can relate.

The Miami Herald columnist, also a best-selling author of satirical fiction, is a fourth-generation Floridian who abhors what a complex of greed and ignorance has wrought in the Sunshine State.

Through 20 years of reportage and column writing, Hiaasen has used his laser-sighted wit to skewer big business, corrupt government, slipshod developers, immigration, lawyers and even tourism.

His sixth novel, *Stormy Weather* (Alfred A. Knopf), is dedicated to hurricanes "Donna, Camille, Hugo and Andrew," whose cyclonic caprice exposed rampant folly while setting the table for a con artists' feast.

"Florida is a mecca for scams. The only thing that's really changed is the technology of avarice," says Hiaasen, who visited Charleston Thursday. "The same con games are being run as at the turn of the century. It's one giant Klondike land sale. Only today there's not as much land, so the techniques of selling are stylistically a lot slicker. They have to be.

"And that's just one component of it. Florida always has attracted con artists. Long ago, it was a haven for outlaws from the West. And it hasn't changed much. Half of America's 'most wanted' guys wind up in Florida, which is fairly hospitable to them. The state has styled itself as a magnet for people, not only from this continent, but from Central and South America—with predictable results."

Hiaasen operates on the assumption that, in most cases, the more grotesque and appalling a situation, the greater the potential for hilarity.

"There are many different kinds of humor. I try to avoid out-and-out slapstick. A more rapier-like satire is useful. That, and what is almost a sort of gallows humor that develops. You go after targets that are obvious. If buildings collapse because inspectors have been bribed and corrupt politicians go along with it, they're gonna take their licks in the novel."

Among the blackguards are those Hiaasen terms "Roofers from Hell," who took advantage of people at the worst (and most propitious) time.

"This storm was heart-rending. And the villains are dealt with in ways I find poetically just. In the Miami area, we had to wait for Andrew to see that we'd been building crackerbox houses. We hadn't had a big one in 30 years. The storm peeled off all our assumptions. Then came people to exploit the disaster. This sort of thing has to be an object not only of outrage but of satire. The book is one way of exposing what's going on."

Hiaasen is especially nettled by the cavalier disregard that many developers and corporations traditionally have displayed toward the rich but declining Florida ecosystems. That, and the questionable notion that "market forces" are a cure-all.

"It (the land) was all a commodity, and it was considered infinite. The idea was that we could keep draining and filling and paving it, never looking at the big picture. But things have gotten better. There are actually some very good, conscientious developers building good homes who don't level everything in their path. Yet despite all the misery and havoc and human tragedy, when there was a drive to revamp building codes after the storm, much of the industry vigorously opposed it."

Hiaasen is quick to note that Hurricane Andrew also was a windfall to a lot of people whose rebuilt homes were decidedly more opulent than the original structures.

"Some folks made out very well. So it cut both ways. The whole point of *Stormy Weather* was to take in all of that. There were a lot of little stories repeating themselves again and again on TV. I took those as emblematic of the event and incorporated them into the novel."

One of the most vivid and funny real-life incidents chronicled in the book is the rampage of monkeys loosed on South Florida when Andrew disgorged them from a complex of wildlife farms and medical labs.

"It really happened. It was wild."

Although scam-meisters make for delicious, if rueful, comic fodder, Hiaasen disagrees with those who believe he harbors a sneaking admiration for their audacity.

"Not at all. A writer covertly or overtly revels in good material. Every reporter who ever held a notebook in his hands knows the difference between good and bad copy. I simply recognized the poststorm madness as potential for a book."

Unlike most conventional crime novels, *Stormy Weather* emphasizes social satire over the customary deduction. In this regard, Hiaasen is a philosophical descendant of the late John D. MacDonald.

"He was a great influence and inspiration, in the sense that nobody can write like him. He knocked me over as a young person. MacDonald was a master of suspense. At the same time he instilled a great sense of place—Florida—which few writers were writing about then, and an indignation about what was happening to it. When he had the character of Travis McGee having a conversation about how the state was being despoiled, it was heresy. Now you hear millions of Floridians saying it.

"Florida is a big, tough, urban state. And MacDonald nailed it years ago. I knew I wanted to write and I recognized that he managed something very tricky: a hard-boiled detective-style thriller that makes you turn the page that is also suffused with social commentary. He was a great inspiration."

Hiaasen, whose first novel, *Tourist Season,* was published in 1986, will see his fifth book, *Strip Tease,* go before the cameras next month. Most novelists whose work is being cannibalized for film treatment are delighted with the money, but a trifle ill at ease with what eventually may adorn the screen. The writer says he's "very cautiously" optimistic.

"I didn't adapt my own story. It was done by Andrew Bergman, a good writer and director. Some of his lines are so good I wish I'd written them. The movie stars Demi Moore, who appears to have put a lot of thought into her role, along with Burt Reynolds and Ving Rhames from 'Pulp Fiction.'

"My novel's not plotted in any linear way. So there will have to be changes. My feeling is that it's better for someone else, someone objective, to make them. I keep my distance. A book is yours, for better or worse. But it's too easy to get sucked into the Hollywood thing."

Meanwhile, what with his twice-weekly column and publicity tour for *Stormy Weather,* Hiaasen hasn't had much of a chance to start on a seventh book.

"I haven't put a word on paper. Nowadays, the publicity on a book starts a month to six weeks ahead of publication. But I'll start fiddling around with ideas after the tour ends in October.

"I like to do about one book every two years. I don't want to wear out my welcome. It's nice to spend 18 months on a manuscript and get it the way I want it. It offers a little more breathing room, even though the work is still torturous. I don't want my books to blur together either. I've been so lucky to have the response I've had."

August 27, 1995

John Berendt's *Midnight in the Garden of Good and Evil*

All cities are mad, but the madness is gallant.

Christopher Morley may not have had Savannah in mind, but what better aphorism could there be to define that stately bastion of Old South charm, spiritual cousin—though few would admit it—to the Holy City.

John Berendt's immensely popular first book, *Midnight in the Garden of Good and Evil: A Savannah Story* (Random House), embodies the same principal. Its appreciative, warts-and-all rendering of the city (and its more colorful denizens) has ascended the bestseller lists, charming all comers.

Well, almost all.

Berendt, a Manhattanite who lived in Savannah for eight years, offers observations both sympathetic and wry in *Midnight.* And while most citizens, reportedly, have felt flattered, some locals consider the book mildly scandalous.

"I was afraid a lot of people would, which did not happen," says Berendt. "The book is not at all condescending. That was people's fear until they read it. But I love Savannah, which is why readers there have responded so well to 'The Book,' as they call it.

"I was very gratified that the response was so positive. I understand one bookstore there sold 3,200 copies alone."

Though several reviewers, and Berendt's publicist, have characterized the book as a hybrid of travelogue and murder mystery, he prefers to think of it as a memoir.

"I think it's really about my encounter with the city and its citizens. But it does have a travel aspect and a true crime aspect."

Midnight evokes the landscape of Savannah and its surround as well as distinctive architectural features and the leisurely pace of life. It had an irresistible appeal for Berendt, certainly, an Esquire magazine columnist who was first drawn to the city in 1982.

Yet the overriding theme and focal point of the book involves the late Jim Williams, a wealthy international antiques dealer who, apart from playing an integral role in the historic city's restoration, was tried on four separate occasions for the 1981 shooting death of Danny Handsford, a 21-year-old "house helper." Williams died in 1990 of a heart attack.

There are scoundrels in this lively nonfiction work, but the book's larger menagerie of eccentrics—including scene-stealing black drag queen Lady Chablis, one of Berendt's more outrageous guides—does not necessarily constitute a rogue's gallery.

"I don't think I had any stereotypes in there. All the individuals in the book are very fresh and sufficiently unique. As for the trials, they become the action, serving as a way of further portraying Savannah."

Berendt, a cum laude graduate (1961) of Harvard, is a New Yorker born and bred. Formerly an associate editor at Esquire, he also wrote for David Frost and Dick Cavett before commencing his column 12 years ago.

Still, eager to escape Gotham's ceaseless metro drone for a more pleasing clime, he was seduced by Savannah after a single visit.

"There's the physical aspect of the beautiful treescape, with the squares, Spanish moss, live oaks, flowering shrubs and marvelous townhouses and mansions. The climate also is delightful. The light is soft and filtered. And it's quiet.

"It was quite a relaxing and stimulating change. Sometimes when you slow down, you can be stimulated. I was able to see things more clearly. People became more vibrant and alive around me, because there was no background noise—not just the low-decibel level but other things. People came into focus a lot more sharply in Savannah than in New York."

In taking a social barometer, Berendt also explored the racial climate, but he disclaims any agenda.

"What attracted my attention was what I focused on. I didn't come down to tell the people of Savannah anything, about race or any other subject. I came to learn. But I did feel compelled to make some references to race relations in the book.

"I put emphasis on the superficial gentility between whites and blacks, which I see as commendable, though there's a gulf between the two that has led to great disparity. I noticed that people were being solicitous and considerate, which means it's more than just saying hello."

Berendt began writing the book in 1985, sans agent or publisher. Though completed in December, 1992, Random House positioned it for publication this year. Meanwhile, the company distributed galleys to its regional representatives and bookstores. Excitement mushroomed.

"Booksellers began to hand sell the book, encouraging customers to read it. But the book was not hyped. Random House shrewdly saw to it that people got to read it early. Done another way, the book may not have made the best-seller lists the way it has."

With Savannah newly immortalized, might Berendt now train his gentlemanly sights on Charleston? Here, where pundits tell us eccentricity is so commonplace as to become conventional behavior?

"I just may."

April 3, 1994

Patricia Cornwell's *Unnatural Exposure*

A serial killer, a lethal virus and the Internet.

In the eighth thriller featuring Chief Medical Examiner and sleuth Dr. Kay Scarpetta, one would have to say Patricia Cornwell has all the bases covered.

This is what culture critics call "playing the zeitgeist." Publishers call it money in the bank.

Unnatural Exposure has all the elements of another Cornwell best-seller, with taut narrative, intricacy of detail and finely honed characterization wedded to one alluring bonus: Never before has Scarpetta been so humanized.

How does a series character stay compelling? Growth, says Cornwell.

"In every new Scarpetta book I learn something about her that I didn't know, another dimension I hadn't seen, particularly in her interaction with other characters. It would cease to be interesting if I had her all figured out, or any other character all figured out. Every little bit along the way, she continues to evolve as, hopefully, her author evolves."

Those already deep into *Unnatural Exposure*, released Monday by Putnam, know that Cornwell has created a harrowing predicament for her indomitable heroine.

After Scarpetta has been called to a murder scene to investigate the remains of the victim—whose head and limbs have been deftly severed—it becomes apparent that the deed may have been done by a notorious serial killer. Also apparent is that the deceased had been ravaged by a rare strain of smallpox-like virus.

Later, Scarpetta receives a personal e-mail inviting her to download a photograph of the corpse. Pixel by pixel, a gruesome image appears on the computer screen, and Scarpetta realizes she is up against a creature more sinister than anyone she's faced. Not only that, she may be infected with the virus.

"I always think of the potentiality for crimes that can be committed through any new medium and the Internet is clearly a road that could lead through hell in terms of the evil that can be perpetrated," says Cornwell, a former police reporter for The Charlotte Observer. "We're already seeing evidence of it.

"Scarpetta is dealing with a diabolical, technically well-versed killer. What happens to her in the story very easily could happen for real."

Several things distinguish *Unnatural Exposure* from its predecessors, says Cornwell.

"First of all, she's dealing with a natural killer who kills in an unnatural way. So you have a cause of death, a disease, that is also the weapon. And that brings you into a whole realm that we haven't been into with her before, where she is basically tracking a monster through a microscope.

"It was very different for me to get into that mindset, and it makes it more of a one-on-one battle for her where she's pursuing a disease as well as an individual she's only encountered on the Internet. The Internet is very important in this book. And it is also very timely due to what is going on in our society."

Also, the latest thriller is considerably more revealing of Scarpetta as a human being. More than anything, she discovers strength through vulnerability. Being placed under guard at the U.S. Army's Medical Research Institute for Infectious Diseases can do that to a person.

"We've never seen her sick in bed before. Much less quarantined and treated like a child by nurses. What kind of patient will she be? Clearly, a bad one. We also see her get drunk at the end of the book, and to some extent disintegrate emotionally as she finally comes to terms with a loss she hasn't coped with over a number of years."

A Miami native who splits her time between homes in Virginia and New York, Cornwell says if she had known in advance that the Scarpetta saga would stretch through eight novels—a ninth already is under way—the writer might never have gotten here from there.

Today, keeping it fresh is her principal task.

"The greatest challenges for me these days are, No. 1, not to get caught up in the expectations people have now and in your status as a novelist, because that can be sort of like Narcissus looking in the pond. It can be paralyzing. You have to keep being in touch with yourself and your own passions and what your standard is for creating a good book. I feel pretty comfortable in my ability to do that. I just try not to look at it from the outside in.

"The second big challenge every year is the research. The reason my books maintain a certain standard or level, I think, is that I work harder every year for the newest one. I don't say, 'Oh, well, I've hit No. 1 on the (bestseller) lists now and I can take a long vacation. If you are going to continue to enjoy what you do and to do a good job you have to work even harder as time goes by. The research gets more intensive and more exhausting every year."

Technical realism and procedural fidelity are as vital as plot and character study to Cornwell's novels. She accumulated invaluable experience as a computer analyst in the Virginia chief medical officer's office, a post she held for six years.

She says her approach to research is a hybrid of journalistic background and novelistic concerns.

"I am still in many ways a nonfiction writer. That's how I was trained. I was first a journalist, then a biographer. My approach has never wavered from what I did back then, which is you get an idea or there's something you want to pursue and you begin looking at those avenues you must go down to get that information.

"Like any other journalist, when you suddenly get something that's behind the scenes that you know is original and fascinating, you can just feel your adrenalin pumping and you want to run home and write about that and say, 'I'm going to show you something you haven't seen before.' The difference, of course, is that I can weave it into fictitious stories. But the skeleton of it and the connective tissue of all of it is fact."

There's connective tissue, as well, between Cornwell and Charleston, a city she hasn't visited in 17 years. Her ex-husband, Charles Cornwell, is associate pastor of First (Scots) Presbyterian Church here and recently was named a senior editor at the local publishing house of Wyrick & Co. They met while Cornwell, then Patricia Daniels, was a student at Davidson College, where he was an English professor. Theirs remains an amicable relationship.

Scarpetta's adversaries may constitute a gallery of the grotesque, but the most fiendish, merciless foe besetting Cornwell is . . . her book tour regimen.

"For most authors as they are coming along a book tour is exactly that, a tour. You get on the road and you go to 20 different cities and you do your book signings and your media. I have to say, it's a nightmare. So exhausting, and many times so discouraging when no one shows up. And I've certainly had my share of those over the years, if not recently.

"The hardest parts for me now are the actual signings. Physically they're more difficult because the crowds are so much larger. You may sign your name 2,000 times in a day. I physically get in shape for them. I have a trainer with me on the road, and we work on my hands and my arms to work on my energy and keep me strong and healthy."

Cornwell wants her readers to know that book tours are a way of life, during which she has to give up everything she is and does for the occasion.

"But it's very gratifying. I love to meet these people face to face because most of the time I work in isolation. And I never forget that I am where I am because someone out there reads those books. We do have a relationship even if we haven't met. It gives me a chance to try to thank them. That may sound pious, but it's very sincere on my part."

Meanwhile, Cornwell still waits for Scarpetta to make the transition to motion pictures. The most difficult part has been to find an actress best suited to the role.

"We continue to work on (a film version of) *From Potter's Field.* In the last two years I've been through two directors and two different studios. We have a new screenwriter now and we hope to pull it all together. We don't have a Scarpetta yet, which is a very demanding part. But it's going to happen. We just want to do it right."

July 20, 1997

Sue Grafton's *P Is for Peril*

Whatever you do, do not put Sue Grafton on a timetable. Especially an inflexible one.

"I don't like being pushed," says one of the leading lights of the contemporary mystery novel. "I'm cranky about that. I work better with the illusion of time and space."

So when Grafton's editor and friend of 18 years switched publishing houses, Grafton promptly moved from Henry Holt to Putnam with her—together with the author's 16th Kinsey Millhone book, *P Is for Peril*, due out in June.

"Whither thou goest, I go," says Grafton, who spoke to The Post and Courier from her home in Montecito, Calif. "We have been working together since 1982. I'm crazy about her. She gives me permission to write well. She leaves me alone to do the job and she trusts me. And she is my second reader after my husband. I always hold my breath to see if she likes it."

The reading public rendered its verdict back in 1982 with the inaugural *A Is for Alibi*, embracing Millhone's quirks, foibles and wit, as well as the private eye's penchant for pounding the pavement rather than a keyboard.

Devotees will have an opportunity to hear Grafton this week when the University of South Carolina's Bicentennial Writers Festival begins its three-day run on Wednesday.

Grafton's visit to Columbia precedes her upcoming book tour, and is being undertaken largely because of her friendship with USC professors Natalie Hevener Kaufman and Carol McGinnis Kay, authors of *G Is for Grafton: The World of Kinsey Millhone* (Henry Holt).

"My only complaint is that Kinsey has a biographer and I do not."

Grafton has said she closely resembles her protagonist and alter ego, save that the detective is younger (36 at last count), smarter (questionable), thinner, twice divorced (Grafton has been married to Steve Humphrey for more than 20 years) and stubbornly resistant to haute cuisine.

Grafton's own reading appetite still tends toward the hard-boiled. Her favorite writer is Elmore Leonard, but she has less than kindly words for mystery novels that are either clumsily written or so conventional they are rendered inert.

"I've read the cozy (mystery) novels, and some of them I like. But I prefer a different tone—dark."

Now published in 26 languages, Grafton is a direct literary descendant of Dashiell Hammett, Raymond Chandler, Ross Macdonald and John D. MacDonald. But she developed her own signature marketing gimmick with her alphabetic book titles.

"It seemed like a keen scheme when I thought it up, though you can't be certain even one book will be published. It's remarkable to me, and I still don't believe it. That's why I'm always humble and lovable. I never relax. I never take the work for granted. I write every book as though it was my first—and my last. That keeps me sharp."

The Millhone books take place within a fairly narrow time frame of the 1980s, which helps account for her more traditional sleuthing methods.

"I backed into that decision," says Grafton. "So now I can't have her make any sudden leap into the year 2001. Besides, I don't think computers and the Internet are that interesting in solving cases. Murder is about human beings, not data. That's part of the tradition of the hard-boiled private eye."

Grafton has three kids and two grandchildren. Her alphabet books are designed to be just as individual as her human offspring.

"I hope not ever to write the same book twice. That forces me to be more inventive each time. I try not to fall into any unconscious patterns. To that end I keep elaborate charts so I don't unconsciously repeat myself."

March 18, 2001

Mickey Spillane's Perfect Life and *The Ship That Never Was*

"The good life begins when you stop wanting a better one."

Mickey Spillane, interview

MURRELL'S INLET—If the broad, chiseled face is any barometer, Mickey Spillane is a contented man. His slice of the good life is a two-story white frame house, a Ford pickup, an occasional commercial and a Yorkshire terrier named Bandit.

And he wouldn't have it any other way.

"You know, money's only good when it can be converted into something useful. I may not have a lot, but I have what I need. As far as I'm concerned, my career is basically over. I can still write, of course—I'm doing young adult books now—but most of the drive is gone. I'm free and clear financially; I live a quiet life. It's what I want."

Spillane, 64, has not abandoned Mike Hammer, the hard-boiled, soft-centered private eye that at one time made this former comic book writer the fifth most published author in history.

But with more than 150 million Hammer novels sold—in numerous languages—since 1946, Spillane has turned his prolific hand to enthralling a new generation of young readers.

"Right now I've got the greatest thing going with kids you've ever seen in your life," says Spillane, who, despite persistent rumors, has no intention of leaving his home of 24 years.

"I've spoken to a few groups of school kids and they're aware of the first two books (*The Ship That Never Was* and *The Day the Sea Rolled Back*). And one thing I learned is that you can't write down to them. They're a lot sharper than you think."

Wooden boats and old ships are a Spillane hobby, attested to by the many models that festoon the memory-rich interior of his waterfront home. Writing mystery stories revolving around them was as fitting as his characteristic pork pie hat.

"Kids love to fantasize. Hey, the underside of a table is a whole world to most of them. The funny thing is that I have so many adults coming up to me who have passed the books along to their children only after they've read them themselves.

"Of course, the sex and violence are very limited, but I still write them in a straightforward style. There's a girl protagonist in *The Ship That Never Was*, and there's a great, typical Mike Hammer ending in *The Day the Sea Rolled Back*. I won a youth literary award for the first one, which makes me feel pretty good."

His young adult stories, primarily for ages 9 to 14, have just enough realism to make them plausible. A science fiction element is present, too. The plotting is more complex than one would suppose.

It's just the *idea* of Spillane writing for kids.

Man of Action

From auto racing to flying, the circus to motion pictures, the Spillane legacy is one of action. He still has energy to burn. The flat-topped hair, though streaked with gray, stands at attention. The forearms roll with sinew, the eyes are clear and as observant as ever.

And, as each yarn is spun, each anecdote told in hilarious (and often unprintable) detail, the arms wave, the knees pump, and the face takes on more guises than a dozen Lon Chaneys.

"I can't think old. That's the thing," he says. "My grandkids help keep me that way. And I'm a kid at heart. They want to play with my toys when they come to visit, but I only let 'em look."

Born Frank Morrison Spillane on March 9, 1918, he attended Erasmus Hall High School in his native Brooklyn, N.Y. He enrolled briefly at Fort Hays (Kan.) State College in 1939, where, primed by years as a summer lifeguard, he became a champion swimmer.

He had begun writing while in high school, but started his professional career in 1940—with comic books.

"Those were great times with Marvel Comics. We did Captain America and a load of other good characters (including Mike Danger, forerunner to Mike Hammer). In fact, I was one of the first 20 guys who helped start the whole thing. And let me tell you something, these people were tops. The great thing about being a comic book writer was that you were working with artists. We were innovators as well as storytellers, and we delivered a first-rate product."

Following war service, during which he got his first glimpse of the Grand Strand as a pilot with the Southeast Training Command, Spillane returned to comics. But in 1946, he wrote his inaugural Mike Hammer novel, the immensely popular *I, the Jury*.

It was an immediate bestseller, despite the cool reception it drew from critics. The book was an augur for lasting success.

By 1951, five of his early novels had topped 40 million in sales. Then years later, the figure had risen to 70 million. Spillane took a hiatus from books in the 1950s to devote more attention to magazine writing and film work, as well as stringing for newspapers, but in the early 1960s resumed his book career with *The Deep* and another Hammer novel, *The Girl Hunters.*

Screen Incarnation

His novels appeared with relative frequency thereafter, and works filmed by Hollywood included *I, the Jury*, *The Long Wait*, *My Gun is Quick* and Robert Aldrich's critically applauded 1955 adaptation of *Kiss Me Deadly*, starring Ralph Meeker as Hammer. Veteran character actor Darren McGavin played Hammer in a string of anecdotal episodes in a 1958–59 TV series, and Spillane himself took a crack at the role in "The Girl Hunters."

"I was the best," he says with a laugh.

A sequel to a 1980 made-for-TV movie starring Kevin Dobson ("Kojak," "Shannon") as Hammer is in production at this time.

Spillane's experience with Hollywood has been mixed.

"When I played Hammer, I was just playing myself," he says. "How could I have been uncomfortable? Of course, I'd done a few major films before playing my own character, and I appeared in just about every TV show of the period as a guest. But the thing is, an actor is a secondary person. I writer is a primary one. An actor has to have something to act, right?"

Yet there was one actor who played a primary role in Spillane's life, a consummate performer and dear friend, the late British star Basil Rathbone, best known for his Sherlock Holmes.

"Of all the nice guys I ever met, Rathbone was the nicest," he says. "He was a 'laugher' and an easy guy to break up during the days of live TV. He was also one of the finest fencers I ever saw. Remember 'The Adventures of Robin Hood'? When he an Errol Flynn dueled to the death in the climax, Basil could have sliced his ears off blindfolded. We used to fence each other now and then and he gave me a set of foils as a present."

Those foils hang in a prominent place in Spillane's living room, hard by photographs of motion picture sets, the sculpture, the beer mugs and tankards, and a pantry that more resembles a miniature general store, complete with pot-bellied stove.

Outside, resting under a carport like a slumbering panther, is another artifact from Spillane's Hollywood days, a sleek white 1956 Jaguar set up for racing. It poises unused, haven for a host of tree squirrels who build their nests underneath.

The donor, John Wayne.

"I'd always loved racing and sports cars," says Spillane. "Back in the early '50s I raced a 1937 Ford up in Middletown, N.Y., and was the first driver to wear a hard hat and use a shoulder harness.

"Anyway, I was doing a circus film called 'Ring of Fear' with John Wayne and the Ringling Brothers people. Every day we'd break for lunch and go to the Cock 'n' Bull. Across the street was a Jaguar dealership, and I used to walk over and stare at this white Jag through the window. I guess I made no secret of the fact that I admired it."

Spillane, who acted in the film, wound up doing an 11th-hour rewrite, salvaging what all concerned agreed might have been an unmitigated disaster.

"It could have been a big bomb; we turned it into a good movie."

Several weeks later, at home after the wrap, Spillane awoke at his customary 5:30 a.m. to find a white Jaguar in the driveway.

"It had a huge red ribbon around it and a simple note that said 'Thanks, Duke.' The way I figure it, they didn't want to insult me by offering me money for the rewrite."

The circus was a preferred playground for Spillane, who "traipsed off" with Ringling Brothers for a series of magazine pieces during the late '50s.

"I wanted to go back to magazine writing for a while," he recalls. 'I'm a writer. I never wanted to limit myself to being just an author."

Then, as now, Spillane writes when he needs the money. He is well known for his rapid-fire typewriter, which has turned out complete novels in as little as two weeks.

"How long does it take me to write a book? Well, that depends on how much I need the money, and how fast. I wrote *I, the Jury* because I needed $1,000 to build my home up in New York. For a young adult book like I'm doing now, it takes about a week.

"But I write a good eight hours a day, talking to my typewriter as I work: 'Morning, honey, how are you today?' You've got to have concentration."

And experiences on which to draw.

"As you get older your style and ability improve. You have more experience and insights into people's lives, emotions and motivations. Sometimes you slip up, though. When I wrote *The Erection Set* in 1971, I found that I had updated and rewritten *The Count of Monte Cristo.* I got quite a start out of that.

"Anybody writing fiction has to remember one thing. The plot isn't the primary structure; it's characterization. Plot is incidental to the changing of a person's character through the course of the story."

The course of Spillane's life, for the most part, has been the keeping of an even keel: feet on the ground, spontaneity tempered with discipline. Twice marred, with four children ("Two of them talk with a southern accent, two with a northern one"), Spillane is relaxed, affable, and just another citizen of Murrell's Inlet.

The new celebrity afforded by his association with the Miller Brewing Co. hasn't affected the relationships with neighbors, though autograph hounds come sniffing down his dead-end street during the tourist season.

"I've been in the public eye for a long, long time," he says. "I don't run away from it. But I do like the atmosphere here, the way people react to me. I like being just another resident."

It's "Hi, Mickey!" Or, usually just "Mick." And the Lite Beer commercials have brought him a brand new constituency.

"Matt Snell (ex-New York Jets running back) and I were the first guys to do the Lite Beer ads. They were test marketing the product in San Diego nine years ago, and wound up using our spot when it went national.

"Now we've got a whole rogue's gallery doing them. They're a lot of fun, and even the big ones when all of us are together take no more than a couple of days to shoot. All the guys have nicknames. I'm 'the guy with the girl;' Dick Butkus and Bubba Smith are 'Laurel and Hardy.' "

NBC Magazine once had Spillane hooked up to a mike during taping. As one might expect, the outtakes were a riot, and the unusable footage made a delicious blooper reel for someone's private collection.

"All the guys clown around, but they're as disciplined as any actors I ever met. There are a lot of tigers among them, though."

There's a gentleness about Spillane that belies his "macho" past, and a surprising sensitivity that expresses itself in a dozen ways, with every waking hour. He is a man people love, and the favor is returned.

"You know, it's the people you meet in life who really matter. Events fade into memory. The things you've done don't stick with you nearly as long. You can have the big bucks. Give me a guy I can talk to."

May 2, 1982

James Ellroy's *Destination: Morgue!*

"Chandler wrote the kind of guy he wanted to be; (Dashiell) Hammett wrote the kind of guy he was afraid he was."

James Ellroy, *Paris Review*

MEMPHIS, TENN.—James Ellroy has no doubt as to his self-identity, or where he resides in the pantheon of detective novelists and crime writers. And that's the scary part.

Ellroy is inimitably unusual, in the most entertaining way, of course. He estimates he has a walk-out ratio of about 1 in 5 at his addresses, during which he delights in provocative remarks, profane effusions, and whatever else pops into his impish head. Sometimes it's calculated for effect, sometimes just serendipity.

"Why do they come? Because they want a picturesque afternoon at a cultural event," he confides, deadpan.

Fans, of whom there are many, couldn't care less. The more outrageous he gets, in print or in person, the more they dig it. It's what they expect from the author called the Demon Dog, who on this day read from his comedic piece on Arab terrorists, "Jungletown Jihad," a jingoistic joust from his new collection *Destination: Morgue! L.A. Tales.*

From the audience: peels of laughter, gasps of consternation.

Grrrrr

With this canine, his bite and bark both have teeth. It is doubtful many novelists, screenwriters or journalists have assembled the sort of experiences Ellroy has logged over the years, some of them unsavory.

The author of such books as *L.A. Confidential*, and *The Black Dahlia*, Ellroy was born in Los Angeles in 1948 ("The year of the rat in Chinese astrology," he reminds us.) Though Ellroy is associated with the city in the public mind, and remains a champion of its police department, he departed L.A. in 1981, living in Connecticut and Kansas City before settling in Carmel, Calif.

It was Jack Webb's *The Badge*, a history of the LAPD given him at age 10 by his father, that laid some of the foundation of his future career. It was within those pages that he came upon the story of the Black Dahlia, as well as the cops and crime figures he would later amplify in his *L.A. Quartet.*

"I've still got a copy and look at it once in a while. I'm astonished at the extent to which that book is a template for my obsessions. People will tell you he (Webb) was the first great auteur of television. But a lot of the early '50s episodes of 'Dragnet' are unwatchable. I enjoy them because they are procedurally accurate, there are occasional exterior shots of L.A. of the era, and because they recount some real crimes."

As for the accuracy of his literary colleagues, Ellroy professes ignorance.

"I don't follow modern crime writing. The truth is, I'm not a crime writer anymore. I'm the only person who went from crime writing to something else and has won mainstream honors. I'm not talking about writing the same old things at a different level of intensity. I started out writing generic thrillers, and now write 700-page historical novels set outside of L.A. My last two books, both novels, *American Tabloid* and *The Cold Six Thousand*, are my best-selling."

In Transit

Destination: Morgue! is Ellroy's second volume of previously uncollected works. The book contains nonfiction pieces plus four short stories, three of them new and constituting a novella. Like his previous collection, 1999's *Crime Wave*, much of it is drawn from his 10-year stint (1993–2003) as a writer-at-large for GQ magazine.

"It's a transitional volume," says Ellroy, 56. "Sort of, 'This is my career to date. Take it or leave it.' It's a primer on me, my obsessions, my fixations, my past life, my interests, plus the new novellas, which are thematically consonant. The Stephanie Gordon murder that I recount in true-crime detail in part one of the book also comes back in part two, fictionally. Add the return and the demise of (muckraker) Danny Getchell (in "The Trouble I Cause"), and what you've got is a quilted book where nonfiction bleeds seamlessly into the fiction, as well as a book built around my obsessions and my themes."

Apart from the reopening of the 40-year-old Gordon homicide case, addressed in "Stephanie," some of the material builds on biographical content that Ellroy first plumbed in 1996's *My Dark Places*, the scaffolding of which was his attempt to crack the still unsolved murder of his mother, Jean Ellroy, in 1958.

The essays "Where I Get My Weird Shit" and "My Life as a Creep" recount his childhood, including the murder, a West Hollywood upbringing in the company of his no less obsessive dad, a drug-fueled coming of age in the '60s and '70s, and a spate of weird pranks, shoplifting, and bouts of vagrancy and breaking and entering. Oh yeah, he also chronicles, vividly, his youthful preoccupation with iconic sex goddesses.

"What stands out to me in these essays is the strength of my fixation with women. It was glandular, it was sexual, it was emotional, it was moral, it was spiritual. I'm happily married now and don't think of them (other women) in any kind of carnal way anymore."

Not to say he's gone conventional.

Primate Primitivo

Ellroy's previously unpublished, three-part novella is told from the perspective of LAPD detective Rick Jenson, who some view as a prototypical "primitive" male.

"He's comedic," Ellroy says, dismissing his critics' distaste for his infatuation with sleaze. "These are comedies. I think they are profound comedies that say a lot about a certain kind of man: a conservative, if not reactionary WASP American heterosexual male living a life of action. All 'Rhino' Rick Jenson knows is solving crimes and loving Donna Donahue. And I identify with that kind of single-mindedness. These are guys who are confronted with a specific stimulus, a crime to solve, and go at it hammer and tong. Rick's also a tragic as well as comedic figure, and profoundly un-PC."

As to that, Ellroy, whose characters mirror his own conservative moral code, does not fret over unreceptive readers appalled at his attitudes, or those who sit on pins and needles waiting, with hair-triggers, to be offended at the slightest provocation, real or imagined.

"We have a great deal of fun in these stories poking fun at homosexuals and people of color. People can either enjoy this or not. I don't care. (Unlike some reviewers) I'm not out to second-guess people's lives. I'm not a cultural critic. I leave it open. There are some specific issues pertaining to crime that I am passionately committed to. There are some aspects of crime that I am expert on. But beyond that I don't follow the culture."

Percolating

Ellroy's next novel will be a sequel to *The Cold Six Thousand*, which probably will come out in about two more years. Meanwhile, he's stumping for one documentary film and looking forward to another. "Bazaar Bizarre," currently on the festival circuit, was made by a friend of his, Ben Meade, with whom he'll also be shooting an adaptation of *Destination: Morgue*.

Ellroy has been involved in the film business as a screenwriter and producer for some years but had nothing to do with Curtis Hanson's film adaptation of *L.A. Confidential.* He's chiefly concerned with the impact adaptations of his work have on his book sales.

"I just got lucky with (the film) *L.A. Confidential.* They're shooting *The Black Dahlia* next year in Prague, in March, with Brian DePalma directing Josh Hartnett and Scarlett Johansson. We'll see what happens. These are wonderful devices for selling books for you."

November 14, 2004

Joe Queenan's *Queenan Country*

Joe Queenan is not mean. Nor a misanthrope. No, really. He just wants to get it out of his system.

Given the cultural and political state of affairs decade after preposterous decade, who can blame him?

Queenan actually has the occasional nice thing to say about people, however wrenching this effusion might be. Yet professionally he retains the reputation of a wag, a scold, a board-certified curmudgeon. He, who once said in all earnestness, "I can never remember seeing a movie where I wanted someone to die as much as Ali McGraw in 'Love Story.'"

Queenan, who lives among nice, mostly ordinary citizens in Tarrytown, N.Y., is a self-proclaimed "sneering churl." As one of our ablest satirists in print, his forte has been skewering the foolishness of movie stars and the inexhaustible banalities of American culture. Name a trend, and he has deflated it with a literary ice pick or a bracing brand of bile.

Gross Affronts

Queenan, whose most recent book is 2004's *Queenan Country: A Reluctant Anglophile's Pilgrimage to the Mother Country,* may seem merciless at times if for no other reason than he is personally involved.

Preening stupidity is an affront to his sensibilities. But however pitiless the attack, it's cruel to be kind, folks. Cruel to be kind. Don't get the idea that Queenan holds a grudge. Not even against an arrant movie such as "The Grudge." His displeasure generally lasts about as long as it takes to exorcise it through his keyboard.

By the time you read it, he's long ago moved on.

“My son and I chose to go to see the movie ‘Poseidon’ rather than ‘The Da Vinci Code’ not just in protest to *The Da Vinci Code* (the book) but because there was a better-than-even chance Kurt Russell would drown in the (disaster) movie. But I wish him no ill will in real life. The pitch in which you write satire is amplified just so you can be heard above the din.

“When I meet people at a book signing or other event, there’s usually a guy in the back who looks like a serial killer or Silent Bob, born with a baseball cap turned backwards and carrying some loosely bound sheets of paper he wants to show you. Later, in your hotel room, you read it and it’s all about him wanting to dismember Courteney Cox.

“These people think that just because you write something disparaging about an actor that you feel the same. They don’t understand that from the time you wrote those lines to the time the book got in the bookstore four years later, you’ve cooled off. But they haven’t.”

Still, his targets usually have it coming. Ridicule, that is, not dismemberment. They’re not villains in his eyes, just incredibly annoying.

Ex-pro quarterback Joe Theismann, for example. Queenan cannot stand him as a broadcaster. “During the game, I want the man held in protective custody at Guantanamo,” Queenan says. “But I don’t talk about Joe at all in the offseason.”

Dripping Venom

Queenan, a former editor at Forbes and Spy, has written for Movieline, The New Republic, GQ, Rolling Stone, Esquire, Vogue and The New York Times, among other publications. His books include *If You’re Talking to Me, Your Career Must Be in Trouble*, *Confessions of a Cineplex Heckler*, *The Unkindest Cut* (a chronicle of his attempt to make a film underwritten by his credit card), *Imperial Caddy* (on Dan Quayle), *True Believers*, *Balsamic Dreams: A Short but Self-Important History of the Baby Boomer Generation* and *Red Lobster, White Trash and the ‘Blue Lagoon,’* the last being an account of his descent into the netherworld of American popular culture.

He has made three short films for England’s Channel 4, *Mickey Rourke for a Day*, *Hugh Grant for a Day* and *So You Wanna Be a Gangster*, and has hosted the BBC radio program *Postcard from Gotham* for three years.

The Philadelphia native says that if he were to revive his “For a Day” forays, it almost certainly would be as Defense Secretary Donald Rumsfeld.

“He’s the focal point of everything, you know. All conversations lead back to Rumsfeld. He does that thing that Julius Caesar did, speaking about himself in the third person. I think it’d be really interesting to take him back in time: Donald Rumsfeld at Woodstock, for instance. But I wouldn't want to be anyone in pop culture for a day. Not now. I don't think we have anyone in movies who has that larger-than-life quality. Sean Penn grew up.

"Then again, I could be Wesley Snipes. Looks like he's in a heap of trouble with the IRS."

In the Works

In the pipeline is a new book. But he can't talk about it.

"I was working on a book about pop culture while taking a falconry course in Vermont for Men's Health magazine. I thought it'd be cool for my capsule bio to say he writes for this and that magazine and he's a falconer. But I realized I didn't want to write another book about pop culture. But now I'm getting back into the mind-set.

"In April, I drove across the U.S., 4,700 miles. What I found out about it, apart from the sense of accomplishment from performing this mythical rite, was that it's a great experience when you get out there and discover this whole country already exists inside you even though you've never been there. It's already in your consciousness. Driving from the East Coast to California, I found all kinds of funny things to write about that didn't have to do with politics or pop culture or Hollywood.

"Except in Kansas City. I've been racking my brain to think of something funny that happened there. I found African alligators in Colorado and visited D. H. Lawrence's Pornographic Paintings Gallery in Taos, N.M. But I found nothing that was weird or funny in Kansas City."

Maybe if Rumsfeld had tagged along.

October 22, 2006

Herb Frazier. Photograph by Seth Hamilton

Pressing Issues

"Since when do you have to agree with people to defend them from injustice?"

Lillian Hellman, *Scoundrel Time*

Thank heaven for the modern muckraker, whistleblower and dragonslayer.

In an age when newspapers are suffering a precipitous decline, the value of topical reportage and commentary that is trenchant, thorough, and as impartial as humanly possible has never been more apparent.

While there are excellent examples of the form, feature film documentaries too often view every issue through an ideological lens. The ubiquitous blog is of questionable veracity and motive. Some cable and network TV news programs (such as those airing on Fox News and MSNBC) are as much theater as journalism, wielding their biases like a club.

Authors of books are not immune to these failings, of course, yet the most professional ones seek a balanced treatment without distorting the issue at hand, realizing there are often more than two sides to a story.

This is not to say that the passionate polemic has no place. It gets the blood pumping. Let's just not call it journalism.

The authors in this section operate from positions of indignation, outrage, personal experience and sadness, from a desire to wave a red flag or offer a cautionary tale that may deflect us from folly. But each of their books embodies, in one way or another, Gandhi's belief that, in matters of conscience, the laws of the majority have no dominion.

Kirkpatrick Sale's *The Conquest of Paradise*

On the eve of the 500th anniversary of Columbus's "discovery" of America, Kirkpatrick Sale is throwing a wet (Indian) blanket on the celebration, a blanket damp with tears—and fouled water.

Sale, author, lecturer and founding member of the environmentalist New York Green Party, was in Charleston during the recent Earth Week observance to address an audience on the subject of his book *The Conquest of Paradise: Christopher Columbus and the Columbia Legacy* (Knopf/Plume).

In an interview with The Post and Courier, he also discussed the "failure of environmentalism as an effect political movement" over the past 10 years.

"This, in spite of all it has done—often immense things—and in spite of all the laws that have been passed. It has failed at the most basic level, and we are losing the war."

But his book's underlying argument is much broader: that it was Columbus who brought with him the germ of an infectious disease, the virus that set us upon the disastrous environmental path we tread still.

The primary culprit, says Sale, is the "affluenza" caused by unrestrained capitalism's capacity to exploit the natural world.

"I wanted to say this during Earth Week, so that people will understand that the task is to go to a deeper level and change the values that this degradation is built upon."

Columbus-bashing seems to be a popular sport in a time of agitation for multiculturalism, but Sale insists that's not what he's doing.

"In order to have an appropriate perspective it's useful for us to go back 500 years to the European culture that brought itself across the ocean and planted itself here, and has become perfected here in the form of the United States. We can take a wide focus and see what that culture ultimately stands for, and what it's wrought."

Best known for his influential mid-'70s book *Human Scale*, Sale sees only a modest chance of retaining the best of western civilization in a synthesis with a new, more benign model.

"My instinct tells me that the ideas of western industrial civilization are so corrupted that there is not anything of value to be found there. Or at least let us lay those things aside and come back to them later after we have embraced an alternative set of values that does not lead to degradation of the planet. Maybe some elements of it will be useful."

Sale insists these alternative values already exist, embodied in the wisdom of the people of nature that were here centuries before the Great Discoverer landed—the Native American.

"There is another way of living on the earth, and these people have shown us this. In nature, I see co-operation as the norm, not competition. Although certainly, it is often unconscious co-operation."

Many question Sale's assertion that the North American continent was a "paradise" before Columbus set change in motion. Was it really? Apart from recent scholarship, contemporary motion pictures afford varying points of view on the nature of Native American cultures and the myths that occasionally surround them.

"Dances With Wolves" gave us a gauzy, romanticized vision of Indian culture and benevolence, in high contrast to the more starkly realistic "Black Robe." Not all Native American tribes were such careful stewards of their environments, living in balance and harmony with the natural world, much less peaceful.

But Sale's argument finds many adherents, on screen and in print.

In many ways it is echoed in the recent book *America in 1492*, a collection of essays edited by Alvin M. Josephy which has been praised for engrossing writing but criticized for serving up "politically correct pieties in place of scholarship."

While some deride as naïve and simplistic the notion that Western technological civilization is the source of the world's evils, both books stress that there is fundamental truth in the claim.

The question remains: Can we dispel the romanticism also enveloping Columbus without diminishing his achievement and blaming this single act for all that has befallen the continent? Is it fair, for example, to flail Columbus and the subsequent evils of European occupation, such as enslavement of native populations, while pretending slavery was previously unknown in America?

Even amid the Columbus-bashing in *America in 1492*, several contributors report that long before Columbus set sail, slavery was practiced by the northwest coast tribes, the Calusan tribes of Florida and the Aztecs, among others.

"The evils to which they refer are associated primarily with Indian empires of Central and South America," says Sale. "I think there's no minimizing these evils, which tend to exist in all hierarchical empires—in which exploitation of peoples and destruction of the environment goes hand in hand. Of course, one reason empires do not last long is environmental decay.

"But you don't find these characteristics in the larger number of Indian societies outside of those empires, where you have the tribal cultures persist even as empires rise and fall."

Sale concedes that European incursion was inevitable. If it had not been Columbus, he says, it would have been someone else from the European continent.

"The disease organism would have arrived here sooner or later. But we, today, have to recognize that we swim in the water of western capitalist culture, and that the water is polluted."

April 19, 1992

Robin Cook's *Critical*

Novelist and physician Robin Cook did not need to see "Sicko," Michael Moore's controversial broadside against the American health care industry, to know that the documentary filmmaker had failed to ask the most fundamental questions.

Why is health care so expensive? And can market forces really bring costs in line?

"No," says Cook, emphatically, challenging the notion that "evil" insurance and pharmaceutical companies alone are responsible for this state of affairs.

"Market forces will not function to bring down the cost of health care because there are many things in the medical arena that simply do not react to market forces. No system is perfect, but it's not just about the dichotomy between health care as practiced in the United States and programs of socialized medicine abroad."

Cook's work is best-selling fiction girded by science fact. His novels have dissected a host of hot-button issues in medical practice, among them stem-cell research, organ donation and genetic decoding.

With his 26th book, *Critical*, Cook uses series character Laurie Montgomery, a New York City medical examiner last seen in 2006's *Crisis*, to examine a fresh controversy: specialty hospitals and the impact they will have on the health care industry. New doctor-owned, for-profit surgical facilities have emerged that he says promise a gold mine for investors, though raising troubling questions about patient safety and potential conflicts of interest.

"These facilities are sort of like the concept of concierge medicine, and they serve to increase the cost of care while providing it mainly to the wealthy and well-insured. It tells me that our system is out of whack."

A resident of Florida and Massachusetts, Cook, 67, is a graduate of Columbia University Medical School and completed his postgraduate medical training at Harvard. He is now on leave from the Massachusetts Eye and Ear Infirmary.

Cook says specialty surgery hospitals often are newer, cleaner and more efficient, and some patients do benefit. Nonetheless, he finds the concept as practiced, with some revenue derived from public monies, to be a violation of social justice.

"We are not offering everyone the same care."

Compounding the problem, in Cook's view, is greed.

"The goal of being a very good doctor has been trumped by the opportunity to make more money, sometimes big money. If a doctor wants to invest in a full-service hospital, the chance of there being a problem with self-interest is very low. But when specialty hospitals started out with these little surgery centers that have gotten to the point of looking like a whole hospital, the equation changes," he says.

"If you're only doing one thing, then there's a large opportunity for conflict of interest. That's the reason specialty hospitals are a problem. Not only does the surgeon get his large pay for doing the operation, but in a doctor-owned facility he also gets paid for having the patient stay in the hospital. The question is, is a specialty hospital really a hospital? I say it is not. If someone has a heart attack, the specialty hospital will have to call 911."

Cook insists the long-term effect that high-profit specialty hospitals will exert on the health care industry is to widen the disparities in care between the haves and have-nots, generally benefiting well-heeled upper- and middle-class people. While not an advocate of any one system, Cook the author, unlike the American Medical Association, does not quake at the term "socialization."

"Money should not be the goal in medicine. It should not be a business. Why is the idea of socialized medicine any different from the idea of socialized law enforcement? Can you imagine what it would be like to have profit-making law enforcement or firefighting services? No politician has ever said we should not have socialized police forces in the U.S.

"I've been a Republican. I didn't even like the idea of insurance in medicine until about 20 years ago. I always felt a direct fiduciary relationship between doctor and patient is better for everybody, but catastrophic circumstances are different. That was back when I thought medicine would respond to market forces. But it is obvious to me now that it does not. People have a right to health care.

Cook says the way we pay physicians today makes no sense whatsoever.

"We pay an invasive cardiologist much, much more than what we pay a primary care physician. You need not be a genius to know the answer to some of the questions facing medicine."

August 12, 2007

Mary Alice Monroe's *Sweetgrass*

Why does a nation increasingly homogenized look so wistfully to the South, a place it once disparaged as backward and inert? Could it be, as Mary Alice Monroe suggests, a reflection of a longing for permanence?

"Why is the lowcountry so interesting? I think it's because in a place where families stay for generations and don't move away, the culture is strong. But it's not just the culture. It's the ritual, the family rituals of birthdays and weddings and deaths. It's such a rich collective identity of the family that you wonder what will happen if it dissipates. Who are we when we lose our place, when we lose community?"

Monroe's eighth novel, her first in hardcover, is foremost a study in family, family ritual and what occurs when this scaffolding breaks down. Like all her novels, *Sweetgrass* (Mira Books) also deals with the natural world, the perils confronting it and parallels in the human realm.

Named for the indigenous plant that grows within its borders, Sweetgrass is the ancestral estate of the Blakely family, which for eight generations has been the steward of the plantation along the South Carolina coast.

But intruding on the whisper of the grasses is a new, harsher sound, that of bulldozers flattening nearby properties. With it comes development, propelling property taxes through the roof.

While some families see an opportunity to capitalize on soaring land values, others, often at odds with parents and siblings, fear they may be forced to sell the one thing that binds them.

The Blakelys are as endangered as the grasses. For Mary "Mama June" Blakely, the struggle to save her home has been more burden than holy war.

Unlike her husband, Preston, who views the endurance of Sweetgrass as an end in itself, Mama June fears the further disintegration of her already fractured family.

Tragedy drove her son, Morgan, to the Far West. Her daughter, Nan, is wed to one of the same developers who would displace them. When misfortune strikes another blow—Preston's debilitating stroke—it is up to Mama June and Nona Bennett, the former family housekeeper whose ties to Sweetgrass are no less strong, to save that which is vital to both families. For Bennett, it is the sweetgrass itself and the survival of a 300-year-old legacy: The land harbors one of the few remaining sources of the grass that she uses to weave her traditional baskets.

Wings and Weaves

"I always write relationship novels—that's where my heart is—but since *Beach House*, I'm always looking for endangered species or something else to tie in with nature," says Monroe, a resident of the Isle of Palms. "I was doing volunteer work at the South Carolina Center for Birds of Prey (in 2003) and finishing my last book (*Skyward*), plus trying to figure out what the next one would be.

"We were releasing hawks one day, and it was really clear how important it was to choose the area correctly. I realized that loss of habitat was a real concern, not only for birds of prey but for all species. That was playing in my mind, and then I was watching someone weaving a sweetgrass basket. I inquired about it and as I learned more about the baskets, I also found that the grass itself was disappearing. I don't think a lot of people in South Carolina are aware that this indigenous plant is vanishing."

And then it clicked. Monroe, who invests a great deal of time in research and preparation, saw all her story elements coming together.

"You have the disappearance of the plant because of development along the coast. Then you have the disappearance of a culture, the art form of baskets that was many years in the making. Then when I related what loss of habitat means to human beings—loss of home—I had a great story. I dove in."

Monroe continues to be associated with a variety of environmental organizations in addition to her other community work. She says that whatever the subject, she is neither lecturer nor teacher, but listener. She quotes the late Joseph Campbell, who stressed that writers are the shamans of modern times, and that it is their task to put their ears to the ground.

"I've always said that a good writer is a better listener. I think as an intuitive writer you just have to go with hunches, and I am 100 percent intuitive, and I was tingling and knew I was on the right path with this story. Then I started the interviews. The academics first, like Dale Rosengarten. Then I went out into the field (speaking with local families). It's not their story; it's fiction. But I was inspired by their struggle to try to preserve a portion of their land and the compromises that have to be made. That is part of the core of the book."

Serendipity also has taken a hand. Monroe notes the recent distribution of real estate reassessments for Charleston County, an occasion for many a tremor and much gnashing of teeth. The fictional Blakely family doubtless will have company.

"Everyone is going to sympathize with them, because that's happening right now."

The Metaphor

In an earlier interview, Monroe addressed her inclination to pen novels with strong settings in nature, and that her inspiration comes from the analogies between nature's struggles and those of people.

"In *Sweetgrass*, the metaphor is really pretty obvious. It's a family saga, a story of a mother's journey. It's two women, actually, two matriarchs, Mama June and Nona. Mama June was the heart of her family, and when she fell apart, the family collapsed. Then the husband has a stroke. Suddenly, this woman has to pull her family back together. So while she's ostensibly trying to save Sweetgrass the estate, she's really saving her family.

"She is weaving together all the disparate pieces of her family into a new whole. So on the one hand, they ask the question: What do we do about Sweetgrass? But what they are really asking is what do we do about our collective identity, and what is family?"

One of the themes evident early in the book is the tension between outrage over rampant development and the persistent difficulty, or inability, to come to terms with the inevitability of change.

"You can't change the fact that a million people are going to move here (the lowcountry). The question is how can we find answers that work for us? There are answers, and the challenge is to face the question," says Monroe. "My concern is that everyone becomes aware of what has to be protected. There are a lot of mistakes being made, even by people with good intentions, because it hasn't been well-researched. There have to be serious organizations like the South Carolina Coastal Conservation League to guide the way, that will consider all alternatives.

"I think conservation easements are the wave of the future. They are here now; they do great work. They are giving families an opportunity to save land. That, in turn, protects habitat and green space in an urban growth area. We need to prepare for the projected population growth."

The issue is one keenly felt by Monroe, who felt compelled to relinquish land of her own.

"My family has a big farm in Vermont. My husband, Marcus, and I sold our piece of it. I wrote the book, I think, to solve that parting for me. How did I feel about my loss of not being a part of the family land? Even though it's still there, and I can visit, my association has been severed. We did it to get a place here. It's just decisions you have to make, so I sympathize with the ones other people face."

Approach Vector

Monroe, in the process of finishing her ninth book, *Turtle Beach*, insists she has an odd way of writing. The preparation she relishes also can be painful.

"I'm in agony, because I'm sure I can never do it again. I know the germ of the idea. But until it clicks, until I 'get it,' I can't begin the first sentence. Then I call it projectile writing. It just all comes out, a very tense and draining time for me. Until I get 50 to 80, maybe a hundred pages in, the characters are rough. Structurally, I know who they are and what they have to do and their motivations. But I can't necessarily speak for them. But gradually I get the feeling for who they are, as with Mama June, the protagonist. As a writer, you're so invested in her.

"The second time through, when I edit, I go in with a very sharp eye for every movement and every bit of dialogue so that the reader knows who that character is right away."

And Monroe says she has so many stories left to tell.

"There are stories I am supposed to tell, and it goes beyond nature to what is deep inside my heart and my spirit. It sounds almost corny, but I truly believe this. My job is to find the parallel. It seems the niche I have created and am able to do is with nature. It's all about trusting your instincts and finding a vehicle. As long as people are willing to listen, I'm going to write the stories."

July 3, 2005

Anthony Doerr's *Memory Wall*

If life is a progression of short stories pretending to be a novel, it has one of its most perceptive chroniclers in Anthony Doerr.

On the release of his first collection, *The Shell Collector* (2001), many hailed the Cleveland-area native as the great young hope of short fiction. Though he has expanded into novels (*About Grace*) and memoirs (*Four Seasons in Rome*), little has changed but his expectations.

"I had no expectations when I was writing *The Shell Collector*, and it was a liberating experience," says Doerr, whose second collection, *Memory Wall*, was published this week by Scribner.

"I like to think this new book is better, more grown-up. I'm a father now and have a small readership that I want to honor with careful, generous work."

Doerr draws on his disparate, often exotic travels and varied occupations—working in a fish cannery, as a cook, on fruit and sheep farms—to craft lyrical tales.

"I want to make every sentence count. My short fiction is about taking on larger issues through the lens of an individual, a single character."

Doerr's stories have captured three O. Henry Prizes and have been anthologized in *The Best American Short Stories*, *The Anchor Book of New American Short Stories* and *The Scribner Anthology of Contemporary Fiction*.

He has won the Barnes & Noble Discover Prize, the Rome Prize and the New York Public Library's Young Lions Fiction Award.

In 2007, Granta magazine also secured a place for Doerr on its list of the "21 Best Young American Novelists."

Now living in Boise, where he serves as writer-in-residence for the state of Idaho, he moonlights writing a column on science books for The Boston Globe.

Like *The Shell Collector*, Doerr's new collection embodies his fascination with the natural world. But here, as the title story suggests, the emphasis is on memory, how it lends coherence and meaning to human experience.

Originally published in McSweeney's, the story earned the National Magazine Award for fiction. Another, "The River Nemunas," was awarded a Pushcart Prize.

"For some time now I've wanted to do something about memory and the fragility of it, how it can change," says Doerr, a 1995 graduate of Bowdoin College in Maine.

"For example, every day we lose hundreds more people who experienced World War II. And we lose their memories. Once something becomes history, it is really malleable, of variable quality and veracity. In a small way 'Memory Wall' is investigating the fragility and malleability of memory, which is why a lot of characters in the collection suffer from dementia.

"The great strength of this story collection is that it can open lots of windows on a single topic, more so than the novel can."

Four Seasons in Rome detailed his family's year in Rome, when Doerr was a fellow at the American Academy of Arts and Letters. The influence on his work exerted by that interlude also is a reflection of the potency of memory.

"Memory and history," he says. "Stories are embedded in the stone in Rome. When I came back to the States, it taught me a lot about America, how new we still are and how we erased the memories of those who were on the land before us. All these things are rooted in history."

Doerr's short stories vary significantly in length, with *Memory Wall* harboring some of his longer pieces.

"There is a cliff you come to when you get to about 40 pages in a story, knowing that it will be hard to get a magazine to commit to something of that length," he says. "But you must make the work as long as it needs to be."

He says his writing process begins with an arresting subject or observation.

"I get really interested in things that seem discordant. Like in the story 'The Demilitarized Zone.' I try to see how I can build that up. Or 'Village 113,' which opens with the Three Gorges Dam in China," he says.

"For me, the way I've always understood such immense things as wars or that dam project and its displacements is through stories and narratives, through individuals."

The author likens reading a story collection on the same theme to asking viewers to watch a sitcom in which all the characters change week to week, and he is grateful to have an audience willing to make that commitment to his short form work.

"Again, it's a small audience. And when I think of (the size of) the readership, I get a little worried. But I'm encouraged by the quality of the work out there, writers like David Means or Andrea Barrett, to name two. So I don't despair at all in terms of quality. That said, I'm still very much a print media guy, and I wonder how things like Kindle will change novels or story collections.

"Will the latter be like an album from which people buy individual songs?"

July 18, 2010

Roger Pinckney's *Signs and Wonders*

DAUFUSKIE ISLAND—Roger Pinckney's venerable white Jeep Cherokee jiggles along a rutted road, passing quaintly restored chapels, abandoned houses overgrown with vegetation, and tidy little homes nestled in the embrace of maritime forest.

The occasional incursion of shiny new development, as at Haig Point, is offset by street signs suggestive of this island's unhurried identity, and drawing power. Turtle Pace Lane says it all.

"People who leave Daufuskie sometimes have a hard time adjusting to the faster pace elsewhere," says author and activist Pinckney, whose new book is the essay collection *Signs and Wonders* (Wyrick & Co.). "Those coming here for the first time don't seem to have quite so taxing an adjustment."

Pinckney, born in Beaufort, celebrates his connection to this still bucolic place, a five-mile-long, two-mile-wide sea island near Hilton Head—alone among its larger neighbors in having no bridge. But it took him 30 years to renew his acquaintance.

Heeding the call of the Y chromosome, Pinckney left the lowcountry for Alaska in his 20s. His odyssey stalled in Minnesota—for three decades—where the avid outdoorsman traded an ocean for lakes and first made a living raising livestock. Writing came later.

Three daughters and a son all were born in the North Star State, but the siren song of the South was never entirely stilled.

In the late 1990s, Pinckney found he was spending up to five months of the year in the area in the course of researching magazine articles. He moved back home for good during Christmas 1998.

> "I wasn't thinking about land or money or voodoo vittles. I was thinking of the magic of the new moon floodtide, 10,000 acres inundated, the feeder creeks and little salt guts crackling with shrimp, and the redfish in the shallows and the cedar hummocks off in the distance and the blue sky beyond and the wind singing sad songs that only those who love this place can hear." (*Signs and Wonders*)

His vivid prose often has a lyrical, even ethereal quality, but Pinckney, a stocky, Hemingway-esque figure, is direct and plain-spoken, with an, um, well-established personality. Which is to say he harbors strong opinions and doesn't mind casting them off the dock for review. Sometimes to the consternation of those whose visions he opposes.

In recent years, it is balancing sparsely settled Daufuskie's traditional way of life with the inevitability of change that, other than writing, consumes his energies. Today, hobbling on a freshly broken toe on his left foot, he rolls a cigarette from a fragrant pouch of tobacco and holds forth not on the past, but on the future.

What is needed, he says, is equilibrium between growth and the imperatives of cultural and environmental preservation.

"Maybe 25 years ago developers thought of property as just raw material, to see how tastefully they could shoehorn in as many houses as they could and develop amenities like golf and tennis and marinas and whatever else would enhance the real estate value. But as open land gets scarcer, I think it's time for a new model. It's no longer about how many houses can we build.

"People come to the lowcountry from all over the world, and they are fascinated by it. What we're doing is destroying what people come here for. What we have a chance to do on Daufuskie Island is to turn that around, to say that if a third of your property is in a conservation easement, that's not going to cost you money because you can put in fewer homes. It's going to make you money because the people who buy the property place a premium on the natural world."

Pinckney is convinced most homeowners or prospective buyers would agree on the financial and spiritual benefits of being surrounded by green space. He believes better towns and better communities make better people and that one key to this is one's emotional response to place.

"We have all kinds of opportunities over here. A lot of permits that have been issued in the past for traditional Sea Pines Plantation-type, high-density development are still in place on some of this green space that you see here. And the reason that it was never developed was just because of economics. But now we have an opportunity to rethink this whole thing. It's an opportunity that won't come again. There is a direct financial benefit in preserving land, clean water, clean air and wild animals. But to me the spiritual value is more important."

It just took a while for Pinckney to put it into words—and action. While working recently on another collection of essays, *The Fish Crow Chronicles*, it occurred to him that he was "the seventh son," heir to a tradition of Pinckneys in the lowcountry that extends seven generations to Roger Pinckney IV in 1767.

"I suddenly realized that all the Roger Pinckneys (of which he is the 11th and his son the 12th) were first sons. But I'm the seventh one in the lowcountry, and you know the seventh son, traditionally, is the warrior poet. When I was a kid, I saw Hilton Head basically go under the plow and saw these islands I loved changing and the Gullah people that I loved being displaced. But I avoided writing about it for a long time."

During his school years Pinckney did not give much thought to following in the footsteps of past voices of Daufuskie, like Albert Stoddard or Billie Burn and her son, Bobby. Even later ones, like Pat Conroy, did not galvanize him at first.

"I avoided my responsibilities as a chronicler, as an advocate for my land and my people because I guess I wasn't physically and emotionally and mentally up to it. For 30 years I did something else."

It was not wasted time. The harsh winters of Minnesota carved him like a rock face worn by the elements, leaving a granitic resolve. Not to say he relishes the role, in 2004, of gadfly or nemesis. Necessarily.

"I want to live a life and not be a lightning rod. But I also want to be able to leave something to my children and my grandchildren, and your grandchildren. I believe in this island culture, which is unique and different from the Southern experience as a whole. I'm a cultural partisan."

> "The wind gathers sand and sends it hissing along the beach. It sounds like dry snow sliding off the tin roof of the barn I no longer own, and suddenly Minnesota's frozen fields and crystalline lakes and brooding spruce seem another world, someone else's life."

Drawn largely from previously published material in such periodicals as Saltwater Sportsman, Gray's Sporting Journal, and Sporting Classics, *Signs and Wonders* continues the coalescing of Pinckney's interior and exterior explorations.

The book is not simply about his life on Daufuskie ("sharp like a feather," in the original Indian dialect), but about being a voyageur in the Land of 10,000 Lakes and other points of nature's compass. Not to mention living for 27 years in a log cabin with only wood for heat.

A previous book, *The Right Side of the River*, had more to do with his time on Daufuskie, whereas *Signs and Wonders* is described by its author as the timeline of his life and the blessings he's received. Other books include the novel *Little Glory*, which he characterizes, gleefully, as strident and politically incorrect, *Blue Roots* and *The Beaufort Chronicles.*

If Pinckney's style is influenced chiefly by that of novelist Cormac McCarthy, his observations remind one of any number of writers, from Twain to Edward Abbey. His muse is much closer: Susan Card (his "angel of shining light"), with whom the author shares a beachfront home.

"I feel that I'm a craftsman and an artist, but at the same time I'm also a technician. I use few words, yet it's all in how you arrange the words, the rhythm you impart to them, the poetry you can evoke. My broader goals with *Signs and Wonders* were to have such a recognizable style and be so good at what I do that (people) recognize that 'This guy's got something to say.'"

What originally drew Pinckney to writing was not his fascination with hunting and fishing, the wild, or a cause to espouse. It was genetics, he says, and the fates.

"My grandmother worked for The State in Columbia, the first female journalist to be able to write beyond the society pages. My father was a storyteller to the point where the Smithsonian came down and recorded him. So I think that that, and the conjunction of the planets, had me destined to do it.

"But, like I said, I really tried not to do it for a long time. When I broke down in Minnesota on the way to Alaska I started by raising cattle and horses. I also raised hay and oats and all my kids in the saddle. My day job was restoring sports cars. I eased into writing by working for newspapers, covering everything from revolutionary Indians to marijuana farms."

Later, his work in the Minnesota secondary school system showed him that people could take control of their community and achieve things.

"I always look for common ground and consensus. But the warrior poet in me also says, 'We want a new way.' I was hired in 1999 by the Daufuskie Island Community Improvement Club to put together a community needs assessment called 'Daufuskie 2–0/20.' We sent a letter and a survey to 1,700 people on the island. It came back in favor of, No. 1, historic preservation, and No. 2, environmental protection.

"When that was distributed, it hit the fan with the real estate people. But we're not trying to stop anything; we're trying to build a community. The payoff is huge when you can strike a balance between the native population, the natural world and development."

> "Down here on Daufuskie, there are 150 of us on 5,000 acres, no bridge, no bank, no traffic lights, no traffic at all. The fast food has hooves and horns and fins and feathers. There's no gas and no law, except the immutable statutes of God and time and tide."

Pinckney does not draw a line between the natural world and the humans who, not always thoughtfully, inhabit it. Just as it is vital to preserve the wild, he says it is foolish to attempt to seal it off from direct (not simply observational) human experience, whether by development or other means.

"There are groups in this country that are locking up the land. And there is some political agitation to lock up the lands of the west. Land locked up certainly has a value. But the real value of wild spaces is their ability or tendency to affect human behavior, to affect the human heart. What good does it do to have it locked up so there's just a little knot of people looking at it? We need people out in it. We need people to experience it. It has to be accessible to the public. Too many places aren't. It's private and you can't go there."

A self-described Jeffersonian, Pinckney says he is of two hearts.

"Part of me says, 'Let's find what works and do it. Another part of me says, 'Let's go beyond that.' I want to see a new American Revolution. If our culture and our nation is to be saved, and there is obviously some doubt about it after 9/11, our bedrock values will save it."

August 1, 2004

David Cox's *Dirty Secrets, Dirty War*

It was a human nightmare. And a journalist's crucible.

March 1976. Following the coup against Isabel Peron, the armed forces of Argentina formally exercised power through a right-wing junta whose leaders would rule until December 10, 1983. They called their repressive governing program the National Reorganization Process.

Using the tactics adopted by the opposition Montoneros (left-wing Peronists) and People's Revolutionary Army as rationale, these military dictators attempted to silence all dissenting voices.

The linchpin of their doctrine of ideological war was the elimination of the "social base" of insurgency, which translated as the detention, torture and murder of intellectuals, middle-class students and labor organizers, though few had proven ties to leftist guerrillas. By the end of the 1970s, the insurgents had been suppressed, but the nation had suffered horribly from its "Dirty War."

Documenting the disappearance and probable death of some 11,000 people at the hands of the military regime, the 1984 Commission on the Disappeared was a grisly testament to political paranoia. But human rights groups estimate that more than 30,000 "disappeared" (arrested and executed without trial) during the 1976–83 purge. This does not count an estimated 1,500 deaths attributed to various guerrilla attacks and assassinations.

Many fled into exile. Few dared voice outrage, save for the Mothers of the Plaza de Mayo, mothers of the dead and disappeared who began holding vigils in April, 1977. Their demands for an accounting were unmet.

As editor of the *Buenos Aires Herald*, Robert Cox, who had immigrated to the country from England in 1959, exhorted the generals to stop the killing, even trying to engage them directly—a delicate and dangerous process. Exhibiting tenacity and courage, he stayed on as others left, fighting to bring the truth to light until the safety of his family finally compelled him to leave.

"We all grew up very quickly in that time," recalls 42-year-old journalist David Cox, who followed in his father's footsteps. "There was the fear of constantly being watched. We were children, but we knew what was going on. It wasn't just when the military came to power in 1976; it started earlier. All these people had been killed. My father, who saw this happening before anyone else, felt he had to stay.

"He spoke harshly to the generals. But when the word came that we were going to be next on the list, my mother pleaded with him for us to leave. At first, he wanted the family to go ahead of him while he stayed and did the work. But even though my mother believed in what he was doing and was partly the source of his courage, what it came down to was her saying, 'We need you with us.' We all came out of it alive, which was a miracle."

Robert Cox retired earlier this year as assistant editor of The Post and Courier after 28 years of service.

His son, a producer with CNN in Atlanta, is the author of the chronicle *Dirty Secrets, Dirty War: The Exile of Editor Robert J. Cox (Buenos Aires, Argentina: 1976–1983)*, published by the book division of Evening Post Ventures in association with Joggling Board Press.

Economic disarray, corruption and public revulsion, not to mention the regime's defeat at the hands of Great Britain in the Falklands War of 1982, finally discredited the junta and led to the lifting of bans on political parties and basic political liberties. But grave damage had been done.

David, who also remembers an Argentine childhood that was "very rich, full of immense wonders," wrote the book his father could not.

"After the experience we had endured, my father wanted a place that would be quiet and good for the family. He went ahead of us, to Charleston. Once the family arrived here, it was quite something to us, so green and tranquil—a dream. This was very powerful, this feeling of calmness.

"When I was still little, my mother asked my father to write this book, thinking that it would do him good because of everything he was going through—and to this day still does go through. He tried. Later I asked him to do the book and hoped he would follow through. It was important to the whole family, but most important for him, because everything he had experienced was so intense and difficult. But it was too painful; he had seen way too much, and just couldn't write it."

The job fell to David to write a story about journalism, about terrorism and about family.

"It is, of course, a tribute to my father, who, in opposing the junta, did something very few did. Because of that, a lot of people still are alive. The hardest thing for me was to sit down and hear his voice on the recordings that had been made when he was in Argentina, recordings made in order to protect his life, for fear that at any moment anything might happen. He wanted to leave some sort of testimony.

"My father kept every single document, which was amazing since a lot of things in Argentina had been destroyed. I felt this enormous responsibility to be able to write it in the most objective way."

David first wrote a Spanish-language account of letters exchanged between his father and a confidante, loosely translated as *Witness to the Truth*, which he says is very different in approach than *Dirty Secrets, Dirty War*.

"It is pure, objective testimony. There is a big struggle in Argentina about the truth of what really happened, though things are coming out more and more. It is now very hard to deny what happened."

When David, himself a former Herald staffer, was in Buenos Aires writing *Witness to the Truth*, he injected himself into the narrative only to the extent of relating what he was experiencing there upon his return. "I spoke to the generals. I also spoke to the victims. I asked them questions I had not been able to ask when I was very little."

With *Dirty Secrets, Dirty War*, he wanted to tell his father's story and stay completely out of it. David felt he had been presented with a great opportunity, not only to describe his family's experience, but the story of all those who had suffered.

"It is my hope that people can take something positive out of this," he says. "It's still very emotional, though. The story still touches us, affecting each one of us in a different way. But I think that the more we make the journey as a family, the easier it becomes. I knew it would be painful, but in many ways it is a relief. For the first time, my brother, Peter, has been able to open up about what he experienced.

"I felt I had to do it, really, for my father. Although this is a family story, I felt this tremendous burden to set my father free, and to tell this story to my generation."

December 7, 2008

Fritz Hollings's *Making Government Work*

"Show me the money."

This familiar catchphrase from "Jerry Maguire," a popular sports movie, applies just as snugly to national political figures immersed in the perpetual campaign, the perpetual pursuit of campaign cash, often to the detriment of the job they were elected to do. But it is only one way in which money, ill-used, exerts a disruptive influence on governance, says former Sen. Ernest F. "Fritz" Hollings.

He considers money the cancer of the age. And he approaches the scourge like a surgeon in *Making Government Work: Lessons From a Life in Politics*, to be released Monday by the University of South Carolina Press. Written with Kirk Victor, who covers the U.S. Senate for the National Journal, the book is equal parts memoir of a career in public service and a cautionary tale on the political and economic quandaries that face the nation.

Hollings says he had no intention of trotting out a tedious "He said, she said" narrative.

"I knew that if I was to write an autobiography, I was going to focus on what was really significant that I know about, something that would be a theme. And that theme is trying to make the government work again. We have a standoff now, and the election in November is not going to change this, not until they cut the money and untie the knot. The campaigns are way too long. Ten years ago, I had to raise $8.5 million, which is $30,000 a week, every week, for six years. Money is the cancer on the body politic. Nothing will get done until you cut the money."

Public service

Trained as a trial lawyer, the Charleston native began his political career as a South Carolina legislator (1949–54), progressing to lieutenant governor (1955–59), governor (1959–63) and U.S. senator (1966–2005). He was a U.S. presidential candidate in 1983–84. Throughout, says Hollings, he has focused on putting government on a sound financial basis and championing economic development.

With policy expertise on the budget, telecommunications, the environment, defense, trade and space, he was the author of the Coastal Zone Management Act (1972), Ocean Dumping Act (1972) and Automobile Fuel Economy Act (1975), as well as co-author of the Gramm-Rudman-Hollings Deficit Reduction Act of 1985. Hollings led in the creation of the Special Supplemental Nutrition Program for Women, Infants and Children in 1972 and passage of the Telecommunications Act of 1996.

In 2008, Hollings sees much in the way of governmental missteps—and inaction. His experience in the trenches suggests some remedies.

"It was said once that we give a six-year term to a senator, rather than to a congressman. Two years to be statesman, two years to be a politician and the last two years to be a demagogue. Now we spend all six years raising money. Big business controls much of the money flowing into campaigns, and this flow has anesthetized the public servant. We have to go to work for the country instead of the campaign. If you limit the money, you limit the campaign. Unlike (ex-Bush administration press secretary) Scott McClellan, who finally came clean, everything I say in the book I also said while I was in office."

Streamlining a Life

At 360 pages, the six-term senator has not produced a volume on the order of former President Clinton's 900-page tome. Approaching it with a sense of economy, Hollings says he wrote most of it from memory. He had to (with the aid of Victor's fact-checking) after losing his voluminous notes to a house fire.

A 1942 graduate of the Citadel, Hollings received a law degree from the University of South Carolina in 1947, beginning a 20-year practice the following year. But little of his early years and education makes the cut. Nor do his years in the military. Hollings served as an officer in the Army's 323rd and 457th Artillery during World War II (1942–45) and was awarded the Bronze Star.

"Even omitting most of this, I had to cut the book short. There's a heck of a lot of good stories I had to leave out. I don't spend much time discussing earmarks. They used to say, 'Rivers delivers,' but I have delivered way more than Mendel Rivers, I can tell you that. And I'm proud of it. But I had to do it quietly. And I left all of that out of the book. But I did put in my failures."

As an example of failure, he cites the federal budget.

"I thought we had balanced the budget under Bill Clinton in 1993 when he came to town, and I helped fashion that tax plan. We had eight years of the best economy and we gave George W. Bush surpluses as far as the eye could see. He said we'll get rid of the national debt. Then he went for tax cuts. And now we have added on an average, for seven years, $514 billion more than we've taken in each and every year. We will have added $4 trillion to the debt by September, which has zoomed up the interest costs over $400 billion, over

$1 billion a day. These are interest payments to obtain . . . nothing. The first thing the government does each day is borrow a billion dollars."

Hollings confronts what he terms an increasingly flawed political system and a government that has gone "into the ditch." It may seem stuck in that ditch, but it can be excavated, he says.

"It can. The willingness to do so is a reflection of the people."

Reality vs. Illusion

Every generation of middle-age adults seems to survey the scene of civilization and conclude that we are all going to Hades in a handbasket. Politically and culturally, Hollings sees peril and promise ahead. Though his emphasis is on the former, he is optimistic we can escape the traps if there is the will to do so.

"I'm trying to get to today's reality in the book. We are going out of business. You not only have lost 3.2 million manufacturing jobs since George W. Bush got in, with a 94,500 net loss of manufacturing jobs in South Carolina, but what hasn't been outsourced—and there is a hemorrhaging of outsourcing of jobs—is being bought up because of the cheap dollar and us running all these deficits.

The French bought up Bell Labs. Japan owns Westinghouse Nuclear. Taiwan has Gateway. China has IBM and all its software. Some 8,600 plants at a cost of $1.3 trillion in the last 10 years have been bought. It's the cheap dollar. It's perilous, and we need to wake up the government. We're in a trade war, and we have to start competing. There's no mystery to it."

Hollings also holds forth on strengthening regulations on free trade and amplifying our communications and education programs to compete more effectively in an information-driven global marketplace.

The chorus rhapsodizing over "free trade," Hollings says, is singing off-key.

"The idea of free trade is like world peace. It's a good goal. But you're not going to have world peace anytime soon. The way to get free trade is to raise a barrier to a barrier, then remove them both. Again, you have to compete. But this is against the rules now in government."

Hollings remains a staunch proponent of "fiscally responsible yet progressive programs" not being mutually exclusive.

"You learn as a governor that you cannot run for governor of South Carolina unless you promise to pay the bills. But if you are running for the Senate, forget about paying the bills; you promise the reverse: tax cuts. Neither party is going to recommend raising taxes again, but they've got to do it. We've got to make it profitable to produce in the United States. Corporate greed is not going to get you anywhere."

As the author or co-author of five trade bills, Hollings knows something of incentives and disincentives.

"Henry Ford helped create our trade policy, protecting American industry. He wanted the fellow manufacturing the car to be able to buy it. He doubled the minimum wage. He put in the first health benefits and the first retirement benefits, furthering the development of the middle class. Now, you try to put in a trade bill like old Hollings did, and they'll come down on your head: the banks, Wall Street, the Business Round Table, even the U.S. Chamber of Commerce. In 1992, I was the chamber's Man of the Year. By 1998, I was a pariah on account of my opposition to NAFTA."

And so on. Hollings, 86, says his worry in the course of writing the book was, "Could I be relevant?"

Making Government Work answers the question.

June 15, 2008

Harriet McBryde Johnson's *Too Late to Die Young*

She is what she always wanted to be, someone forever striving after the wind, playing an active role in the saga of her own composition.

In the lexicon of life being written by Harriet McBryde Johnson, certain words are deprived of their negative potency. There is no operative phrase such as "in spite of," no well-meaning but counterproductive nicety so fashionable in this age of euphemisms.

The Charleston lawyer is as forthright, as funny, as direct as they come, with pointed opinions (and shafts of barbed wit) that bristle from a quiver of ideas—and objections.

The proof, for those who haven't met her, is in the memoir *Too Late to Die Young: Nearly True Tales From a Life*, released this month by Henry Holt and Co.

A congenital neuromuscular disease may have rendered her unable to walk, dress or bathe without assistance, but it has not impeded her in what matters to her most, be it championing the disability rights movement, representing her clients, running for office, engaging in spirited debate, travel, or savoring the sensual delights of her native Charleston.

She is a vivid contradiction to the prevailing assumption about the disabled. With this book, she lets us "peek in her basement."

"(The prospect of) doing the book was not all that enticing at first. Where was I going to find the time?" says Johnson, first approached after her essay in The New York Times Magazine, "Should I Have Been Killed at Birth?"

"But I think there is good to be had from sharing experiences and perceptions. I am not Mahatma Gandhi, nor a candidate for sainthood. I enjoy writing, and it is something I am pretty good at, though all my stories begin with the spoken word. I wanted to communicate at several levels with this book. It was something of a vacation from my normal writing, which is strongly analytical, and in which being personal and colorful is frowned upon.

"Different people are looking for different things in the book. Since the Times story, reaction has been all over the map."

If others choose to superimpose their presumptions as an overlay to her stories, that's their option. Johnson takes an anecdotal approach, setting a tone from the start.

She deflects the reader from any maudlin state of mind by writing, "God didn't put me on this street to provide disability awareness training to everyone" or to "feed the public appetite for inspirational pap."

Johnson always has refused to be reduced to a "stock figure in melodramas about courage and determination." In her 20s, Johnson had come to feel set apart not by realities, but by perceptions, hers as well as others'. And now?

"I think it's true that every human being is different. But with a visible disability, most of society puts you in a box. And it is considered significant in a way that other things aren't. So I do think perceptions remain the most powerful differences there are.

"To a certain extent, it's necessary to size people up pretty quickly as you go through life. We make inferences based on somebody's age or their occupation, their (political) party affiliation. That's not a bad thing. The problem is when it evolves into a full-blown stereotype, when it's a whole cluster of characteristics that become a whole bag of assumptions about disabled people or people defined as terminally ill, and where it gets real hard to break through. Where assumptions are not stereotypes, it's pretty easy for us to adjust them, without a lot of angst, when we meet someone who doesn't fit our preconceived notion. But when it's a stereotype, people resist changing."

For more than 25 years, Johnson has been active in the struggle for social justice, her law practice centering on benefits and civil rights claims for poor and working people with disabilities. In popular parlance, if not the law, the landscape of the language has changed.

But supposedly kinder, gentler terms such as "differently abled" are not used by people with disabilities, Johnson says.

"They're usually used by those who, it seems, cannot face the reality. I've never heard a person in a wheelchair say they were 'physically challenged.' Within the disability rights movement, as with other liberation movements, there's been an effort to reclaim language and make it our own. So a lot of us on the more radical end use words like 'crip' just as gays and lesbians use the word 'queer.' But those words aren't quite acceptable outside the group, certainly not in a journalistic or professional context."

Johnson says that there exists a consensus within the movement that there are correct ways to refer to disabilities that are neutral.

"'A person with a disability,' for example, or someone simply saying, 'I have a neuromuscular disease,' not 'afflicted,' not 'suffering from,' or 'I use a wheelchair' rather than 'I'm confined to it.' Those are the ones who really make me crazy, because a lot of my clients who are newly disabled fight using wheelchairs and other things that would be helpful, and they'll actually say, 'I'm not ready to be wheelchair-bound.' It sounds so horrible.

"Well, many of these folks aren't bound to it; they can walk a little bit. But a wheelchair would enable them to get out a lot more and go a lot farther a lot faster. So that language does have an effect on behavior and how people feel about themselves."

One reason Johnson chose to write about herself—there's also a novel, *Accidents of Nature*, in the works—was that she could do so without worrying what someone was going to think.

"In a way, it's very freeing not to have to worry, 'Am I being totally fair here?' I can just go ahead and say it."

And say it she does.

Johnson's even tones do not mask the passion with which she addresses the concept of life as a "treasure of infinite value," her own right to live and her opposition to assisted suicide. It's a particularly hot-button issue of late, what with the saturation coverage of the Terri Schiavo case.

But what of the converse: someone's right to die? Who holds dominion over a life, if not the individual?

Johnson has not seen "The Sea Inside" or "Million Dollar Baby," current films that deal, respectively, in a direct and indirect way with assisted suicide. She has, however, read about them extensively.

"That's a very long and complicated batch of questions, and I guess if we're talking about the common media framing of the issue, basically what we see in a lot of these literary presentations is an underlying cultural assumption that when people with disabilities want to kill ourselves it's a rational decision, while with other people who want to kill themselves, the presumption goes the other way.

"There are many, many unbearable losses, but if you want to kill yourself because your spouse has died, you had a horrible disgrace, you lost your job—any of the reasons that people do it, the response in the culture is to reach out to you and to help you transcend. But any time you want to have a nuanced moral dilemma, make the person a quadriplegic, and the presumption goes the other way."

The reality known within the movement and in the literature of social sciences, Johnson argues, is that losses of physical capacity can be transcended, too.

"People do get past it, and they rate their lives as good or better than it was before. But because there's this presumption that 'Oh, I wouldn't want to live that way, no one would want to live that way,' it becomes a totally different dynamic.

"With all these assisted-suicide dramas there is that underlying assumption that this is an unbearable loss. And that's a stereotype. Even a movie that doesn't take sides still takes sides."

But do people have the right to kill themselves?

"People have always committed suicide, and they always will. I don't judge them morally. But the question is, should we have a different social response when the reason is disability, and I don't think so. As for Terri Schiavo, I just have to say there was a lot of hypocrisy and illogic on both sides of that argument. I was for feeding her for totally different reasons than the Christian Right. Hers was a good example of a story presented as two sides, left vs. right, and that's not at all the way I would frame it."

Johnson frames it as an issue of discrimination. Had Schiavo not been disabled, her husband would not have been able to go to court and authorize her killing, she says.

"Because she took nourishment from a feeding tube rather than by a spoon, it was easier. I think that's unjustifiable. Twenty-six disability rights organizations, including the Chicago-based group Not Dead Yet, were signed on for continuing to feed Terri Schiavo. How often did you hear about that? It's because it didn't fit the dominant template. It's a good example of how the movement and the popular culture define things differently."

Make no mistake, *Too Late to Die Young* is not narrowly focused. Johnson invokes many recollections and deals with a variety of subjects, such as her closing essay on the subject of pleasure. In fact, she says she made a game of seeing just how much she could cram into one book. Many are stories she has told for years to many a "captive" audience. There is also Johnson's fervor for politics. Among the chapters she most enjoyed writing was "What the Hell, Why Not," about her adventures and misadventures during an eleventh-hour campaign for Charleston County Council.

"My hat's really off to people who do it for real, people who are really serious and do the work, whether you like them or not," says Johnson, a longtime Democratic Party stalwart and a former delegate to its national convention. "It's a phenomenal undertaking to say I want to serve the people and do all this crazy stuff. I already loved politics and this community, but running gave me a new appreciation for what it involves.

"Obviously, there's a lot wrong with the political process, and money matters way too much. But still, one person, one vote. I get a kick out of seeing people line up and push buttons."

Less appealing to her are voter apathy and the inroads being made by what she terms "the conservative social agenda."

"It has become so much more powerful. I don't think public attitudes have really changed, but I do think social conservatives have done some phenomenal grass-roots organizing. At the same time, some things have really evolved, and ground has been gained against that social agenda. What we need now is rational discourse and the ability to think farther ahead than next week."

April 17, 2005

Will Moredock's *Banana Republic*

Will Moredock knew he was going to kick up some dust. After having spent three years in Myrtle Beach to assess the changes development had wrought on the social, political and environmental landscape, his conclusions were sure to upset those with vested interests. At least.

Moredock's book, *Banana Republic: A Year in the Heart of Myrtle Beach*, acknowledges the near inevitability of the city's exponential growth, but offers a scathing indictment of what he views as the runaway pace of development and what it costs the vast majority of residents.

Like many, the Charleston publisher and writer had fond childhood memories of Myrtle Beach dating back to 1954. His family journeyed there almost every year of his youth. Today, he sees a hideous neon inferno that too often lives down to the moniker of "Redneck Riviera," with a preponderance of low-wage subcultures that make a huge demand on limited municipal resources.

"I moved there in 1999 to write a book," he says. "I got out for my sanity."

A 1978 University of Georgia graduate, Moredock was a staff writer for The State in Columbia from 1986–89, and was founder-publisher of Point magazine (1990–1992) until returning to get his master's in journalism from the University of South Carolina. A former winner of the S.C. Fiction Project short-story competition, Moredock also was a news editor for Creative Loafing in Charlotte (1997–98).

The subject of Myrtle Beach was close to his heart, and it was a story he felt needed to be told, even if some dismissed it as a diatribe.

"Less than a century ago," Moredock writes, "dreamers, builders and speculators created Myrtle Beach from nothing, on a desolate South Carolina shore, to be a resort for small-town and working-class Southern families. Today, it draws more than 13 million people annually from around the world."

But growth is out of control, Moredock asserts, and there is no political will to contain it.

"The book was something I knew a lot of people would relate to. I knew I had a market for it, but the book I wound up writing was not the one I started to write. I was going to write about life on the boulevard and boulevard culture, but after being there for just a few weeks, it was my idea to capture a year in the life of the place. I was confronted by the fact that most of what Myrtle Beach is about is this huge development boom that's sweeping over the community, transforming its politics and alienating a lot of people."

The evidence of unplanned, uncontrolled growth is everywhere along the Strand, insists Moredock. It's a principal reason he wrote the book, though he disagrees with those who have called *Banana Republic* no more than a polemic against development.

"One of the reasons I wrote the book was to sound the alarm and to say the entire lowcountry is going to be like Myrtle Beach in 20 years if somebody doesn't put on the brakes. At this point I don't see anyone doing so. Money is driving the thing, and ultimately, in this political system, money carries the day.

"But the book involves much more than a critique of unrestrained development. It also deals broadly with the huge influx of youth, the hedonistic boulevard subculture, the role of religious tolerance (or intolerance) in the culture, the sex industry, and what all of this means."

Moredock says it may be difficult for people who see only Myrtle Beach's outward paean to pleasure to believe it is still, at base, an average Southern town in which things may have gotten out of hand. "Take away the beach and the canyon of oceanfront hotels," he writes, "take away the strip clubs and the golf courses, the roller coasters and the 2,000 restaurants, and Myrtle Beach is essentially a medium-sized Southern town—'Mayberry-at-the-Beach,' as some have called it—a town of neighbors, of Christians, of cultural and political conservatives."

Really?

"Yes. I think I describe it fairly well. The fact that there is so much of a Christian Right backlash going on there proves to me that it remains a conservative, rock-ribbed, Southern Protestant culture. But rather than going after real culprits (of social problems), they're going after gays, black motorcyclists and strip clubs.

"These are the byproducts of this overdevelopment. The city fathers made the decision decades ago that they were going to make Myrtle Beach into a worldwide resort beach, and they flung the doors open. A lot of people have come in that these conservatives don't like, but they can't turn back the clock."

Moredock fears the genie is out of the bottle and may not agree to be confined again. And while he would have liked to have assayed some positive signs, to his mind they were few and far between.

"Of course, millions of happy memories are established there every year. People keep coming back, so they must be enjoying themselves. But it's been nothing less than a disaster for locals, except for the few who have gotten wealthy from development. The town keeps sucking in these hordes of low-paid workers for low-paying jobs, and it's a huge strain on the infrastructure and the entire community to provide them with services.

The proponents' argument, says Moredock, is, "Look at all the money it's brought into the community, and the jobs."

"Well, most are people who are working very low-paid jobs and wouldn't be there at all if not for all the development. They're creating problems for those who have been there for generations. It takes a lot of taxes to support all this."

Add homeless people to the problem of increasing numbers of runaways, and the situation is only going to get worse, says Moredock.

"A lot of people go there with $10 or less in their pockets hoping to get one of the jobs they hear about. People flood in only to find they're working for $7.50 an hour. When their car breaks down, when they get laid off at the end of season, there they are, wards of the city, or living on the street."

The powers that be have made some effort.

"There is some transitional housing for workers, but it's a drop in the bucket. It's the same problems resort towns are facing throughout the country."

Some still take pride in their community, however garish and traffic-choked it may be viewed by disdainful outsiders. Yet Moredock's exploration seemed to uncover few willing to carry the banner.

"It's all dominated by tourism. It's taking pride in the numbers: the number of people who come, the number of dollars that are spent, all indicating growth. As for local individuals taking pride in some historical or cultural feature, I'm not aware of that.

"I think the Highway 17 Bypass in North Myrtle Beach is the tackiest, gaudiest strip I've ever seen. There's room for everything in a democratic society, whether one likes it or not. But when it comes to planned development, when the big money hits town, ordinances go out the window."

Moredock has little but scorn for the majority of local politicians.

"The problems facing Myrtle Beach provide an opportunity for grandstanding and demagoguery, but I have seen no serious, concerted effort to rein it in. The first thing a serious municipality would do would be to institute some stiff impact fees, which, of course, is anathema to politicians."

Myrtle Beach Mayor Mark McBride, currently campaigning for the U.S. Senate, was unavailable for comment, but Myrtle Beach City Councilwoman Susan Grissom Means believes Moredock paints the city with too broad a brushstroke.

"Of course, I am aware of the book but have not read it," Means says. "Some of what he writes about probably applies to Myrtle Beach proper—I know he was particularly critical of the development company Burroughs & Chapin—but most of what he criticizes would apply to the larger Grand Strand and not to the city of Myrtle Beach itself.

"So some things, like Horry County, I cannot comment on and City Council has no control over. I do not think we have had uncontrolled growth. I think we have been very careful in the growth that we have seen and in the annexations that we have done in the last four years since I've been on the council.

"Even though we don't have huge developer impact fees in place at this time, we do have large ones in place for water and sewage connections, one of the things we have to be so careful about because of the capacity we need to serve the community. Our tax rates here are some of the lowest east of the Mississippi, so I also disagree with his statement that taxes are out of control."

Moredock concedes his book has a moralizing tone, and he refuses to apologize for it.

"I'm a moralistic person, I've been told. Some of my Presbyterian upbringing comes out in this book, certainly, but I do think people have a responsibility to society and to one another, and I don't see much of that being exercised in Myrtle Beach.

"There are people who work in some capacity for the city who are on the sidelines and want to save it, but they don't know how."

November 16, 2003

Herb Frazier's *Behind God's Back*

Try to imagine that moment when a person who has known only the bonds of slavery is told, "You're free." What would be the reaction? Elation, perhaps. But in many cases, confusion or bewilderment as well. "Free to do what?" "Free to go where?"

It's understandable why a man or woman, suddenly left to their own devices, might choose to remain close to the place where they had lived most of their lives.

When freedom came at last to slaves on the rice plantations of lower Berkeley County, many stayed to farm the land and raise their families. Often it was in settlements quite near the plantation gates, there to write their own histories.

Four generations have gone by, and now the descendants of those families reveal their joys and sorrows in author Herb Frazier's *Behind God's Back: Gullah Memories of Cainhoy, Wando, Huger, Daniel Island, and St. Thomas Island, South Carolina*, to be published Tuesday by Evening Post Books.

The book marks a collaboration between Frazier, public relations and marketing manager for Magnolia Plantation and Gardens, and Columbia-based artist John W. Jones, a painter who has sought to bring attention to the everyday lives of Gullah people.

The idea originated with the Coastal Community Foundation of South Carolina, which commissioned Frazier to write the book.

"But it also had a personal component for me, having grown up in Charleston," says the author, formerly a reporter for The Post and Courier. "Cainhoy and Huger are words that I heard mentioned in our family's history, too. My grandmother, Mable McNeil Frazier, who raised me, lives in Cordesville just north of Huger. I later learned that my aunt Blossom Mack was from Berkeley County, so I bumped into a little of my family there as well."

Behind God's Back compiles varied accounts of the experiences of Gullah people who struggled through the passages of Emancipation, the Great Depression and into the middle of the 20th century, trying to sustain a measure of African lifestyles in rural communities near Charleston. Arguably, more than any other black community in the country, the Gullah people of the coastal area of the Southeastern United States have managed to preserve a greater portion of their cultural heritage.

The question is, "How?"

"The simple explanation is because of the geographic isolation," says Frazier. "Also, because African-American communities, rural and urban, tend to be close-knit and closed off socially."

Days Gone By

In approaching the descendants for their recollections, primarily individuals in their late 80s and 90s, the author had a distinct advantage.

"People recognize my name from the newspaper, so in many cases, they knew of me. I think that helped. I also think the way you approach people is important. You can't be too aggressive. You need to be more of a listener than a talker. I usually started the conversation talking about growing up in Ansonborough and where I went to school and church, and that my parents live on Wadmalaw Island.

"I'm from here, so I bring a level of appreciation of, and insight into, what people are about to share."

Frazier says that as one referral led to another, the project took on a life of its own.

"The people I talked to told it straight, without any embellishments. I think they were honest in their portrayal of the character of the area in the 1930s, '40s and '50s in terms of how people got along and what they did to get along, how they raised their families."

Key guidance and assistance was provided to Frazier by activist Fred Lincoln of the Cainhoy-Wando community and from Colonial-era expert Suzanna Smith Miles, a historian formerly of Mount Pleasant who now lives in Gettysburg, Pa.

The stories in *Behind God's Back* also are drawn from whites who live in the communities of Cainhoy, Wando, Huger, St. Thomas and Daniel Island.

Their memories offer another perspective on the sometimes stormy interaction between blacks and whites, most notably the Cainhoy gunfight of 1876, when "black Republicans stood their ground during a political rally to achieve a rare victory against white Democrats in the turbulent period of Reconstruction."

From a personal standpoint, Frazier always harbored a desire to write something about the area more substantial than a newspaper story. This book filled the bill.

"That inspired me on one level. On another, I realized what I was doing was giving a voice to people who ordinarily are not asked or sought out for their opinions, or their stories. We as journalists so often focus on elected officials and community leaders. But these are just regular people.

"This was a process of inverting the pyramid and putting the emphasis on them. Within their own communities, however, they carry a great deal of respect because of their age and experiences and leadership positions in the church. These older people have a wealth of knowledge and experience they will take with them when they die. It's important for younger people to sit and listen to these stories that people in their families have.

"We don't live the same way now. Communities don't come together to build schools like they once did, nor do they sustain themselves like they did when they could live off the land."

Transformation

In some respects, the book echoes the issues raised in Justin Nathanson's "Bin Yah," a locally produced documentary film exploring the impact of suburban sprawl on historic black communities in Mount Pleasant.

It was Northern industrialist and philanthropist Harry Frank Guggenheim (1890–1971) who erected a retreat near Cainhoy, where he hunted and entertained celebrity guests. He also owned nearby Daniel Island.

Following Guggenheim's death, Daniel Island's rural character underwent a brisk metamorphosis into an upscale neighborhood annexed into the city of Charleston.

Together with other residential and commercial growth on St. Thomas Island and nearby Cainhoy, this transformation has longtime landowners wondering whose ancestral properties might be the next to succumb.

If more land is lost, writes Frazier, some fear that already imperiled Gullah traditions might be further diminished or even lost. The Coastal Community Foundation is concerned with precisely this trend and how the residential and commercial growth accompanying the 1992 completion of the Mark Clark Expressway (Interstate 526) has and will continue to alter the area's character.

"When Gullah people lived way out in remote areas, they referred to themselves as living 'Behind God's Back,'" says Frazier. "You had his protection. But when the expressway opened, that isolation was breached."

Frazier does not say that the proposed extension of I-526 to Johns Island is a good idea or bad idea. But like many, he casts a wary eye.

"When you look at what happened on the east end of 526, that could very well be a harbinger on the James Island and Johns Island end if it is extended. I'm not saying this should not happen. I'm saying there are questions people need to ask up front so that development does not go on unchecked."

February 13, 2011

Dick Cavett. Photograph by Barbara Friedman

Watering the Wasteland

"They call television a medium because nothing it serves up is well-done."

Fred Allen, *The Big Show*

Allen, the great radio (later, TV) star whose topical comedy show delighted listeners for almost 20 years, applied the skewer to the boob tube quite nicely.

It wasn't all mindless pablum, however. The Golden Age of live drama resided in the early years of TV, as did such seminal comedy programs as "Your Show of Shows" and "The Ernie Kovacs Show"—irreverent, inventive, brilliantly written and performed material that remains influential today.

Television news in its infancy was about sober reportage, not pyrotechnics and theatrical excess. Overwhelmingly, its inaugural generation of reporters, editors and anchormen arrived before the cameras as trained newspapermen. It wasn't showbiz. Not yet. Then came ratings.

For all of that, then or now, TV never has capitalized on its enormous potential. Are remarkable programs aired? Certainly. Is the talent level for entertainment productions at its apex? Absolutely (notwithstanding the witless drones of Reality TV).

Some of the writers profiled here not only brought intelligence and style to bear in their careers, but often a refusal to knuckle under to network pressure to soft-peddle controversial subjects. Others, working under the protective umbrella of commercial-free PBS, pretty much had free rein. All stretched boundaries in an effort to edify as well as entertain. They deserve our respect.

Dick Cavett's *Talk Show*

An acting teacher, observing then-unknown Marlon Brando walk on-stage for the first time, hadn't a clue who he was.

But an indelible impression had been made.

"Before he even spoke," the instructor recalled, "it was as if a leopard had entered the room."

Quoted by Dick Cavett in his engaging new book, *Talk Show: Confrontations, Pointed Commentary, and Off-Screen Secrets* (Henry Holt), the line may remind many of how they felt when tuning in to his provocative programs: as if a mind had entered in the wasteland. And a wit as well.

Host of "The Dick Cavett Show," which aired on ABC (1968–75) and on PBS (1977–82), Cavett also helmed talk shows on the USA, HBO and CNBC cable networks. Since 2007, he has written an online opinion column for The New York Times.

A youthful 74 and as intellectually spry as ever, he is far from entering his anecdotage.

Cavett understood better than most that the art of the interview is the art of conversation, sage counsel he received from his one-time boss, Jack Parr, then host of "The Tonight Show."

"It was priceless advice," says Cavett, who spoke to The Post and Courier from his home in New York. "At first, I was startled because I wasn't sure what he meant when he said, 'Don't do interviews.' I thought, is he suggesting I do a musical show or that I should sing or do magic? But obviously he meant to make it a conversation. Don't make it a thing that smacks of clipboards, David Frost and 'your most' or 'your favorite' questions."

Finding His Voice

After dabbling in acting and reviving the magic act he incanted early on, Cavett's chutzpah helped secure a post in 1960 as talent coordinator for "The Tonight Show." But it was his sharp command of language that won a position on the show as a staff writer, a post he continued to handle with aplomb after Johnny Carson took the reins.

Cavett tested the waters as a stand-up comic in 1964 before joining the staff of "The Merv Griffin Show." On-camera appearances on that program and others led to a morning talk show deemed "too sophisticated" for its time slot. Enter the inaugural "Dick Cavett Show," a late-night offering scheduled opposite . . . Johnny Carson.

Cavett says that writing for a comic with a strong, singular voice was relatively easy, at least for him, but that learning to give wing to his own voice was a different matter. It took some time before Dick Cavett could be heard in the lines he wrote.

"It seemed so strenuous (to develop)," he says. "At first, it was like someone had given you a sleeping pill. You sit at the typewriter, where you are quick to dash things off in order to survive as a comedy writer. I did it faster than most, which made me unpopular with the older fellows on the staff. But writing in my own voice was more difficult."

The fifth DVD collection of installments of "The Dick Cavett Show," the "well-kept-secret DVDs" as he refers to them with rueful good humor, is called "Hollywood Greats."

The book harbors a similar pantheon of immortals: Brando, Groucho Marx, Katharine Hepburn, Orson Welles, Fred Astaire, Lucille Ball, John Wayne, John Huston, Robert Mitchum, Bette Davis, et al. To audiences of their era, they seemed almost otherworldly.

"At one point, I thought, 'Who are their counterparts today?' Meryl Streep and Al Pacino are wonderful actors. But there is something of dimension missing. That may have been one of the things that was most intriguing to viewers, to hear how these iconic figures would talk, how they would be, when they sat down with me."

Even Cavett was star-struck in some measure. "It was hard not to be. I'm a kid from Nebraska whose life was transformed by saying, 'Fine show, Bob,' to Bob Hope behind the University of Nebraska Coliseum. This, as he got in his car to return to his glamorous life. And my thought was, 'I want to go wherever he goes! I don't want to go back to Lincoln High School and study the principal exports of Argentina.' I can feel it now as if it happened moments ago."

Surprisingly, Cavett has had little occasion to revisit his talk-show interviews on tape before writing his columns for the Times or the new book.

"Not a lot, no," he says, "and there are still some I never saw once. I'd have something to do the night that it aired and thought I'd catch up with it someday. Recently, I pulled out some of the episodes we shot during two weeks in

London, and it was a who's who: John Gielgud, Ralph Richardson, Glenda Jackson and others of that stature.

"I really ought to take a month off and try to watch some of these things. Though many have been transferred, there are still a lot of them that are languishing on 2-inch tape, which is a dangerous gamble. I need to find a patron to rescue them out of that condition."

Enduring Moments

The book's pieces on Richard Burton are as engrossing as listening to the late actor and his "Welsh organ tones." Cavett got the best from Burton—urbane, erudite, self-deprecating—in his several appearances on the show, but audiences were denied one mesmerizing moment to which only Cavett was privy: Burton, crossing the stage long after a performance of "Camelot," stopping and delivering the prologue to "Henry V."

"Oh! I just got a little chill now as you described it," says Cavett. "And with the 'ghost light' being the only light. Burton was a prodigious drinker, but he was not drinking then. I realized later just how lucky I was for Burton to be on the show during that period."

The John Wayne who emerges in Cavett's recollection is an order of magnitude different from the image. Introduced to Wayne on the set of his final film, "The Shootist," Cavett, who like many worshipped The Duke as a boy, met an actor whose sensibilities surprised him. Wayne a great fan of Noel Coward? Who knew?

"I wondered how I could get anybody to believe that or not accuse me of inventing it out of whole tissue." Sometime after the show he did with Wayne, Cavett got a letter from the former's daughter-in-law, saying, "Thank you for letting people see the man that I knew."

"He was an actor, not a cowboy. I don't think I took the opportunity someone urged on me once to ask Wayne why neither he nor his four strapping sons ever served in the military. But I know that haunted him horribly for the rest of his life. He felt it was an awful mistake, and he tried to make up for it."

Talk Show is not wholly about celebrities, however substantial or lofty. It also contains Cavett's views on the sorry state of discourse ("It's Only Language") and politics, as well as his takes on cultural watersheds and absurdities, heroes and villains.

"What My Uncle Knew About War" is a terse, potent piece that laments the romanticism of war.

"I cringe every time I hear those phrases from politicians: 'Those who gave their lives' or 'made the sacrifice.' You didn't sacrifice your life; it was ripped from you. You did everything you could to hold on to it. And a sacrifice is something you give in order to gain something more valuable, isn't it?"

Near the close of the book, Cavett quotes Jack Nicholson, who remarked that when Brando passed from the scene, "The rest of us moved up a notch."

Perhaps the same will be said for Cavett.

December 5, 2010

David Steinberg's *The Book of David*

David Steinberg's *The Book of David* is the funniest book of the Bible that failed to make the cut.

Now hold on. No blasphemy intended. And no burning bushes, either. The longtime comedian, comedy writer and director's first book is strictly a memoir, albeit in mock-biblical language.

Truth be told, Steinberg always felt the Scriptures could use a little punching up, humor-wise. His contribution is a look back at 40 years of irreverent observation, a testament, as it were, to a sharp eye, a keen ear and an ability to articulate a cockeyed view of his experience.

Steinberg, you may recall, was the first stand-up comic to take God to task (respectfully) for vague and cryptic language, a cheeky jibe at the Almighty that convulsed fans of TV's old "Smothers Brothers Comedy Hour" in 1970, one of the most subversive programs ever to give network brass palpitations, and upset more than a few of inflexible bent.

"I don't think any of us really realized just how Calvinistic the culture was back then," recalls the native Canadian, 65, a fixture in American TV for decades.

> And lo, the Smothers visited young David (no slingshot) upon the populace to smite all pretension and conformist residues. And visited upon him was the terrible wrath of WASPish displeasure. And he rejoiced.

"I didn't enjoy it as far as Tom and Dick (Smothers) were concerned, of course. I didn't want them to be thrown off the air. Imagine: the No. 1 show in the country, the pressure they were getting from the White House and elsewhere to get the show off the air. When I did my 'sermons,' we didn't realize that there had never been anything humorous on religion on national TV, ever."

Curiously, it was Steinberg who played the Phoenix, getting his own TV series (in 1972) from the Smothers wreckage.

"One of the executives at CBS loved the Smothers brothers and loved the show. And Tommy Smothers was also one of those angels that moved you forward. He loved other comedians; he didn't feel they were competition. He just loved talent. I could not have gotten more support than what he presented me. He kind of set me up."

An early member of Chicago's fabled improv troupe Second City, and the performer whose appearances on "The Tonight Show" with Johnny Carson were second in number only to Bob Hope's, Steinberg is among the most successful sitcom directors at work, having shepherded multiple episodes of everything from "Seinfeld" and "Friends" to "Mad about You" and "Curb Your Enthusiasm."

As a performer, he's been likened to a hybrid of Lenny Bruce and Woody Allen. But Steinberg, who as an actor never dreamed of doing stand-up, is just as distinctive in his own way. And he's championed many a young talent in recent years on his TV Land gig "Sit Down Comedy with David Steinberg."

"It's one of my favorite things to do. Almost all of those guys are proteges of mine, though I didn't know they all were going to be such successes. It's such a treat."

Still, many of the younger guys don't quite "get" the greats of the past.

"Younger comedians don't seem to see the ideas that were behind people like Lenny Bruce. What I learned from him is that he didn't care if he only had a third of the audience. I found that amazing. How does it feel when two-thirds of the audience is scowling at you? In that way he never lost himself, and never sold out. I learned from him you don't need a big audience to carve out who you are. My audience are people like me. That way you're not talking down and you're not talking up. That way you're a more authentic version of yourself."

Popular wisdom holds that it was cultural pride that compelled Steinberg to be one of the first Jewish stand-up comics not to Anglicize his name for the stage. Maybe so. But it also may have been about thumbing his nose at a certain Miss Krog, the second-grade teacher (real name omitted) who said the Winnipeg wit would never amount to anything.

"That was why I would never change my name. How would she know how well I was doing? But now there are so many David Steinbergs out there it drives me crazy."

Ultimately, the surprise of *The Book of David* is that it's his first book.

"I've been writing my whole life. But I never sat down to write a book. I've been busy. When I finally started on this one, I tried the conventional approach, writing about everybody—I'm been lucky to know the brightest and most talented people in the industry—but in every story, I was the funniest thing about it and everyone else sounded like dolts. So I determined to do the next best thing: Redo the Bible in some way."

How has this affected his relations with the deity?

"I still like the rituals of Judaism, but my relationship with the deity is like this Dean Martin and Jerry Lewis relationship, with God as the cool Martin."

July 8, 2007

Carl Reiner's *Just Desserts*

Jaunty as ever, Carl Reiner still wears life like a feather in a hatband.

Even in the company of such young lions of the cinema as George Clooney, Brad Pitt and Matt Damon, his co-stars in the "Ocean's" caper films, Reiner owns a flair that's impossible to miss. He is not simply respected among them, but revered. And with reason. For more than 60 years, he has been a figure in high relief (not to mention comic relief) in the landscape of American humor.

Whether as playwright, producer, TV scripter, screenwriter, director, actor or author, this effervescent showman, 87 and still bubbling, has entertained three generations of audiences with breezy aplomb—and a wicked ear for the absurd.

At the moment, Reiner has a satirical "novellelah" (*Just Desserts*) aloft and a new children's book (*Tell Me Another Scary Story*) on the runway, but the temptation is to reminisce about all those venerable vehicles stored in the hangar: the memorable TV shows and features in which Reiner's gifts can be revisited at whim.

The 12-time Emmy Award winner may be best known as the egocentric Alan Brady, a self-styled comic genius who lorded it over the beleaguered writing staff portrayed in "The Dick Van Dyke Show" (1961–66). Yet Reiner was also the creator, producer, principal writer and frequent director of the series, based on his own real-life experiences as a writer-actor on two hit television programs of the '50s: "Your Shows of Shows" (1950–54), a TV landmark widely regarded as the most innovative comedy program ever to fit on the small screen, and its successor, "Caesar's Hour" (1954–57).

"I thought to myself, 'I live in New Rochelle, N.Y., I work on a comedy-variety show and commute to New York," recalls Reiner. "So I wrote 13 shows for a pilot series based on this called 'Head of the Family.' It almost sold, but didn't. So I set it aside and wrote a film. (Producer) Sheldon Leonard saw I had these 13 shows written, and my agent said, 'Give them to him.' I didn't want to fail again with the same thing, but then Sheldon ('The Andy Griffith Show, I Spy') suggested casting Dick Van Dyke."

Reiner also inaugurated his directing career on the Van Dyke show, a major hit that would catapult Van Dyke and Mary Tyler Moore to stardom and prove hugely influential. But soon he would make the move into features, starring opposite Eva Marie Saint in Norman Jewison's hilarious "The Russians Are Coming, the Russians Are Coming" (1966) and the following year in an adaptation of Joseph Stein's play "*Enter Laughing*," which was based on Reiner's own semi-autobiographical 1958 novel of the same name.

He directed the films "Where's Poppa" (1970) and "Oh, God" (1977), then played an instrumental role in launching the film career of Steve Martin, directing and co-writing "The Jerk" (1979), "Dead Men Don't Wear Plaid" (1982), "The Man with Two Brains" (1983) and "All of Me" (1984).

The native New Yorker had cut his teeth in several Broadway musicals of the 1940s and enjoyed the lead role in "Call Me Mister" before being cast by Max Leibman on "Your Show of Shows," a pivotal career break. A half-century later, he still draws on the experiences and training from that series. Featuring Sid Caesar, Imogene Coca, Howard Morris and Reiner, "Your Show of Shows" was a proving ground for a bevy of writers whose protégés would populate the writing staffs of just about every significant sitcom of the 1960s, '70s, and '80s, even as their mentors conquered other fields.

"YSOS" also inspired the affectionate 1982 movie send-up "My Favorite Year," produced by former "YSOS" writer Mel Brooks, and the play "Laughter on the 23rd Floor," penned by yet another "YSOS" graduate, Neil Simon. Its influence can be seen today, which is quite a legacy.

"It is," Reiner says. "Television was a college in those days. We had 60 minutes to do a show, and the length of the show was always determined in dress rehearsals. It was training without knowing we were developing that discipline."

Reiner's most recent book, *Just Desserts: A Novellelah*, was released in September by Phoenix Books, and Dove Books has scheduled an October release date for the Halloween-timed *Tell Me Another Scary Story . . . But Not Too Scary.* Illustrated by James Bennett, it's the "interactive" sequel (complete with a read-along CD) to Reiner's 2003 book, *Tell Me a Scary Story . . . But Not Too Scary.* A third one is in the pipeline.

Just Desserts, a romp with serious overtones, assays what happens to a romance novelist when he e-mails God. This, with some suggestions on not waiting for heaven or hell to reward the virtuous or punish the vile. He gets a favorable reply from the deity, who thinks it's a good idea. But is this really God, or the unacknowledged "god" that Reiner, a nonbeliever, says is in all of us?

"I'm never happy until I have a project I am doing," says Reiner, soon to be joined by Mel Brooks for a Library of Congress installation of their 2005 book, *The 2,000-Year-Old Man Goes to School*, an outgrowth of the classic routine.

"The new children's book, which was inspired by my grandson, is exciting to me. And that's what keeps you going. It's having something to get up and do every day. If I have nothing to do, I get bored. I had a good role model. My father, who was a watchmaker, was always doing something. The ethic of never just hanging around, always being involved in some project, was invaluable. My kids are exactly the same way."

Son Rob has had remarkable success as a feature film director and occasional actor since the '70s, following his own breakthrough in TV's "All in the Family." As for Reiner's other kids, Sylvia Anne (Annie) is a poet, playwright and author, while Lucas is an actor-director.

"I've really enjoyed watching Rob's career," says Reiner, proud of each of his offspring. "From a very young age, he wanted to be a director. Not me—I only directed to protect what I had written."

Reiner, the writer, was the real Rob Petrie, the comedy scribe immortalized by Van Dyke. And Alan Brady? "He was a combination of all the rotten-behaving star comedians I ever met."

Writing has been, and always will be, Reiner's first love and greatest reward. Especially books.

"It's because you are alone with your reader. When doing Broadway shows or movies or TV, you need an awful lot of help. And your writing doesn't always get interpreted the way you want. But in a novel, you talk directly to the reader and tell them exactly what you want them to know. It's so personal."

October 4, 2009

Larry Doyle's *I Love You, Beth Cooper*

Perhaps it was those seven formative years he spent with United Press International, covering the early AIDS epidemic and the Challenger shuttle disaster for a news agency slowly going bankrupt.

It would be enough to steer anyone toward humor, even its darker side. But Larry Doyle's first novel, *I Love You, Beth Cooper*, is agreeably light in tone.

Witty, too, as becomes a writer who, during a particularly fertile period, was the executive editor of Spy magazine and one of the subversive minds behind "The Simpsons" and "Beavis and Butt-head" series.

Doyle, who lives in Baltimore with his wife, Becky, and their three kids, has created quite a stir with his first book, one optioned in manuscript form by filmmaker Chris Columbus. *I Love You, Beth Cooper* began its life as a screen treatment, and ends it, circuitously, as a Doyle screenplay.

"It is really easy not to write a novel," says Doyle, who persevered despite mighty distractions. "But I'd wanted to do one since I was 18. A literary agent in New York, Sarah Burns, finally convinced me to do it. I had sent her an outline for a movie, and she said, 'This is a novel. Write it up and send it to me.' And I had a hell of a time writing it—it was really fun. It's something I wish I had done a long time ago."

There were, of course, other commitments.

Following his stint as a medical and science reporter for UPI, Doyle briefly was editorial director of First Comics, which he departed to pen the newly revived "Pogo" comic strip. That led to a gig at National Lampoon, which promptly folded (he assumes full credit), and then Spy ("during the last of the funny years," crows his publicist). Doyle next invested four years as an editor-writer for New York magazine, during which time he moonlighted with episodes for "Beavis and Butt-head" and "Rug-rats."

Doyle was a writer and supervising producer of "The Simpsons" for another four years, capturing two Emmys and an Annie Award. He was the writer and executive producer of the film "Looney Tunes: Back in Action" and produced eight new "Looney Tunes" shorts for Warner Brothers. He also wrote the movie "Duplex," starring Ben Stiller and Drew Barrymore, which he considers an irredeemable disaster.

Doyle's other magazine credits include GQ, Rolling Stone, Harper's and Time. He is a frequent contributor to The New Yorker's "Shouts and Murmurs" section and also writes "The Doyle Report" each month for Esquire.

I Love You, Beth Cooper taps into his own vividly recalled years at Buffalo Grove High School (no fictional stand-in allowed), the setting of a novel that chronicles 17 exhilarating hours in the life of debate team captain Denis Cooverman, a guy undergoing accelerated adolescence.

"I have the advantage of being a man and, therefore, never growing up," Doyle says.

The coming-of-age story certainly is among our most durable. But also among the most frequently and badly rendered. Doyle was determined to give it fresh perk and a deeper dimension.

"I hope it seems fresh. What I was trying to do is both a coming-of-age novel and a commentary on the genre, and on teen movies. I wrote a character who hadn't experienced anything and had him go through every teenage ritual I could think of. This story is somewhat unusual for me in that it is very light," adds Doyle, who helped readers immerse themselves in the tale by compiling an iTunes iMix of all the songs featured in the book.

"The story dictated that I keep it moving, so it doesn't have that first-novel problem (of turgid prose, or of crippling fealty to form). When I decided that my book did not have to rival Thomas Pynchon's *Gravity's Rainbow*, I was relieved of the responsibility of writing the Great American Novel."

That said, Doyle promises his second novel will be impenetrable, pretentious and larded with academic jargon.

"Everything I know about everything will be in it."

June 17, 2007

Bill Geist's *Way off the Road*

Somewhere on the continuum of wanderlust, whose poles are inhabited by "On the Road with Charles Kuralt" and Jack Kerouac's *On the Road*, Bill Geist continues to discover America.

Not the U.S. of A., one hastens to add, of celebrity worship or political punditry or "reality" TV, but the actual reality of more or less ordinary citizens doing extraordinary things.

For 20 years, the former New York Times columnist has plied the byways and backroads of America as a roving correspondent for CBS News's "Sunday Morning." On the occasion of his milestone anniversary, Geist has published his seventh book, *Way off the Road: Discovering the Peculiar Charms of Small-Town America*, to be released Tuesday by Broadway Books.

"For me, the show keeps getting stronger and stronger and serves to drive me farther away from celebrity journalism and people who are selling something," says Geist, a breezy, slightly cockeyed observer beloved of five million viewers a week. "None of these people in the book are what you'd call 'normal,' but unlike so many people in, say, New York and Los Angeles, they're the kind of people who don't take themselves too seriously. Everyone is kind of equal, and of equal interest, in my work."

Geist, an Emmy Award winner who also has contributed to CBS Sports coverage of the Olympic Games, Super Bowl, World Series and NCAA basketball's Final Four, is the author of such disparate gems as *Little League Confidential; The Big Five-Oh: Facing, Fearing and Fighting 50; City Slickers; Fore! Play; Monster Trucks and Hair-In-A-*Can; and *The Zucchini Plague and Other Tales of Suburbia.* But his proudest accomplishment may have been finishing third in the Illinois State Fair Bake-Off.

Geist is hard pressed to assay his most memorable adventures, or the most intriguing eccentrics he has met, but those chronicled in the book afford a distilled series of highlights. The Church of the Holy Barbecue, for one. Or the TV news anchor in Muleshoe, Texas, who presents the news from her bedroom. Then there's the Mike the Headless Chicken Festival, feasting on Moonburgers in Moonshine, Ill., the prospect of roadkill stew in Kansas, and Sundown Days in Hanlontown, Iowa, where once each year people gather to experience the wonders of the sun setting between railroad tracks.

"There are several categories of favorites. I've done a lot of personal things from home, like when my wife suggested I do a take-off on Martha Stewart's Christmas spectacular. I also managed to cover four Olympics without really going to any events; at the Winter Olympics in Japan, I covered the capsule hotels, whose 'rooms' are basically coffins. But the big category covered in this book is the *On the Road* things, like the 93-year-old newspaper publisher and pilot in Loyalton, Calif., a one-man staff who delivered his papers by air to subscribers who lived on ranches. Not to forget the Prairie Dog Sucker, the Frozen Dead Guy and the many unusual variations on American entrepreneurialism."

Try getting *that* from "American Idol."

Geist says that while he has sensibilities very different from those of the late Charles Kuralt, there are similarities (Kuralt, a Tar Heel, would have appreciated Geist's take on a new law in Wilson, N.C., banning indoor furniture on outdoor porches). So, are they spiritual cousins?

"In some ways, yes. And it was Kuralt who actually hired me back in 1987. He literally called me from a pay phone, telling me to come along and do it. 'It'll be fun,' he said. That was all I needed to hear. It turned out he wasn't well, and was going on the road less and less.

"At the time, I was writing a column for the Times called About New York, so the work just expanded from subway tokens to airline tickets. It's not easy going all over America, but like Charles promised, it's great fun."

Geist, who is contemplating writing a novel, notes that one of the secrets to the show's success is that he hasn't gotten it all figured out. He just knows that no one person or notion speaks for the whole country, and that its citizens do have more on their minds than many might suspect.

"Our best ideas come from people in small towns who write us a letter that begins, 'You won't believe this, but . . .' "

May 13, 2007

Brian Lamb's "Booknotes"

Before "Booknotes" premiered on the C-SPAN cable network in April 1989, host Brian Lamb was not exactly what one would call a big reader.

Suddenly, the former Navy public-information officer, once a civilian staffer in the Nixon White House Office of Telecommunications, became the most committed of bookworms.

In eight years, the hour-long "Booknotes" has become television's preeminent forum for the discussion of nonfiction books and authors, and Lamb has read every one of the 428 books he's spotlighted on the program.

This doesn't even count his companion series on C-SPAN 2, "About Books," which at two hours running time showcases author readings, panels and other book-related events, including fiction.

Now Lamb, C-SPAN's founder and chief executive officer, has a tome of his own. "Booknotes" (Times Books) features 120 edited excerpts from the series, chiefly dealing with authors ruminating on the writing process. Already in its fourth printing, the book has climbed onto The New York Times best-seller list.

"I'm very anxious to learn. It is why I read these books and spend a lot of time doing it. It's like an education all over again for me," says Lamb, 55, a native of Lafayette, Ind., who received a B.A. in speech from Purdue University.

"I suppose a lot of me is wrapped up in this program, but I hope it follows through on its basic mission, which is to let viewers make up their own minds about whether this is a good or bad book or guest."

With an estimated 60,000 hardcover books being published annually in the United States alone, the majority of them nonfiction, choosing which authors to feature on the TV series is a time-consuming, collaborative effort of the "Booknotes" staff. Deciding on a linchpin for Lamb's book—which is divided into Storytellers, Reporters and Public Figures—was more straightforward.

"Books come over the transom every day and you get hundreds of them in a year's time. But I have a lot of help on the program. You kind of look for political balance, diversity, age balance—all these things.

"As for my book, we looked for some kind of a voice. We started out thinking it would be arranged by varied subject matter. But when we looked back at what was most fun over the eight years of the program—all that you learn about authors and how and when and where they write—that seemed to be the better emphasis for the book. And it helps us talk about what we do. We have an opportunity to focus on something that commercial television can't."

C-SPAN, or the Cable Satellite Public Affairs Network, was born in March of 1979. One thing to keep in mind when watching the network, Lamb says, is that it has the advantage of not having to worry about ratings. It has none. No one knows how many people are watching the network at any given time.

"We have a different mission. Everything we do here, whether it's the government hearings we cover or the book programs, we never have to worry about numbers. This is an enormous luxury. It's the reason you get what you get on 'Booknotes.' Our approach to the program is to focus on the author, on the hardback nonfiction book, with the aim of giving viewers a new face, a new author, and a new idea 52 Sundays a year."

The "Booknotes" series began as an effort to give due attention to Neil Sheehan's Vietnam War volume, *A Bright Shining Lie: John Paul Vann and America in Vietnam*. The theme of both the series (and the book) remains the same: the power of ideas and the written word.

"Maybe I'm naive, but I think the power of the printed word still is paramount in the idea segment of what's going on in this world. I've been in Washington, D.C. for 31 years, and it's my experience that print is paramount here. People in government usually run to the TV camera every time it's offered because it's the way for them to get to the average folk. But the ideas are laid down on paper in newspapers, in magazines, in books. That's where the power is here. Print sets the priorities."

There is one other constant to the program: Lamb's great stone face.

Sometimes he'll be traveling and meeting people and chance to overhear someone say, "Look, Helen, he actually smiles!"

"I'm not at all like you see in the interviews. And I don't mean there's a big hidden personality here, although I'm much more animated and I hope to goodness I have a much better sense of humor than it looks like on the show. But the reason I do it the way I do it, both on the call-in shows and on the 'Booknotes' program is that I don't want me to be what you see.

"I think this is a bit of an experiment. No one else in this business does it like we do, which tells you that it doesn't sell in the marketplace, or at least they don't think it does. We're trying to prove that you can pull off TV without the focus being on the host."

Lamb is not an avid fiction reader, but the Arlington, Va., resident jokes that lots of people working in Washington, D.C., think that some of what he puts on the air is fiction.

"Much fiction has a great deal of insight and value to it, but there are so many nonfiction books that impact Washington, and almost everything we do here is focused on the political system and how decisions are made in the government. This restriction on fiction only applies to the 'Booknotes' program, not to 'About Books.'"

Lamb's shows are at least as entertaining as a good novel, devotees agree. And frequently just as colorful.

August 24, 1997

Josephine Humphreys. Photograph by Wade Spees

Palmetto's Progress (The Locals)

"Mastery is not something that strikes in an instant, like a thunderbolt, but a gathering power that moves through time, like weather."

John Gardner, *The Art of Fiction*

Familiarity breeds . . . association.

When dealing with local and regional authors, a journalist is advised to stay at a certain remove. It is fine to be cordial acquaintances, but becoming too friendly with the people you write about on a more or less regular basis can be perilous. Hurt feelings are the least of it. Being too chummy also can exert a subtle, unconscious effect on your article—or worse, a conscious one—which shortchanges the reader.

Better you should maintain that professional distance. But this is not a simple matter, especially when there are authors in your city and state who you not only admire and respect, but have taken an immediate (or gradual) liking to. Genuine rapport is rare, and demands to be appreciated.

I've known some of the people represented in this section for many years. They have been unfailingly generous with their time and candid in interviews. So it's a tricky high-wire act to negotiate. I managed it, in part, by reading a local author's latest work but never writing a review of it. Articles only. That may seem a bit strange. But my functional job title was book review *editor*. And it was protective armor. An article is (or should be) pure reportage; no opinion should insinuate itself into the text. By contrast, a review passes judgment, and I always placed my responsibility to the reader of the newspaper above any other consideration. If I could not be rigorously honest, no holds barred, I was not about to write a review. And even a good book may not be to any one person's particular taste.

On the other hand, one of the delights of the job is in witnessing how those writers you met at the beginning of their careers have grown, their talents deepened, their voice evolved. I am happy for them, and grateful they are in my life—just a few (metaphorical) blocks away.

Bret Lott's *How to Get Home*

Clarity and simplicity are virtues in fiction, if not absolutes. But simplicity of storytelling does not necessarily imply a lack of depth or complexity.

Quite the contrary, says Bret Lott, for whom precision of meaning is critical. Not only in his own writing, but in his work with students at the College of Charleston.

"The older I get, the longer I write, the more clarity and simplicity are important to me," says the Mount Pleasant novelist and short story writer, whose second collection of stories, *How to Get Home*, will be released Monday by John F. Blair, Publishers.

"It's driven home to me every time I teach. And I'll always be a teacher, even if I hit some magic lottery one day. Every year I have a new fleet of students come in and they all want to know how you do it. I give them all the same answer: just be as clear as possible. No coyness, no tricks, no word games or puzzles for the reader."

Too keen a taste for embroidery generally reveals itself in unnecessarily broad strokes, and a kind of writing that lends itself to cliché, Lott says.

"Embellishment is more showboating of the author than fidelity to the characters. What I'm striving for is the truth of these characters, not drawing attention to myself. The need for clarity hasn't changed, although as I get older things become more complex, and simplicity and complexity sort of intersect each other in ways that make it more difficult to be clear.

"Still, you strive for simplicity, which is not the same as being simple, or simplistic. I tell myself, 'I know nothing. I want to find out.' My job as a writer is to try and discover, not to have something to say beforehand and tell people about it. That's not what fiction is about. I try to break down my own prejudices and preconceptions about the world. And simplicity lends itself to that."

How to Get Home is Lott's sixth book. Included in the collection are "War Story," originally intended as a chapter of his last novel, *Reed's Beach* (1993), and *After Leston*, a novella which continues the story of the character of Jewel Hilburn, memorably limned in the novel *Jewel.*

After Leston likewise was intended as a section in *Jewel*, but was excised.

"You hate to waste something," says Lott, 37. "It was 91 pages long and represented three months of my life and some good writing. It didn't really fit into the novel, though. So I started reading, cutting and shaping and got it down to about a 55-page novella, which was first published by a small literary magazine."

Raymond Carver, with his spare but incisive sentences, was one writer who exercised considerable influence on Lott. But the disciple thinks it's a mistake to pigeonhole the master.

"Carver didn't like the term 'minimalism.' He preferred 'precisionist' with regard to his work—that is, the precision with which an image is rendered, the precision of a sentence.

"As I said, the older I get, the more complex life becomes, the harder it is to write with precision about it. I think that's why each book I write is harder to do than the one before. You would think it'd get easy."

Isn't that as it should be?

"Yes, what's the challenge otherwise? You'd just be cranking them out blindfolded. Why would you continue to write when you had mastered it? If you were able to master it, I'd move on to something else."

Lott says *How to Get Home* is distinguished from his first collection as much by his growth as a person as his development as a writer.

"To me the difference about this second story collection has to do with the fact that the stories are longer and have what seems to me more depth. I was a 25- or 26-year-old kid when I wrote that first group of stories. I look back and think they were good at that time of my life. But these new stories reflect something more."

It is further set apart, he says, by way of representing the most pleasant working experience he's ever had with a publishing house.

Lott, who spends two weeks every six months teaching at Vermont College, published his first five books within seven years. And though he still feels obliged to produce work at a demanding pace, the fact that this is his first book in three years matters little.

"It really doesn't seem that long. And it didn't take me any longer to write *How to Get Home.* There's another book I wrote between that and *Reed's Beach*, a memoir that Harcourt Brace is publishing next Father's Day called *Fathers, Sons and Brothers.* So I was actually writing two books at one time, which is why there was this big gap."

Lott also has just completed a mystery novel set in Charleston and North Charleston. It was a refreshing change of venue, so to speak, to play around with genre conventions. And Lott, who's always savored a good mystery—Tony Hillerman being a particular favorite—thoroughly enjoyed himself.

"It actually has a plot. I had a great deal of fun writing it because something happens. It's the same kind of people I always write about, but in this case they're trying to solve a crime in which they're implicated.

"My last novel was about the death of a child and not at all fun to write. Interesting, yes, and valuable for me as a human being to have done. After that I wrote the memoir. Then I simply decided to have some fun. Who knows, I could see writing some more of these if this one gets published."

July 21, 1996

William Baldwin's *A Gentleman of Charleston and the Manner of His Death*

Dynamic and colorful, Francis Warrington Dawson was, with only mild exaggeration, trumpeted as "the most powerful man in the South," a writer of such passionate opinions that he once penned a 22,000-word book review.

A Civil War hero-turned-Charleston newspaper editor, the once-prosperous Dawson was suffering an inexorable decline in his finances and influence—like the Holy City itself—when, on March 12, 1889, he died at the hands of a neighboring physician keen on seducing the Dawson family governess.

The quick acquittal of his killer, and the painful coming to terms with the past on the part of the women in Dawson's life, are part and parcel of a "salacious" tale of genteel Charleston, one McClellanville author William Baldwin tells with relish.

Dawson lives again, as the fictional Capt. David Lawton, in Baldwin's historical novel, *A Gentleman of Charleston and the Manner of His Death*, the first book of original fiction ever published by the University of South Carolina Press.

Baldwin, 61, takes no small measure of pride in the distinction of being USC Press's first published novelist. But the book, which he began in 1996, is one he felt compelled to write.

"I was compulsive about writing it," he says. "For one year (1997), I did nothing but read about Dawson, 40 hours a week. I read what Dawson had written himself, what his wife had written and what others had written about them. There was a tremendous amount of material. The Dawsons were so larger than life, and they knew it.

"But I always felt like Alex Moore, an old friend of mine from when he ran the (S.C.) Historical Society, and Curtis Clark, the new director of USC Press, were taking a chance with this book because in a sense, it's pretty controversial. They just chuckled, but I'm surprised they published it."

Larger than life

A Gentleman of Charleston gradually was whittled down from its initial 600 pages to today's tidy 203. But the "central" figure of the novel—some, like Baldwin's wife Lil, might argue its female characters reign—pivots on the life of an outsized man.

Dawson, a London playwright, enlisted in the Confederate Army at age 20 after the bombardment of Fort Sumter. He seems to have participated in almost every major battle.

Dawson originally moved to Charleston as assistant editor of the Charleston Mercury. He became a national figure as both writer-editor and later owner of the then-Charleston Daily News, which he and co-owner Bartholomew R. Riordan consolidated (with the Charleston Courier) in 1873 as The News and Courier.

Though best known for his novel *The Hard to Catch Mercy,* Baldwin is a skilled and experienced writer of nonfiction, which might make his decision to render this true story in fictionalized form seem curious. He says it was for reasons personal and logistic.

"At 400 pages, the manuscript was still (dominated by) the Dawsons. Everybody in the book except a prostitute and the narrator are real people. I realized this just made things so static; I didn't have control of it. I couldn't just treat the Dawsons as fictional characters, and I couldn't see them as my invention. So I gave them all new names, and then the book was mine. That's when I began to trim it down."

This, of course, begs two questions: How much is factual and how much is embroidery? Where does Dawson end and the fictional Capt. David Lawton begin?

"As far as Lawton and Dawson goes, it's pretty much on the money. Again, all but two are real people. From all the material I read, which contained so many love letters, it seemed like everybody was in love and they were always reading romance novels.

"You can argue that it's romance novels that gets Dawson killed. I asked myself, 'What is the central theme of all these people's lives?' They were all in love. So when I knew I had to go out and promote the book, I decided to look an audience in the eye and say, 'This is a book about how the messy business of sex is a manifestation of God's love for us.' And it is a messy business. In the course of this little book, it gets a couple of characters killed, and four more have nervous breakdowns."

A Gentleman of Charleston, which in some respects satirizes the Gothic romance, plays with the novel form on another level: The novel is being written as one is reading it.

"The first full chapter is an homage to Kate Chopin, the Louisiana feminist. The very last chapter in the novel is an homage to Joseph Conrad. I want the novel to be read as a fun read and to sell well, obviously. But on another level, it's a novel about the process of writing, and it's a novel about late 19th-century literature. The Dawsons appear in at least four other novels, and pages of them are incorporated into the text, which I found entertaining."

On His Mantel

As is his custom, Baldwin, a one-time architectural student, commercial fisherman and building contractor who now moonlights as a portrait painter, prefers to have several irons in the hearth.

Together with Elizabeth Turk, a professor of photography at the Atlanta College of Art, he also is publishing *Mantelpieces of the Old South: Lost Architecture and Southern Culture*, likewise being released this week by the History Press of Charleston. The book is at once an outgrowth of research performed for his 1984 book, *Plantations of the Lowcountry*, done with Jane Iseley, and a showcase of work from the Historic American Buildings Survey collection, a Depression-era work program.

"My son and I edited it down to about 800 photos out of 15,000, and Elizabeth took that down to 20. They tell a story with some 30 pages of text. We wanted something beautiful and romantic, and I think we have it."

He is no less enthusiastic over *A Gentleman of Charleston*, and the way he achieved his principal aims, not the least of which were capturing the texture of a time and place, examining the social codes that governed class, race and gender relations—and having fun. But these, while important, were not paramount.

"Partly, *The Hard to Catch Mercy* was about the spoken word. It was all about oral history. In this new book, I wanted to say something about love in all its different manifestations. I also felt like I wanted to do something about the written word, which is the kind of thing publishers says never to breathe in public.

"They prefer a coming-of-age story full of violence. Well, this is a coming-of-age novel, except the age I was coming to is 61."

October 30, 2005

Josephine Humphreys's *Nowhere Else on Earth*

Romantic illusions aside, it is not often that the writing of a book leaves an author transfigured.

Josephine Humphreys could not have anticipated that the nine-year process of producing her fourth novel, *Nowhere Else on Earth*, would deconstruct not only her approach to fiction, but her entire world view.

"To write this book I had to change gears totally and re-educate myself in a major way regarding history," says Humphreys, whose novel will be released September 4 by Viking. "Actually, I had to change my whole view of the world—or let's say that it did change. That's why I love this book, and that's why I love the time that I've spent doing it."

The book hasn't been the only catalyst of change in Humphreys over the past decade. Her children having grown up and gotten married was just the most obvious signpost of transition.

"But the book drew me into a past world, a distant world that changed the way I looked at Southern history, at history in general, at fiction, and at community life, race, family, romance, education. What else is there?"

Humphreys's long-awaited new novel was inspired by actual events. Set in North Carolina during the Civil War and the early Reconstruction years, it is the story of Rhoda Strong, a 17-year-old half-Scottish, half-Lumbee Indian girl living with her family in a remote rural community on the banks of the Lumbee River.

Strong longs to recover what the war took from her—a normal life and the possibility of love. But forces far older than the hostilities between North and South still exert their power, heralding new conflicts even as the war slowly, agonizingly draws to a close. In the end, Strong must choose between her family and her love for heroic outlaw Henry Berry Lowrie.

"She is a woman who has yearned for the standard dream of love, family, home and happiness. These are important things, and often the most important. But Strong faces a situation in which other things take precedence and become more pressing and important. There are higher causes."

The genesis of *Nowhere Else on Earth* rests with a train trip from Charleston to Providence, R.I., one which left an indelible imprint on Humphreys. She sat next to a 17-year-old bride who was traveling north to meet her husband's family. The young woman was ill at ease over the prospect of encountering her in-laws for the first time, certain they would not approve of her because of her background. She was part-Lumbee Indian, a somewhat mysterious tribe that has been repeatedly denied federal recognition as Native American.

Unfamiliar with the Lumbee and puzzled by their exclusion from tribal status, Humphreys hungered to learn more. For the rest of their time together, Humphreys sat transfixed by the bride and the story of her people.

"We were both 17, and she was so beautiful and bold. She came from a world I had never seen, had never heard of and could not have imagined. Hearing her story and the story of her people, which is what she really told me, resulted in a crack running down the middle of what I thought I had known."

Though each of Humphreys's books is distinctive, Nowhere Else on Earth embodied a radical shift for the author.

"The major difference, of course, is that it is an historical novel based on a true story. That second part altered my whole way of writing. I used to write fiction starting with the blank page and an empty world and filling it with people that I made up.

"And I used to write without a plan for the plot. I had no idea what was going to happen from day to day, and that was fun and entertaining and did not involve the kind of obligation that suddenly arose in this book to access the past and figure out how to make it into fiction."

Thanks to its story, the book came alive for Humphreys far more than any other book she has written.

"That's partly because I'm aware of it having an origin in reality. So I was able to think of the characters not simply as people I made up but as having an identity and a being separate from me."

She used to hesitate to do that.

"I really didn't want to think of them as real. I didn't want to kid myself, though in some ways I would have liked to be able to. Writers who do begin to think of their fictional characters and stories as real have an advantage over those who are rational about it.

"I liked this narrator better than any other character I've ever had, though she has some similarities with some of the other characters and narrators of my books. There's a 17-year-old girl at the center of every one of my books."

Humphreys says the character of Rhoda Strong had been niggling at the back of her mind for a long time, demanding attention.

"I started this book every time I sat down to write, going back to 1981, but had always quit and started a different kind of book. This time I told myself I wasn't going to quit until I did finish, and if I failed, that was OK.

"In fact, Rhoda may be the 17-year-old girl who has kept surfacing in all my books. But she has more depth and more resilience and more of a willingness to learn than the other characters did. She's more eager for change and more watchful of the world around her. And she has a harder problem."

Early reviews suggest that the remainder of Humphreys's cast of characters are no less compelling.

"That's the other advantage of taking so much time, although spending nine years on a novel doesn't seem that long to me. I did have in my mind a fuller idea of each character than I've had in the past."

Which proved as daunting as it did invigorating.

"I could, I think, sit down and write two or three more sequels to this book because I know in my mind what happened to the other people, and what they would have done. And I wouldn't mind doing it if I didn't always have something else I wanted to do that seems more important. Right now there's another story that I would prefer to do, another historical novel. I found a man who I want to fictionalize and a time and a place that I want to live in for a while."

While writing *Nowhere Else on Earth*, this idea was the last thing on her mind. Humphreys was feeling the burden of the question: "What is a novelist allowed to do with the truth?"

Her finished product allayed that concern.

Humphreys is too busy to fixate on the signposts of an author's maturity, a culmination she feels no urgency to achieve.

"I don't think I'm a writer yet. There's always so much to learn, and always so much that I've not gotten right that needs to be better. Stories that I wanted to tell in full but only got skimmed, people I wanted to get to the bottom of that I could really only show the surfaces of.

"The great thing about writing is that you never feel that you've done a great job. You keep at it. But you don't want to feel pressured. I feel that at this age, which is now 55, that I have more time than ever to go slow and to learn. At some point, if I ever really wanted to publish a book to prove that I was writer, that need has just evaporated. I don't feel that at all anymore. I don't feel any kind of ambition in that regard."

Yet pride, she avers, is a useful thing.

"I sort of enjoy pride in other aspects. You have to be proud of your life in at least one or two or three ways. Something has to strike you as having been worthwhile and that you did well. I think I was a good mother. My kids are happy, and they were always a lot of fun to be with.

"I don't want to hang all my worth as a soul on the things I've written, or on any single aspect of my life."

Still, *Nowhere Else on Earth* owns a gravity that, to many, makes it a cut above. If Humphreys could disengage herself from the author's mantle and see her new book through others' eyes, with what might she be most impressed?

"The actual story. The truth that lies under the fiction. The people, the characters, and how they and their deeds came together at this point in the history of North Carolina to speak to us across this century. These people are pointing out something to us that needs to be remembered, thought about and reconsidered."

August 26, 2000

Robert Jordan's *Crossroads of Twilight*

His is a vivid daydream, alive on paper. Not an alternate reality.

For those who suspect Robert Jordan is so consumed by his books, so immersed in their universe that the fanciful has more substance than the tangible, be assured this is not the case.

He still takes out the garbage. And no fictional creations attend him as he does so.

The richly imagined novels of his *Wheel of Time* cycle may possess prodigious detail, and characters that seem to breathe on the page, but the author recognizes the warp and woof of the real quite well, thank you, and embraces the knowledge that, in time, the party will come to an end.

The Charleston native is as grounded as one of the most successful writers in the world can be. Hyperbole? Do millions read your books with the same fervor accorded Tolkien? Do 500 people a day show up for your book signings, from Sacramento to Sydney? Are your novels translated into 20 languages? Are you not only the standard bearer for a major publishing company, but the standard by which others in the fantasy genre are judged? Are there thousands of Web sites devoted in whole or in part to discussing your work?

We thought not.

Balancing Act

The measure of the man is his equilibrium. Global renown may have fattened his purse, but not his head. Jordan has not been shanghaied by adulation down the unworthy paths of ego. Three of the 10 books in the Wheel of

Time cycle have scaled the summit of The New York Times best-seller list. *Crossroads of Twilight*, his latest, is the first to open at the crest. He is gratified. He is not, however, calling for an attendant.

"You want the reader to be drawn into the world you create, to be immersed in it," says Jordan, relaxing in his study. "But if I, as the writer, got that deeply into my world, it would produce very bad writing. You would lose the flow of what you are doing. I'm not suspending disbelief. I know I created this. What I'm after is getting other people to suspend knowledge that they are reading a book and, for a little time, to feel that this thing is real."

Frame of mind is key.

"I focus on sitting down to each book as if this is 'It.' Like nobody has ever heard of Robert Jordan. I've got this one book that I've got to try to make good enough that people will know who Robert Jordan is. I know that's a strange way to look at it, but it is very useful for trying to make the book good. It also helps me not worry about what's gone before."

In the wake of book nine, *Winter's Heart* (2000), Jordan confided that he might prefer that the 10th volume be the capstone of the story. But there will be two more books, at least.

"I tried, but I had a problem with that from the beginning. I knew the last scene of the last book in 1984. When I started writing I knew where I was going. But some things had to be pushed forward. The story hasn't expanded; it's just taken me more time. In *Crossroads of Twilight*, things are reaching that stage where everything really is balanced on the point of a pin, or of a sword, if you prefer. There are a lot of things that could go in many directions. Good or evil can win in any number of different places and different levels."

If the book marks a departure from its predecessors, it rests with one particular device.

"One big departure is that each of the major segments of the book begins on exactly the same day, and it's a very significant day in terms if these books. The characters are reacting to the effects of that one significant day, as well as reacting to what is happening around them."

While Jordan hopes to bring matters to fruition in two more volumes, some of the more devoted fans would be only too happy if he took 10 more books to complete the saga. When such ardent calls fall on the ears of the folks at Tor Books, Jordan is moved to cry, "Don't listen to them! Don't listen!"

"I have spent 18 years of my life on this, and I would like to finish it. I thought I was signing up for a 10K run. I knew it was not a stroll in the park. I knew I was doing something that was going to be longer than usual. But when I first started I thought that 'longer than usual' meant five or six books.

I honestly thought I would finish it in five. But I discovered it wasn't a 10K run. It was a marathon, and I want to cross the finish line.

"Because these books are the way they are, I have to finish it for them to mean anything. After I complete the cycle I can take a breath. I can really go on a vacation."

Of a Piece

It is a mistake to view *The Wheel of Time* cycle as a series. Rather like J. R. R. Tolkien's *The Lord of the Rings*, to which it is most often compared, *The Wheel of Time* is a single novel built of multiple books.

"I'm doing something that hasn't been done, I guess, since (English novelist Anthony) Trollope. I am writing a very long, multi-volume novel. You can read the first book, *The Eye of the World*, and stop, and feel you've read something that has enough resolution that you don't feel you have to read more. But you still have to start there."

Jordan cautions readers not to attempt to pick up the story in midstream, much less get one's feet wet with the most recent volume. Not until having read books one through nine.

"You cannot start by reading *Crossroads of Twilight*. If you do you will be bitterly disappointed. In 10 pages you'll give up. You have to start with *The Eye of the World*, which has been continuously in print in hardcover for 13 years. There aren't many books that can match that."

The 11th book, thus far untitled, is due out in late 2004, or perhaps early 2005. Currently, Jordan is at work expanding an earlier tale.

"I wrote a novella called *New Spring* for a collection that was put together by Robert Silverberg for an anthology called *Legends*. I had to compress the story quite a bit to get it down to novella length. I happened to mention to my publisher that had I put everything I had wanted into the story, it would have been twice the length. He asked if I'd be interested in rewriting it as a novel. So I'm going to do that. It's in progress now. I hope to have it finished in a few more months."

When *The Wheel of Time* stops turning, Jordan will not lack for fodder. He's already been pondering a new project for the past seven or eight years.

"There's nothing on paper yet, but a load of stuff in the back of my head. It will be very different. Another fantasy, but in a different world, a completely different universe with completely different characters. It will not in any way be a sequel, or even related to *The Wheel of Time*, except that it will also go into the clash of cultures, the meeting of cultures that are widely different, a subject which has always fascinated me."

And the prospect excites him. The depth and detail will be there; it's how he writes. But the Herculean length? No. He is trying to plan how to structure this new set of books so that it can be done in six volumes.

Given the respect and artistry accorded *The Lord of the Rings* by director Peter Jackson, does Jordan feel that a film version of *The Wheel of Time* is now more feasible?

"I do not know whether it could be done in that way. I have just had an option offered from a production company called Manetheren Films, which was spawned for the purpose of producing the books as a miniseries or a series of miniseries on some place like HBO or the SciFi Channel. We'll see how it goes. It won't be the first time that someone has bought an option. NBC bought an option, then all the people involved in buying it went elsewhere. But the check cleared."

Certified

"Robert Jordan" is a trademark as well as a benchmark. Few writers experience this status, not that Jordan betrays any of the outward signs of celebrity.

"I have reacted (to it all) with continual surprise. I like it, of course. Who wouldn't? But I didn't expect it. Any writer hopes for success, and by success I mean acclaim, wonderful reviews and going up the best-seller lists. But only an idiot would expect it. There's another side to that, which I think some writers never get hold of. And that's the fact that one day it will go away. People like the books I am writing, and a lot of people have bought them. At some point I will write something that they don't like so well.

"But you hope you keep climbing or that you will have several peaks during your career. What I am most concerned with, frankly, is trying to make each book better that the books that have gone before. If I haven't learned at least a little bit in the last 18 years then I would be a very sorry writer. I would like to be as good as I can be."

Very occasionally, Jordan meets a reader who believes the author is imbued with some arcane potential, that the ability to Channel the One Power (of the books) is not only an actual faculty, but something he can teach them to do.

Jordan chuckles, ruefully.

"I have more often met people—just as frightening in a way—who think because of these books I am some sort of guru or sage, and that they can learn great wisdom from me. I just write books. I tell stories; that's all. The books demand as much as the reader is willing to give them. My main concern is to write them in such a way that they will not merely stand up to repeated readings, but still offer something the second time through, or the fifth."

February 9, 2003

Note: "Robert Jordan" was the nom de plume of long-time writer and editor James O. Rigney, Jr. He died in 2007, one month shy of his 59th birthday. He never got to "cross the finish line" with *The Wheel of Time*, but, with copious notes and outlines, ceded that honor to others in his stead.

Charles Seabrook's *Cumberland Island: Strong Women, Wild Horses*

Ambling through the sun-dappled interior, the first thing you notice is the silence—broken only by the wind sighing through live oaks, the call of a bird or the rustle of some small creature in the bush.

Just at the edge of awareness is the sound of the surf whooshing onto a broad, lonely beach that shoulders up to a bulwark of dunes.

As stealthily as a ninja, a white-tailed deer breaks from cover, crossing the wide footpath and disappearing into shadow. Splashes of color—cardinals, tanagers and pileated woodpeckers—show vividly against a canvas of green. High above the graceful contortions of the trees, with their drapery of Spanish moss, an osprey wheels. With luck, you may glimpse the majesty of a wild horse.

You are in the restorative embrace of Cumberland Island, a complex and varied ecosystem of maritime forest, saltwater marsh and beach that encompasses the Cumberland Island National Seashore, accessible only by boat from the small coastal town of St. Marys, Ga.

It is 9,000 acres of wild America cut through with hiking trails and blessed with 18 miles of undeveloped beach. It is also a battleground on which the forces of development, environmentalism, descendants of the Carnegie family and the National Park Service contend. One man's paradise is another's purgatory. Who is best-suited to be the island's caretaker?

Squarely, implacably, in the antidevelopment camp is biologist and resident Carol Ruckdeschel, the most recent in a progression of women who have helped define the history of Georgia's largest and southernmost barrier island. Their story is told in *Cumberland Island: Strong Women, Wild Horses*

(John F. Blair) by Atlanta Journal-Constitution environmental writer and native Johns Islander Charles Seabrook.

"In my 31-year newspaper career, I have traveled around the world and covered many fascinating stories," says Seabrook, a graduate of the University of South Carolina and a former *News and Courier* reporter. "But Cumberland Island, with its history and characters, is one of the most compelling stories I've encountered. It was ripe for a book.

"I first visited the island in 1972, after President Nixon signed the bill declaring it a national seashore. The idea for a book started percolating around 1998 or 1999. I was doing some stories for the newspaper on the same conflicts and issues I'd covered over the years, and my research was more or less complete. Most of the previous books I'd seen were of the coffee-table variety, but I wanted any book I undertook to be the best, most in-depth I could do. The characters involved were just too colorful and rich to not do them justice."

Originally inhabited by the Timucuan peoples, a coastal tribe today found mainly in Florida, by 1610 the island was the locus of Spain's second-largest mission on the East Coast. Sea Island cotton was an important crop during the plantation period, which gave way to a clutch of mansions built by the Carnegie family in the 1880s.

Only ruins remain of the once-proud Dungeness, a four-story house constructed in the 1790s by the captivating Catherine ("Caty") Greene Miller, widow of Gen. Nathanael Greene, and rebuilt by Thomas and Lucy Coleman Carnegie a century later. It was "Caty" Miller who had the most pronounced initial impact. Her cultivation of Sea Island cotton, coupled with her friendship with cotton gin inventor Eli Whitney, was instrumental in establishing the crop as the dominant resource in the South.

There was also the slave Zabette, who gave birth to four light-skinned daughters fathered by her owner, Robert Stafford, each of whom was dispatched north to be educated and raised in a rarefied social swirl, accompanied by their mother (who posed as a maid). Her secret was not discovered for many years.

The Carnegie dynasty planted its flag on Cumberland Island after being rejected for membership on Jekyll Island. "Miss Lucy" Ferguson, granddaughter of Thomas and Lucy Carnegie, became legend for her resolute work ethic and the imprint she placed on the island's landscape.

In her own way, Ruckdeschel continues the tradition, though not without detractors, as well as allies.

"Certainly the most compelling aspect of the island is its natural splendor and serenity, and that it is subject to such intense, sometimes bitter, conflict," Seabrook says. "But when you start looking at the people behind those conflicts, there is such a rich assortment of characters. How can one place attract so many such people and produce such strong women? The men, in a way, almost seem to be inconsequential in its history.

"What these women, and others, have in common is their intense love of the island. Especially with Lucy Ferguson and Carol, the thing that struck me about them was their back-to-nature experiences and their independence. A self-trained biologist, Carol is an officially designated and respected sea turtle researcher, so she can drive her vehicle on the island for turtle control. She is one of the few people who live there year-round. She minces no words. At the same time she can be one of nicest persons you ever want to meet. Charming. No pretensions; she leads a truthful life."

Seabrook lives in Decatur, Ga., with his wife and two children. Three brothers and a sister remain on Johns Island, a place that, like Cumberland, is enshrined in his imagination yet can provoke a sense of unease. Its future also will be shaped by competing interests.

But Johns Island is not owned by the National Park Service.

"There is, right now as we speak, a first-ever massive management plan, which officially designates a portion of Cumberland Island as a wilderness area," Seabrook says. "The wild area is the source of most of the conflicts.

"The Wilderness Society wants the wilderness to be managed like a wilderness area. On other hand, the retained-rights people such as some of the Carnegie descendants have a right to live in the homes they are in now until they die or their grandchildren die. These rights are almost tailor-made for each individual. And they want the same rights the Carnegies had when they owned the island. The battle goes on."

The beauty remains.

August 7, 2002

Sidney Rittenberg's *The Man Who Stayed Behind*

On October 21, 1949, the day the People' Republic of China was declared, Sidney Rittenberg sat rotting in cell 11 of Beijing's No. 2 prison, a pariah condemned to six years of solitary confinement.

The six years would become 16 for the Charleston-born linguist, falsely accused of espionage and subversion. Ironic, given that Rittenberg had been the darling of the Chinese Communist Party, a loyal and impassioned leftist who believed ardently in Mao Zedong's revolutionary goals.

More than any American of his era, Rittenberg knew the corridors of power in 20th-century China. Mao, Zhou En-lai and, later, Deng Xiao Ping, were not inscrutable icons to him, but personal acquaintances.

If ever a man was caught in the gale of history it was Rittenberg, whose 34 unbroken years in this vast, eternal land are the subject of the forthcoming memoir, *The Man Who Stayed Behind* (Simon & Schuster), written with Wall Street Journal senior writer Amanda Bennett.

Currently a consultant on China with a number of American corporations, Rittenberg's experiences will be related in a "60 Minutes" segment to be aired on CBS in April. He was in Charleston last week to deliver an address at the College of Charleston.

"Going to China happened quite by accident," says Rittenberg, 71, grandson of state senator Sam Rittenberg and the son of the late lawyer and writer Sidney Rittenberg, Sr. "During World War II there was an urgent need for people in the services who could speak Far Eastern languages. I was stationed in Oregon in 1945 when the Army sent me to China as a language expert attached to Army Headquarters, first in Kunming then in Shanghai with the office of the Judge Advocate General.

"It taught me a great deal. I traveled to many little Chinese villages and was immersed in the language and culture. I determined to learn to communicate with those people, to speak Chinese not as a foreigner. I found that being there as an American who accepted the locals on their own terms won respect and appreciation from everyone. I felt that there was a great opportunity to be a communicator there, to be like a telephone wire over which Americans and Chinese could make good, clear contact."

Rittenberg received his honorable discharge in January 1946 and remained in the country as a famine relief observer for the United Nations. For six months he toured provinces such as Hunan—the rice bowl of China—then in the grip of a terrible famine.

"There were days when we were never out of sight of corpses. I'd never seen anything like it: strings of refugees lining the roads who would go as far as they could and then just drop. No one had the time, energy or means to do anything with them.

"This experience was a real eye-opener about Chinese politics and the state of that country. It was very common among U.S. military personnel in Shanghai at this time to hear that nothing but communism was going to save the country, that it was too far gone. The corruption, the violence, the disdain for human life, this disparity between the way a tiny handful of privileged were living and what you saw all around you, made it all inevitable."

The civil war pitting the Nationalists under Chaing Kai-shek and Mao's socialist insurgents had by this time begun to escalate. Having already joined the Party, Rittenberg's sympathies were unequivocal.

"I sympathized with the communists even before I got to China. I had been part of the radical left-wing student movement while in college at Chapel Hill. Above all, my father demanded of his children that they be honest. I was shocked by the injustice I saw around me, which led me to the left."

Rittenberg resigned from the U.N. in June of 1946, fully intending to come home and attend graduate school. But when Chinese officials asked him to stay and help establish an English language school in Beijing, he leapt at the chance.

"After several years in this capacity, I thought that I would serve as a liaison in normalization talks between Washington and Mao. Then, suddenly, I was in jail. I went from being on top of the world to the bottom of it."

His initial imprisonment, beginning in January 2, 1949, was at the behest of the Russians.

"We were in the mountains outside of Beijing. The communists were already negotiating for the surrender of the city, and while these were going on I was suddenly just whisked away. I had been their favorite little foreigner. But Stalin didn't like the idea of any American being on friendly terms with Mao and Zhou En-lai and the other Chinese leaders. He was having enough trouble with them as it was."

The Chinese told him from the beginning that they knew he hadn't done anything wrong. It didn't matter. Rittenberg spent the first 12 months of his captivity in total darkness.

"The pressure was agonizing in solitary. The only time I saw anyone was to be interrogated or to have drugs administered to me. The problem was simple: you couldn't get out unless you confessed. But I had nothing I could confess, and no made up story would have been convincing. The Chinese just wanted to keep you on ice."

Meanwhile, neither his family nor the U.S. government had any idea what had become of him. Rittenberg was released in April, 1955. Though in wretched physical condition, he was not embittered by his ordeal. Quite the opposite.

"They were very repentant. And of all the options offered me, which included going home, I chose to go back to what I had been doing with the schools. Politically, I was even more committed, because I had decided that the reason I had such a hard time for six years in solitary was because I hadn't been a good enough communist. I would train myself to be pure and totally dedicated. I stayed. I met my wife-to-be, Yu Lin. The next year we were married, and we had four children. Everything was fine.

"I was now reading the classified literature that party functionaries read. And I saw Mao and Zhou En-lai and so forth from time to time. I was liked, a friend they felt relaxed around. I was sort of like a privileged mascot."

But Rittenberg also was a purist. He insisted that the Chinese make good on the promise of the revolution—namely, a humane, authentically democratic socialism. This stance led to a second, even longer imprisonment.

The Cultural Revolution had broken out in 1966. Rittenberg, Yu Lin and their friends decided that it was a pivotal moment in time. They believed the one-party dictatorship was crumbling. China now might be transformed into a town hall democracy with elected leaders.

"It all began very much like the 1989 student movement. The tensions that had built up under the picture of seeming socialist equanimity all of a sudden blew up. It was a remarkable experience that turned into a terrible holocaust. But in the beginning, it looked like something very different. I threw myself into support of exactly the kind of student groups that surfaced in 1989. I campaigned widely, speaking and pamphleteering against one-party rule, against slavish discipline, against following dogma, and believing I represented the views of Mao, his wife, and their group."

Ten more years in prison as "an enemy of the state" forced Rittenberg to re-evaluate. When he was freed again in 1977, it was with the knowledge that the entire "democratic" movement has been a delusion.

Again, the Chinese were contrite, officially citing his more than 30 years of contributions to the country. He was free to leave. Two years later, he did, with the trophy of another privileged position. To this day, as consultant for U.S. businesses, there is no one in Chinese government or industry that the Rittenbergs cannot see.

When Rittenberg at last returned to the U.S. in 1980, he was accorded a graceful re-entry by the State Department, and treated respectfully by the media as a man of conviction. After periods in New York, Charleston and Chapel Hill, N.C., the Rittenbergs settled in Woodinville, Wash., near Seattle.

Rittenberg had weathered the two wars, the Great Leap Forward, the Cultural Revolution, the Gang of Four upheaval, heaven knows how many other shifts in power, and Nixon's overtures leading to normalization of diplomatic relations. Why, finally, had he left?

"I think the answer really is that I finally saw that the system in China wasn't working and couldn't work. The reason it doesn't work, I realized, was built into the system itself, from its very inception."

Despite all that befell him, Rittenberg felt neither wounded nor betrayed. Rather, there was a sense of liberation. The veil had fallen away. So many things were finally explained.

"I had not been able to explain these contradictions to myself before because I could not challenge my basic premises. The Cultural Revolution was the real turnaround for me. But it wasn't until I got out of prison the second time that I saw the unvarnished reality. What I felt badly about was having taken part in the political movement that persecuted so many people."

March 28, 1993

Anne LeClercq's *Between North and South*

What will future generations have to replace the social, cultural and political histories embedded in personal correspondence? By its very nature—terse and impermanent—will the ubiquitous e-mail ever duplicate the literary verve, the thoughtfulness, of letter writing?

Can you imagine a publishing house releasing, years hence and with all fanfare, "The Collected E-Mails of Bill Gates"? Doubtful.

Letters are fast becoming a lost art. Fortunately, learning from them is not.

In producing her new book, *Between North and South: The Letters of Emily Wharton Sinkler, 1842–1865* (University of South Carolina Press), Charleston author Anne Sinkler Whaley LeClercq spent years poring over the letters written home by her great-great-grandmother, a Philadelphian transplanted to Belvedere Plantation in South Carolina, and editing them into a cohesive body of correspondence which captures a time and place.

"I'm a collector, an historian and a librarian," says LeClercq, director of libraries at the Citadel's Daniel Library. "I'm overwhelmed by old letters, not only the volume of them but by the burden of trying to understand the past. I'm humbled by people's personal letters. In some ways it's an invasive thing, and you have to deal with that as well.

"Discovering these letters has been a source of inspiration for me. I had 50 of them when I wrote my first book, *An Antebellum Plantation Household.* By the end I had discovered 125 letters in attics, and from cousins in Philadelphia. It's social history in this case, not political history. It's the warp and woof of life, the kind of thing we don't have today because we don't write these letters."

Like her contemporary Mary Boykin Chesnut, Sinkler related stories of colorful characters and noteworthy events, albeit seen though the eyes of a Northern-born urban woman who took on the responsibilities of a rural plantation mistress.

LeClercq's book is the 10th volume in the *Women's Diaries and Letters of the South* series published by USC Press. Carol Bleser serves as series editor. LeClercq undertook the book in honor of her mother, the late gardening guru and author Emily Whaley.

"When I moved home in 1996, Mom was working on her first book and I stayed with her for six months. She was a link to my great-great-grandmother. Mom and I were kindred spirits in seeing what the past might contribute to the present.

"I finished the book last year, with the help and encouragement of Alex Moore at USC Press. He showed me about 10 more things I had to do. I thought I was finished when I handed him the manuscript, but that was far from being the case."

The narrative begins in 1842, with 18-year-old Emily Wharton's marriage to Charles Sinkler of Eutawville, who owned Belvedere Plantation on the banks of the Santee River.

"They were married in September after arriving in Charleston aboard the ship Southerner, having faced hurricane winds en route to Adger's Wharf. They lived in Charleston during the fall of 1847, when she gave birth to a daughter, Arabella. But Emily gave birth to all her other six children in Philadelphia. She thought it would be hazardous to have babies on the plantation. She went home every July to get out of the terrible heat and would return in September. She was always coming and going through Charleston."

Charleston and Philadelphia, two port cities tied to cotton, owned a close connection during the antebellum period, says LeClercq. But life was immeasurably different in the rural reaches. Though hardly a life of deprivation, the environ was foreign to a cosmopolitan lady from one of young America's foremost cities.

"I think life was tough there. All the letters written home to her parents in Philadelphia speak of how cold it was, just 50 miles inland from Charleston. There was a fireplace in every room, but the water in every washbasin was frozen. She also wrote to her brothers Henry Wharton, a Philadelphia lawyer, and Frank Wharton, a university professor in England, and to her sister Mary, who lived in Paris."

To revisit the 1840s in South Carolina is not unlike visiting a third-world country today, at least in terms of the potential hazards to one's health, says LeClercq.

"Life was that different. We are terrified of smallpox and anthrax and other diseases right now, but Charlestonians and lowcountry people with smallpox, cholera and tuberculosis were almost commonplace in the mid-1800s. Emily caught whooping cough shortly after she came here to live and was desperately ill. Whole plantations were quarantined in that era, and she never came to Charleston without checking the published lists of what people were dying of. Still, while the events of September 11, 2001, and the anthrax scare that followed gave me a real sense of foreboding, I look back at my great-great-grandmother and see that never in her letters does she speak of being terrified."

Her family in Pennsylvania was not quite as sanguine, especially with the onset of the War Between the States. Emily Sinkler remained at Belvedere throughout the Civil War. One of her sons, Wharton Sinkler, fought for the Confederacy, and LeClercq has his letters as well.

"I don't have letters from her mother and father, but I know her family was frantic for her safety in 1865. She told them not to worry because they were off the beaten path. Or so she thought. Sherman's March passed within 20 miles of them, and they could see the fires in Columbia.

"Emily's sympathies certainly were divided. Her husband, Charles, had fought in the Mexican War with the U.S. Army, and he subscribed to the journal the *Unionist.* Charles Sinkler was a slaveholder, but he called all his slaves to his side 1863 to tell them of the Emancipation Proclamation—and to tell them they were free to go. His neighbors thought he had lost his mind. I believe there were many Unionists in the South during the war. And I think she was one of them. But she was not a political person like the Grimke sisters, and certainly not an abolitionist."

Yet Sinkler developed a profound interest in religion and African-American culture. She sought to circumvent a South Carolina law prohibiting schooling for slaves by establishing a church where she taught reading through song and prayer. Built on the plantation in 1842, the church survived until Belvedere was flooded a century later.

Her letters may not have evinced an astute political sensibility, says LeClercq, but Emily Sinkler was a perceptive observer attuned to her surroundings.

"She had an acute eye for what was happening around her. She looked closely at slavery and was apologetic in trying to explain to her family this strange institution she found herself surrounded by. There are a lot of qualities I've discovered in this woman that are worth regarding. She sang the operas of Puccini and Rossini when they came out. She read Dickens and Bronte when their books first came out. She realized how very important it was to be 'with it' in your culture.

"It's not just about reading the classics. You are not part of your culture unless you're immersed in it."

December 9, 2001

Dori Sanders's *Her Own Place*

Second novels, like a star athlete's sophomore season, can be a matter or living up to a writer's established standard, and surpassing it. Expectations are high; the challenges are proportionately higher.

And it doesn't help when you lose the first draft of your book on an airplane.

Her first novel, *Clover*, made York native Dori Sanders a publishing and media celebrity. A second book, *Her Own Place*, to be published by Algonquin Books in May, bears the full weight of critical and popular anticipation.

But is she worried? Well, yes.

Sanders, as well known for her peach farm as for her prose, says she approached her follow-up novel with pure, unadulterated fear.

"I am still approaching it with fear. It was the most difficult thing I've ever tried in my life, attempting not only to live up to *Clover*, but to improve on it. I wanted it to be so good that maybe I tried too hard. Then I misplaced the first draft on an airplane during a publicity tour for *Clover* in the summer of 1991. It was at about that time that I said to myself, 'I don't know if I can write a second book at all.'"

She managed, much to the delight of her growing legion of fans.

Sanders's status as an overnight literary sensation continues to baffle and bemuse the fifty-something author, and even after more than a year of countless interviews and speaking engagements, she's yet to adjust to all the attention.

"It's like to kill me. Nothing had prepared me for this sort of thing. It isn't that I'm such a private person. But I *am* a country person, and suddenly having all these people want to meet you is unbelievable. It's not real. I still can't get used to it, someone wanting to meet Dori Sanders.

"You think you'll get comfortable with it but you don't. I was in Columbia recently to give a talk at the new main branch of the Richland County Public Library, and had to pretend the people were customers at my peach shed. Fortunately, I'm far-sighted, so I couldn't see the people close up. I'm comfortable with those who are far away. But if I didn't give out that nervous laugh of mine, my voice would be quavering even now."

Sanders's writing "routine" is unchanged. Although her publishers have prevailed upon her to use a word processor, most of her writing can be found—in time-honored tradition—on "anything and everything: torn paperbacks, a peach basket, a piece of wind-blown paper. And I'm writing at all times and places, like in a truck, on the tractor, or just strolling around."

The protagonist of *Her Own Place*, Mae Lee Barnes, lives on a South Carolina farm. As World War II rages, this war bride, abandoned wife and mother and community volunteer strives to construct a life on her own terms. She is not alone in her metamorphosis; an entire generation of rural and urban women find the boundaries of their existence irrevocably broached.

Clover was dominated by a child's voice, and a child's sensibilities. *Her Own Place*, by contrast, harbors a wholly adult narrator. Barnes is carried from her teens to her 60s in the novel.

"It was more of a challenge because she is more complex," says Sanders. "Her love for the land is what makes her so interesting to me. She has children, but equal to her love for them is her regard for the land. Farming is mean, hard work for a woman to do. But people do not realize how many women in South Carolina of that time actually were the go-getters as far as buying land was concerned.

"They wanted a piece of land no matter what the cost. For many years I have admired the struggles and challenges so many women face as they come into their own. What made them achieve it, at least in my farming community, was when they ventured out to work at munitions plants during World War II. It gave them a streak of independence; they had their own money and their own jobs. They had a share. I want people to see how they took a grip on life and secured a place for themselves. And, once they took it, how they went on from there. That's what I wanted to explore in my fiction. In a small way, this book pays homage to them."

At the same time, Sanders hopes readers will identify with Barnes in her role as mother.

"I think they will. Personally, I felt so envious while drawing a character that's a mother. I was married a long while, but never had a child, so it's a vicarious outlet. I wanted to draw a woman with character and strength, who was secure as a person in her own right, and as a parent."

Many a writer falls into the trap of fashioning a second novel in the image of the first, not only in style and tone, but in characterization. Sanders almost slipped into the same abyss, but escaped.

"That the book is in five parts may reflect my own struggle writing it. Good gracious, it was much more difficult than my first book. I wanted it to be just so. But then I was advised to just tell a story. I stopped all my struggles at that point and decided to just look back on real life as I knew it and tell that story."

Sanders is writing the final draft of a cookbook, also to be published by Algonquin, called *Farm Cooking Back Then and Now.* It's a compendium of recipes devised (often under duress) by her great aunt Versula, who worked on a plantation. Sanders has been pestering and cajoling all her older relatives and friends in an effort to re-create that aunt's culinary wisdom.

"The book will be chatty and talky with a lot of peach recipes."

In the meantime, there remains the possibility of a feature film based on *Clover*—Walt Disney Studios still holds an option—and Sanders's crowded public speaking schedule, which sports as many as 23 appearances in a single week.

"Lately it's been more like 15. I've had the 'help' of my sister, Virginia, who retired from American University as director of admissions for international students. It's 'Oh, yes, Dori can do it,' or 'Oh, yes, she'll be in the area.' Now she has me doing three a day.

"But I don't read from *Clover.* I only tell stories of how I became a writer and what it was that shaped my writing career—I was and am a reader! I didn't have a TV growing up."

What she wants to impart is fundamental, yet far-reaching.

"Most of all I want underprivileged children to see that someone who has lived a rural life and still does, someone who is ordinary, can still achieve great things. All of us are important. You can't be false or fancy, but if we put our best foot forward we can succeed."

March 7, 1993

Anne Rivers Siddons's *Sweetwater Creek*

It would be less than candid to deny that many books of so-called "women's fiction" set in the lowcountry share certain similarities, such as the lush subtropical environ and the obligatory "dark secret." That doesn't mean these novels should be pigeonholed as indistinguishable, or that broad assumptions can be made about their readers.

"How did we get to the place where everything is categorized, that has to fit into a slot," asks Anne Rivers Siddons, who resists the whole notion of labeling writers and their work.

Siddons latest novel is *Sweetwater Creek*, released Tuesday by HarperCollins. With this, as with all her books, she says she does not write to suit a perceived category of reader, regardless of where her story is set or the facets of her characters.

"For me to try to write to an audience would be death," says Siddons, who splits time between her homes in Charleston and Maine. "I have no idea who I'm pleasing. I know they're mainly women, but beyond that, I have no idea who they are. If I'm not writing for myself first, I don't think people will like what I do."

She sympathizes but does not identify with writers who have become such cash cows for their publishers or so cosseted by rabid readers that they feel locked into certain genres or narrative styles.

"It must be hard for writers who can't get out of the box or take risks in subject matter when they want to. What I write always seems new to me at the time. I don't know how to take a risk in that other way. I don't know what I could do that would be different. Except that I have always wanted to do a ghost story."

Not this time out, though the new novel and its protagonist are designed to be haunting.

At the tender age of 12, Emily Parmenter knows loneliness all too well. Left to her own devices after the disappearance of her young mother and the death of her older brother, Parmenter lives on a fading plantation where her less-than-accessible father and distracted brothers raise hunting dogs—Boykin spaniels first bred in South Carolina.

Instead of succumbing to sadness or withdrawing into inner flights of fancy, she finds magic outside of herself, in the dolphins who frolic in Sweetwater Creek, in the cacophony of ducks and in an almost mystic bond with the dogs she trains—especially her own spaniel, Elvis. This is how she holds the hurt of the world at bay. But that world is about to intrude.

Enter Lulu Foxworth, well-heeled daughter of a grand plantation owner, who has fled the Charleston debutante season to spend a summer amid the serenity of marsh and river. Foxworth harbors enchantments of her own, and the relationship she forges with Parmenter will open the portals to discovery. Of many kinds.

Siddons, a Georgia native, has said that her relationship with the South is affectionate but realistic, "like an old marriage." She wants to write about the South as it really is, not romanticize it. No less so in *Sweetwater Creek*.

"If a reader picks up a book about a home in Tuscany, and all she gets is the story of a woman and her basement, then that reader will be disappointed.

Similarly, it's almost impossible not to romanticize the lowcountry a little bit, especially when you first come to it. It is an almost mythic place. But I'm trying to see the abrasive sides of it as well, because they are certainly there and they give the place salt and bite. I don't think this new book is an out-and-out love story to the lowcountry. There are hidden shoals. And it's a tough place for a young girl like Emily to make her way—someone who is so alone, with no one to guide her until Lulu comes along.

"I loved her, and I loved the story, which is also a story of loss, of how resilient the very young can be, and how easy it is to take something away from them, so that they feel lost without even knowing why. What she had was a dead brother and a dog, then Lulu comes along and changes everything."

As for Lulu, Siddons says, "Not every South of Broad debutante is ridiculous. A great many rich women can be lovely. But Lulu also has an obsession."

Many books deal with the nature of female friendships, the bonds of family, the challenge of loss, the ambivalence over a new love and other timeless themes. Allowing for the considerable difference between writers in terms of talent, voice, experience and technical skill, how can a novelist give fresh perk to things that have been plumbed since the first novels came off the presses?

"I think it has to come out of something that touches you deep inside. You wouldn't do a women-bonding story just to do it. And who needs another Southern coming-of-age story? Most of us tend to write about things that are within our experience: a friendship, a love, the necessity to reinvent one's self just to survive. These are more women's concerns than they are men's. Once women go through these experiences, we are not the same people. This, because we live so close to the skin of our emotions."

Unlike Parameter, Siddons says, she had a wonderful childhood. Nonetheless, she felt a special kinship with the character.

"I did, and I can't imagine why. Maybe it was time I addressed the subject of loss in youth. I had written of loss in adulthood, but it is at this point of youth where loss toughens or destroys us."

Siddons is hearing more than a few comments from friends and fans who believe this is one of her best books. She can only assume this means the story is striking chords.

"Some people tell me it's my best. When I finished it, I felt satisfied. I felt the book was truly over, that it had ended the only way it could, and should. Always before, I had the urge to fiddle with a final draft. This comes out of a dissatisfaction, not necessarily with the individual book, but in not being able to do it as perfectly as you can see it.

"The moment a book is born in my head is the first and only time I see it whole and plain and clear. I can never achieve that again, but it's something to work toward. I came close to it with this one."

August 14, 2005

Padgett Powell's *Edisto Revisited*

At his best, Padgett Powell is one of those writers who make colleagues wish they had pursued another line of work.

When it comes to crisp observation, pungent turns of phrase and edgy humor, Powell is a formidable novelist and purveyor of short fiction. Best known as the author of *Edisto*, he returns to the lowcountry in *Edisto Revisited* (Henry Holt & Co.), his fourth novel.

Since 1984, the year Powell was catapulted into the literary spotlight by *Edisto*, the Gainesville native has taught graduate and undergraduate courses in writing at the University of Florida.

But this self-styled loner shares little of the school's high-profile glamour, preferring an unadorned lifestyle and simple candor.

"I used to write about race and sex. And now I write about sex," says Powell, 44, who lived on Edisto Island from 1970 through 1975. "It took me four books to realize that I was writing about loneliness. I'm terrified of it, which functions in many of the things I do."

The fellow who wrote *Edisto* 12 years ago in some ways seems a distant relation to the seasoned writer who toils today. But that acute sense of loneliness remains unchanged.

"He's somewhat distant, in that he had no kids, no money, and no friends. And today I have kids and money and no friends. I've just never really established many friendships. Growing up, I lived in 17 houses by the time I got out of high school. I don't know the number of high schools.

"As a result, I became the perpetual new boy, who is recognized by having no friends. And I have a character caustic enough to keep it that way. It's hopeless. So I've tried to be professional as a writer and devote myself to other things."

Powell's writing, by contrast, engages everyone from associates to total strangers. And he is among that relative handful of authors who infuses his work with the music of language without getting windy and florid.

"It's difficult to say how I do something because what I do I seem to do naturally, without thinking about it. For one thing, everything I write is very tightly linked, and it's germane to whatever storyline or problem is obtaining, except when that which is not germane is more interesting that the storyline.

"If you can keep a thumb on that pulse, things will cohere. In terms of rhythm or 'music,' I sort of hear things out loud. I write as if I'm speaking. I make no distinction. All writing must end in sensory experience, as has been said."

Inevitably, critics have invoked the names Flannery O'Connor, Tennessee Williams and Truman Capote in discussing Powell's fiction. It is an obligatory comparison that Powell graciously accepts.

"Life is categorizing. That's how people negotiate their time on earth. Recognizing categories or effecting categories and defining things through them. So to be assigned to the club is going to happen. And it's a good thing that it's a good club. I also think the entire world sort of holds its breath—some not so deeply—waiting for the new Faulkner.

"That's why anybody out of the South with ostensibly Southern concerns and affects is going to give pause. Genius seems to be discovered every two and a half weeks by The (New York) Times. He or she could rise from their midst at any time."

Simons Manigault, the protagonist of *Edisto Revisited*, has survived the adolescence conveyed so skillfully in *Edisto* and, as the story resumes, is out of college and looking for work. Only he's doing everything in his power to delay undertaking the career prescribed by his father.

"Simons has got a pretty nice situation, though. He's got a good woman and he doesn't mind building beach houses. He's doing OK."

Until Patricia Hod, a newcomer, and pure devilment, arrives.

"She's devilment, all right. Hod's an Upcountry girl, a cousin from the Piedmont, and she's a lovely, firm thing with whom he gets along. And the family doesn't wade in to object too much."

Manigault's triumphs and travails are rendered in the characteristic style—sardonic wit wed to clear-eyed seriousness. But there are significant differences.

"*Edisto* was so preposterous in its fictive premise that only a young writer would presume to do it. An older writer would take a good look at it 50 pages in and say this is not a good idea. No one's going to believe that this boy is 12 years old. You'll see some of that maturity or fatigue or whatever it is in the new book. It's probably more tenable that this is a 20-something year-old man speaking."

Powell, the recipient of the Prix de Rome of the American Academy of Arts and Letters and a National Book Award nominee, currently is working on a volume of short stories.

"It's some short fiction I've collected that I am going to pack up and send to the publisher. There's more of it than we knew lying around, and it may be a fun book."

The contrast between the stories—at a remove from the square, red-blooded republicanism of Simons Manigault's world—is pronounced. And the work is sufficiently weird, says Powell, to induce questions of sanity. At least among his characters.

"It's entertaining to me to contemplate losing one's mind. It leads you to speculate on the ease with which one might 'go over.' A jailbreak of the wits, as I put it in one story. And the wife may be the first to know that the cannon is not tied down."

Before he or the creatures of his imagination go completely bonkers, Powell will, in addition to the normal author tour, make 13 stops on a reading tour, beginning in Iowa City and culminating in Savannah.

Then it's back to the haven of Gainesville, his wife, the poet Sidney Wade, and their children, Amanda and Elena. And a comfortable "isolation."

March 31, 1996

Elise Blackwell's *Grub*

"The profession of book writing makes horse racing seem like a solid, stable business."

John Steinbeck, *The Acts of King Arthur and His Noble Knights*

Authors may enjoy an exalted perch in the firmament of high culture, yet all too many writers of serious fiction know well the vagaries of grubbing for a living.

To "grub" is to "scrounge"—struggling to find a publisher, to get paid an equitable sum, to get read. And to sell sufficiently well to get published a second time.

Elise Blackwell's new book is aptly named. *Grub* (Toby Press) is a notably lighter but still mordantly funny update of George Gissing's famed 1891 novel *New Grub Street.* Gissing's satire of the literary marketplace of Victorian London was a caustic study of the writer's plight in contemporary society, dealing with the drudgery of research, the fleeting pleasures (and excruciating pain) of composition, the demands of deadlines. But its themes had a broader significance: the literary game as a microcosm of modern commerce.

Blackwell, a professor of English at the University of South Carolina, has produced a character-driven tale billed as an "engaging, compassionate" novel that reveals what the publishing industry does to writers and their books, and what writers do to themselves and each other "for the sake of art and in pursuit of celebrity." She echoes much of what Gissing rendered in unrelievedly dark terms.

"Mine is less somber and more humorous, but still a bit nasty," says Blackwell, whose previous book was *The Unnatural History of Cypress Parish.* "It retells the Gissing story almost exactly. All the major characters have a parallel in my novel, with the same initials. What I've done is update it to the contemporary commercial marketplace, and altered it to have all my characters be novelists. But the story also is applicable to the other arts, not just publishing."

For those prone to rhapsodizing on the rule of market forces, Blackwell has this retort: "I was a bit angry when I wrote *Grub*, in part because the publication of my Louisiana novel (*Unnatural History*) was 'interrupted' by Hurricane Katrina—I wrote *Grub* between the writing and revision of that book—and in part because I was concerned about the fate of some of my friends in the publishing world. I saw a lot of great first novels go unpublished because it was decided that the market wouldn't be large enough. I also saw people who had published underperforming first novels and might be unable to publish second ones.

"Other friends shared horror stories about books that did get published. A lot of the individual stories in my novel are comical, like the horrible book tour one of my characters endures in Vermont."

Blackwell saves her skewer for her most serious target, what she terms the "huge apparatus" of people making money off aspiring writers: manuscript doctors, agents promising to secure agents, and, most colorfully, the writer's nag—someone paid to harass the novelist into picking up the pace. "A lot of these people couldn't make money off their own writing," she says, "so they do it off the work of other writers."

Grub is hard on agents and publishers, but harder still on writers themselves, Blackwell says. "I make fun of some of the trends in literary fiction, including my own two books, which were *very* serious."

Blackwell's first book, *Hunger*, was named by The Los Angeles Times as one of its Best Books of 2003. Her stories have appeared in such journals as Witness, Seed, Global City Review and Topic. The Louisiana native is working on her latest novel, *Water Damage*, focusing on the art world.

Meanwhile, she will take a break to stump for *Grub*, which is dedicated to every writer with an unpublished novel, though with electronic publishing and so-called vanity presses, it seems we've almost attained the realization of the dread prediction, "When anyone can publish a book, everyone will."

"It's true. I read a survey that says 1 in 4 Americans claim to be writing a book, which sends shudders down the spine. But the market for literary fiction is particularly tough. I do know writers who make the mistake of trying to ride the next wave, as some of *Grub's* characters do. You don't know when that wave will collapse, especially when it takes you a year to write a novel and maybe another year for it to come out.

"The plight of the contemporary writer is nothing new. Literary production can decide the fates of friendships, careers, lifestyles, even marriages. What's striking is how similar today's market is to the one in London in the 1890s."

Gissing's original was prophetic in one respect: He didn't profit from his book's success. Needing money, he sold the copyright for 150 pounds. Blackwell hopes to do better.

August 26, 2007

Harlan Greene's *The German Officer's Boy*

The very phrase, "Night of Broken Glass," still can provoke a shudder.

On the 7th of November, 1938, Jewish teenager Herschel Grynszpan walked into the German embassy in Paris and shot third secretary Ernst vom Rath, the son of a high-ranking diplomat. Rath died two days later, sending Adolph Hitler into a frenzy.

Within hours, government-orchestrated mobs of anti-Jewish protesters in Germany and Austria erupted into "spontaneous" demonstrations against the Jews of Europe. This infamous "Kristallnacht" is considered to mark the onset of the Holocaust.

For novelist and nonfiction writer Harlan Greene, the background of the event overtook the foreground. In his historical novel *The German Officer's Boy* (Terrace Books), the Charleston author explores what really may have happened that day the young Polish Jew walked into the embassy and provided the pretext for the "Night of Broken Glass."

For years, some historians have suggested that Grynszpan and vom Rath were engaged in a love affair gone bad. Greene took this as his starting point and, in the process, tried to take Grynszpan at his word.

The jury's still out on Grynszpan, says Greene, author of several books of nonfiction and the novels *Why We Never Danced the Charleston* and *What the Dead Remember*.

"The thing about Herschel is that in life, he was so self-contradictory; some versions of events have him saying he was gay while another holds that his attorney told him to say that, because it really did stop the show trial arrayed against him. But Herschel contradicted himself constantly. So what I tried to do in my book is let him do everything for the reasons he said he did it. He did say he was doing it as a dramatic gesture to save his people, but he also said he did it because it was a love affair gone wrong."

Greene says this might be the real genesis of his book.

"In every 'nonfiction' book I read (on the subject), the authors weighed in with their preconceptions, whether being gay was good or not good, or Herschel saying so was crafty, and I could see that these preconceptions colored their interpretations. I don't believe that's what historians should do. It's only fair for me to weigh in with my preconceptions; I admit I have my own ax to grind. At least I say upfront that I'm doing it in the realm of fiction."

Greene opted to write a novel to afford himself the freedom of movement to speculate. There were also logistical concerns.

"I did not have the apparatus to do another history. I don't speak German and I couldn't travel at the time. But I'm no stranger to history. I would read about Herschel in books of nonfiction, and they couldn't reveal to me what was going on in his head. What we believe we did know of him didn't all make sense to me. So even before I sat down to write, I was trying to figure out why would he do what he did."

Greene says the book had been niggling at the back of his mind for years. "It was also written over time, and its publication took a fair amount of time to do. I kept running across Herschel's name in the footnotes of other books. I was always vaguely interested in the topic of the Holocaust, and would read about it as a general reader might. I just sort of stumbled across those books over a period of five to six years, laying out the background in my subconscious. I'm obsessive by nature. And for me, the background of these events took over. It was the germ of an idea that just kept growing."

What most intrigued Greene about the story were the obscured corners of the narrative.

"It was the unknowable part of it—his childhood and family relations—plus the fact that this young and probably very scared young man managed to do something no one else did, which was put a stick in Hitler's spokes, forcing him to do something he didn't want to do."

Greene tried as much as possible to make his Grynszpan a reflection of the man. He extended the same gesture to his characterization of vom Rath.

"I tried to work in every little bit I knew about him, too. He was of a very dignified Prussian family who probably weren't anti-Semitic. He was, to some extent, the more sympathetic character."

Greene, an archivist at the Avery Research Center for African-American History and Culture, has another novel in progress, a work again based on fact and fiction titled *September Heat.* For now, he's just delighted that *The German Officer's Boy* made it to bookshelves.

"What I often do in my work is to try to rescue people from the past, or from being misconceived in time. I can't change their life. I can't make them less unhappy, but I can at least try to write them back into the historical record. It's trying to remember the dead, making sure they're not stereotyped. With Herschel, you can't really tell what's fact and what's fiction."

So he made of it a novel, which he hopes achieves the same end.

November 6, 2005

Ben Moïse's *Ramblings of a Lowcountry Game Warden*

A game warden needs more than commitment to duty and a thick skin. Ideally, he or she must possess the tenacity of a bulldog, the cunning of a commando, the knowledge of a naturalist, the impulse of an educator and the flexibility that comes with seeing not only the big picture, but the human scale of things.

Not to mention being well-versed in a sometimes dizzying array of laws and regulations, plus having the ability to deal effectively with maddening bureaucracies and an assortment of wily (or not so wily) violators.

It's all behind him now, having retired in January 2002, but Charleston's Ben McC. Moïse, a game warden of distinction for 25 years, can recall his adventures and misadventures clearly, and in great detail.

His memoir, *Ramblings of a Lowcountry Game Warden* (University of South Carolina Press) was conceived as a hair-raising, rib-tickler of a book, one he is pleased to see in print after four years devoted to the project. Consider it an act of moonlighting, an adjunct to his favored avocation: raconteur.

"Everybody said, 'Ben, you ought to write a book.' I can't say that it had never been on my radar screen before. Everybody thinks he has something to say, and I like to think that some of the things I had done over 25 years were worthy of repeating, that in book form they might be either entertaining or instructional. But the notion of starting it was a little daunting."

Today, he's basking in the glow.

"The neatest thing was when Alex Moore, the acquisitions editor at USC Press, brought to my front door the first hard copy of the book," says Moïse, whose next goal is to try his hand at short fiction. "Then I knew that it was real. To hold it and realize that you'd done it, was one of the most important moments to me. That, and knowing I'd finally mustered up the discipline to sit down and write it."

Moïse was a bit surprised, yet gratified, that USC Press took him on as an "untested" writer. Never mind that he had been an outdoors writer and book reviewer for years. Or that well before he realized his dream to work as a South Carolina game warden, his career path was as colorful as some of the characters in his book. Moïse, who now devotes himself largely to travel and hosting oyster roasts, enjoyed the seasoning of a host of jobs.

"My poor wife Anne never knew sometimes from one day to the next what I was going to be. I'd arrive home and announce that I had taken a job as a stevedore on the waterfront, or had just accepted a post as a special projects writer for a newspaper, or that I'd had discussions with friends of mine and had decided to go into the catering business or pursue my interest in a cassette tape tours idea."

All of which he did.

"I think sometimes you have to explore a lot of different avenues first to get perspective. The value of that experience to me is that I had already crossed a lot of bridges. I knew by the time I got into law enforcement that it was where I wanted to be. South Carolina has resources that are more than just enjoyable; they are part of our heritage. I thought they were worth saving."

It did not hurt that the job allowed him "a lot of latitude, a lot of freedom."

Moïse says the book is titled *Ramblings* for a reason. The original manuscript was a hundred pages longer, but his editors coached him to write a tighter narrative, "still rambling but not all over the landscape."

Some episodes recounted in the book, the chapter "Murphy's Law" being a prime example, were not nearly so amusing in the throes of action as they are in retrospect, says Moïse, who joined what is now the South Carolina Department of Natural Resources in 1978. His work along a long swath of the S.C. coast was performed during all seasons, all hours and in all weather conditions. Patrolling the waterways, he interacted with a diverse cast of watermen, lawyers, country judges and hunters, as well as stalking a rogue's gallery of poachers.

But it wasn't all a matter of writing tickets and confiscating illegally deployed nets; part of his task was to educate those who ran afoul of the law, or strenuously disagreed with it, on the wisdom of short-term limitations for long-term benefit.

"You had to keep in mind that you were dealing with people, some of whom could lose their livelihood. Although I ran into a few real bad people, a lot of them were good people who just did bad things. If they are made to understand the beneficial effects of certain regulations, which, for those who make their living harvesting these resources, also are for their own well-being, they will tend to abide by them.

"But they are so suspicious of the bureaucracy, and not without reason sometimes. They (resist) those regulations they can't understand or believe have no meaning."

In assaying his evolution from "game warden" to "conservation officer" to "law enforcement officer," the last demanding advanced technical expertise, Moïse concludes with his observations on a growing population's impact on the lowcountry—a coda, and a cautionary.

February 10, 2008

Dorothea Benton Frank's *Porch Lights*

Dorothea Benton Frank is the Bard of the Beach, attuned to wave and sky and the innermost thoughts of all the lively, shy and wistful souls who tread its sands. Set on her native Sullivan's Island, Frank's latest novel, *Porch Lights*, combs the coast for another tale of love and loss, parents and children, mysteries and mirth. But the added heft that came with her previous work, *Folly Beach*, is a trend, not an aberration.

"I think the last book was kind of a turning point for me," says Frank, who divides her time between the lowcountry and Montclair, N.J. "I can sit down and write stories about men and women in great detail, all day long, and it's fun.

"But I began to have a sense, as a reader, that when I read a novel, I want more. I want to learn something from a book. I like to be entertained, of course, and I'm not trying to write historical fiction, but I want to give readers more to talk about after they've read my book."

Frank says that some readers felt Folly Beach's narrative style was "too complicated," but the author insists she tries to keep a "very tight ensemble" of characters.

"Everybody had a reason to be there."

Where *Folly Beach* was lent resonance by the legacies of Charleston Renaissance figures Dorothy and DuBose Heyward, the evocatively titled *Porch Lights*—suggestive of soft breezes and indigo nights—serves up that gloomy old Sullivan's Island literary godling, Edgar Allan Poe.

But the Heywards are a hard act to follow.

Poe on the Porch

"I didn't really know how well *Folly Beach* would be received and how well the Heywards were known outside of the region," says Frank, already at work on her 14th novel, tentatively titled *The Summer of Their Discontent*. "But when I discovered that Dorothy actually adapted *Porgy* for the stage and not her husband, I figured if I hadn't known this, then a lot of other people didn't either.

"In the same way, Poe has always been thought of as a deeply weird little man—and he was—but his whole life was riddled with death and poverty and loss. He never earned more than $6,000 his entire career."

Frank says she always has thought of Poe as an interesting character, and wanted to learn more. She credits Citadel professor Jim Hutchisson's book "Poe" ("riveting," Frank says) for opening a number of windows into the writer's life.

But the master of the macabre is a background player in the contemporary story illuminated in *Porch Lights*.

Tragedy and Balm

The story revolves around the McMullen family, treading water in the wake of tragedy.

When New York firefighter Jimmy McMullen loses his life in the line of duty, the lives of his wife, Jackie, and their 10-year-old son, Charlie, are shattered. An outgoing boy with a curious mind, Charlie retreats within himself.

All Jackie can think to do is return to the embrace of family and her childhood home on Sullivan's Island. There to welcome them is Annie Britt, the family matriarch, excited by the prospect even though relations between her and her daughter have grown less than cordial.

Enter Britt's estranged husband Buster, the former's best chum Deb, and Steven Plofker (the widower next door), not to mention the legends of Poe and Blackbeard the pirate, and you have the makings of one memorable summer.

"I have a wonderful relationship with my children," says Frank, "but I wondered what would it be like for mothers who don't have a great relationship with their kids. How awful would that be? This is what has happened with Annie and Jackie.

"One of the ways that women love is by cleaning the house or cooking for you. They do all these things to show that they love you. Annie is always nesting, but her daughter finds the whole thing intrusive and insulting. It takes time."

The story is told in the alternating voices of mother and daughter, still in Frank's preferred first person, which she likes for its immediacy.

"It's a more interesting way to show how people don't really understand each other, though they eventually do. This tragic loss of Jackie's husband is what draws them all together, but it's a struggle; I don't always like these tidy endings."

June 10, 2012

The Reviews

"Impersonal criticism is like an impersonal fist fight
or an impersonal marriage, and as successful."

George Jean Nathan, quoted in *Peter's Quotations: Ideas for Our Times*

It's an adage of the stage that a good review is but a temporary stay of execution. Gallows humor aside, it is the negative review, or at least one with negative content, that can be most useful to an artist—once he or she gets over the sting, and provided the review is perceptive, fair and constructive. It is not enough to say something is lacking. The skillful critic shows why, that is, if there's a forum left for it.

This final chapter has been composed with a tinge of melancholy, as legitimate book reviews appear to be an endangered species.

Much has been made of late about the demise of critics, a development some meet with hand-wringing and woe. Or indifference. Others celebrate it with glee, as if a self-important corps of the malicious, presumptuous and untalented have had it coming for years. Who needs them? Who are they to pass judgment? After all, isn't the final vote up to the consumer? Isn't a review just another opinion?

Not if you believe in sustaining standards of excellence in a relativistic world. Not if you think a reasoned critique by someone who has studied an art form for decades is inherently of value.

The fact is that many gifted people have been downsized or laid off by the nation's newspapers and magazines, dismissed as irrelevant or unnecessary. And we are the poorer for it.

In a review of genuine merit, good critics bring an understanding of all the arts to bear. They make connections. They assay an artist's development or promise. Like any discerning reader, they do not read for entertainment alone. They scrutinize every aspect of a book. Why? Because it's their job.

But even if this were not so, it's the natural inclination of critics to hold a work to a higher standard. They expect more. They're annoyed when a publisher foists junk on the populace with a covert smirk, believing the reading public too dumb to know the difference.

Critics try to separate the wheat from the chaff (you don't have to be able to lay an egg to smell a bad one). The best reviewers feel a responsibility to the audience but shrink from telling readers what to think.

How to be personal without getting personal? That's one of the chief skills a critic must learn early on. It is your perception, your judgment, your voice. Wield it, but in aid of something more than self-indulgent prattle. Don't get too cute. Don't reveal too much. Be demanding but fair. You have wide latitude, but stick to the subject.

And know that you can make a difference. Like a film critic going to bat for an exceptional but little-known independent movie, the book reviewer championing a quality book that lacks the requisite crowd-pleasing content or the financial push to find its way into public consciousness can make or break the book. Local booksellers and shop owners also perform this function, but their reach may be limited.

In the end, a review should be of worth in and of itself, offering its own set of pleasures and provocation. But it should be done with a measure of grace and an abiding love for the book.

The Cult of the Amateur. By Andrew Keen.

Americans tend to be of two minds on the subject of experts, exhibiting an unquestioning deference to the authoritative voice, yet also having an innate aversion to the musk of elitism.

Of course, many a self-proclaimed "expert" is nothing of the sort. They are merely better at promoting their view, savvy enough or shrill enough to work the media, get a lucrative book deal or trump competitors on the talk show circuit. In such a climate, skepticism is the best defense against the expert and new wave of populist amateurs.

That said, training, experience and expertise do matter. Those harboring these qualities appear to be an endangered species.

While it suffers the customary weaknesses of its form—overstatement for effect, an excess of Sturm and Drang—Andrew Keen's scathing *The Cult of the Amateur* is a provocative and useful attack on the decline of reasoned discourse and professional standards in contemporary society. His culprit: the digital age—MySpace meets YouTube meets Wikipedia. Or rather, "ignorance meets egotism meets bad taste meets mob rule."

Keen, a Silicon Valley entrepreneur, culture critic and founder of Audiocafe.com, invokes T. H. Huxley's "infinite monkey theorem," which suggests that if you supply an infinite number of monkeys with infinite typewriters, some monkey somewhere will create a masterpiece. Keen regards the old joke as a dystopian vision of the consequences of a "flattening" culture that is blurring the lines between audience and author, creator and consumer, expert and amateur.

"Today's technology hooks all those monkeys up with all those typewriters," Keen writes, with inflammatory emphasis. "Except in our Web 2.0 world, the typewriters aren't exactly typewriters, but rather networked personal computers, and the monkeys aren't quite monkeys, but rather Internet users."

Keen does not so much address the old cautionary "when anybody can publish a novel, everyone will," a prophesy that electronic publishing and vanity presses have made a reality. He reserves his ire for the Web diary, or "blog," an estimated 53 million strong, and counting.

"At the heart of this infinite monkey experiment in self-publishing is the blog. Blogging has become such a mania that a new blog is being created every second of every minute of every hour of every day. We are blogging with monkey-like shamelessness about our private lives, our sex lives, our dream lives, our lack of lives, our Second lives. . . . If we keep up this pace, there will be over 500 million blogs by 2010, collectively corrupting and confusing popular opinion about everything from politics to commerce, arts and culture. Blogs have become so dizzyingly infinite that they've undermined our sense of what is true and what is false, what is real and what is imaginary. These days, kids can't tell the difference between credible news by objective professional journalists and what they read on joeshmoe.blogspot.com."

For these benighted Generation Y souls, Keen says, every blog posting is just another person's perception of the truth. But then, there's always been a cacophony of opinion in the marketplace of ideas, and it always has been up to the informed citizen to separate the real from the fictive, be it in reportage, entertainment, books, the Web or conversations held over the backyard fence. It is also disingenuous to imply that every blogger is careless, unacquainted with rigor or a twit, though many are. The same holds for authors of books.

Keen also chooses to downplay the fact that, from time to time, political blogs have beaten the pants off print and TV journalists in getting the news out quickly and accurately.

YouTube, which eclipses the lesser blogs in "the inanity and absurdity of its content," is the easiest of easy targets. And Keen dismisses it with an authorial wave of the hand. Not so the online encyclopedia Wikipedia, on which he piles an avalanche of scorn. On Wikipedia, he maintains, everyone with an agenda or an axe to grind can rewrite an entry to their liking.

"And contributors frequently do. . . . Anyone with opposable thumbs and a fifth-grade education can publish anything on any topic from AC/DC to Zoroastrianism. Since Wikipedia's birth, more than 15,000 contributors have created nearly three million entries in over 100 languages—none of them edited or vetted for accuracy . . . perpetuating the cycle of misinformation and ignorance."

Keen succumbs to even greater hyperbole here. In the first place, by its very nature, Wikipedia strives to be self-correcting, and on a minute-by-minute basis, something to which the vaunted Encyclopedia Britannica's print volumes cannot aspire. As for agendas, has he explored one of the more contentious academic journals lately? Even the most respected expert is not infallible. Should we expect Wikipedia to be?

While one may argue convincingly that art cannot be democratized, or at least that "fine art" can't survive it, and that the impulse to see the value of all art in relativistic terms is both politically correct and misguided—people may be created equal, but their opinions and accomplishments are not—Keen hyperventilates on the destructive powers of the Internet.

"Our cultural standards and moral values are not all that are at stake," he warns. "The very traditional institutions that have helped to foster and create our news, our music, our literature, our television shows, and our movies are under assault as well. Newspapers and news magazines, one of our most reliable sources of information about the world we live in, are flailing, thanks to the proliferation of free blogs and sites like Craigslist that offer free classifieds, undermining paid ad placements.

"Old media is facing extinction. What will take its place? Apparently, it will be Silicon Valley's hot new search engines, social media sites and video portals. . . . Democratization, despite its lofty idealization, is undermining truth, souring civic discourse, and belittling expertise, experience and talent. . . . It's the law of digital Darwinism: the survival of the loudest and most opinionated . . . The monkeys take over."

Some of Keen's points are well-taken, and disturbing. But with inflated rhetoric overtaking sober analysis (the better to sell books that shout down the competition), he also manages to make a monkey of himself.

September 2, 2007

Sex and Destiny: The Politics of Human Fertility. By Germaine Greer.

In *The Female Eunuch*, Germaine Greer crystallized much feminist thought of the early 1970s with the assertion that women had been "castrated" by a repressive society which denied them not only the full exercise of their abilities, but control over their bodies.

It was an extraordinary book, infused with the sort of reasoned, clear-headed observation rarely encountered in the doctrinaire rants that have passed for scholarship among many radical feminist authors. Unfortunately, Greer's sense of humor and generosity toward men—which made *The Female Eunuch* not merely palatable but fair—have been supplanted by a caustic, in some ways unaccountable, dogmatism.

Formerly a champion of the sexual revolution, and one of the women's movement's most flamboyant, appealing and intellectually sound voices, Greer has reversed course drastically. In *Sex and Destiny*, she effectively repudiates many of her previous and most significant stands. In their place we are presented with a new Puritanism: a gospel of abstinence, emphasizing the reproductive function of sex.

Although the thesis of *Sex and Destiny* certainly contains elements of truth, Greer's all-encompassing application rings hollow. She states flatly that western capitalist nations suffer from a kind of moral and sexual decadence, that we not only are obsessed with the hedonistic pleasures of recreational sex but also are profoundly hostile to children and motherhood. She argues further that we have tried to export these twisted precepts—along with dangerous birth control devices—to poor Third World countries, thereby corrupting their innately more healthy mores.

Greer attempts to support her arguments with an enormous store of anthropological data, historical facts, personal anecdotes and page after page of intellectualizations and rhetorical fencing.

But *Sex and Destiny* simply doesn't hold up.

In part, she has made the crucial mistakes of confusing myth with fact and of placing an excess of confidence in highly conjectural prehistoric anthropology, the same problem undermining such books as William Irwin Thompson's *The Time Falling Bodies Take to Light* (1981). This is a common trait among many feminists who (understandably) decry the biblical mythology of patriarchal dominance, yet seek to replace it with an equally dubious myth, that of the Great Mother and supposed matriarchal cultures of antiquity.

Many of Greer's basic assumptions are patently untrue, riddled with contradictions or laughably absurd. Even at the height of the sexual revolution of the late '60s and early '70s, few people took permissiveness as far as the author herself. And in the last few years, as recent surveys reveal, Americans have vigorously embraced the traditional values of monogamy and fidelity in marriage. As for the birth rate, it hasn't reached the levels of the Baby Boom of the 1950s, but it, too, is on the way back up.

So much for Greer's contention that the West is a sterile environment locked in the grip of commercialized, consumer sex.

When it comes to discussing sexual practices in developing and underdeveloped nations, Greer is equally disposed toward drawing overstated and questionable conclusions. She condemns western efforts to proselytize about birth control as genocidal and she so romanticizes the Third World's "pristine," primitive condition that she dismisses life-saving, modernized health facilities as unwanted and corrupting examples of the West's "chromium-plated technology."

In Greer's opinion, we in the West can learn much from other societies' natural approaches to contraception. She says that instead of relying on the pill and IUD—which place women's bodies in jeopardy while enriching pharmaceutical companies—we should employ such alternatives as the rhythm method and *coitus interruptus*. Although these techniques have been widely criticized as unreliable, Greer maintains that they do in fact prevent pregnancy when properly practiced. Besides, she adds, if and when they fail, there's always abortion, which "can very well be the chosen method of birth control for more and more women."

Even better than these methods, Greer goes on, is the old concept of chastity. For her, chastity has a double virtue: it "endows sexual activity with added importance by limiting its enjoyment to special persons and special times," and it also conserves energy that might be better directed toward political and artistic activity. Indeed, Greer contends that sex has become "the new opiate of the people."

In making this argument, Greer seems to have come full circle from her earlier beliefs. When she wrote *The Female Eunuch*, one will recall, her espousal of active sexuality for women was based on the conviction that sexual repression—rather than releasing other energies—caused women to assume passive roles in all areas of their lives.

There's nothing wrong, of course, with writers changing their views or rethinking their previous positions. That's healthy, and useful, generally a sign of growth. But Greer's turnabout is a disheartening, retrograde and, dare one say, almost paternalistic attitude. Her views on the sex act and familial-political relations between the sexes are one thing. But in denying the worldwide social and political impact of overpopulation, of denying, in fact, even the existence of a population problem, Greer's book bears potential for great harm.

June 17, 1984

Orson Welles: A Biography. By Barbara Leaming.

Orson Welles died of a heart attack last week at the age of 70, leaving a legacy of more than 60 films, a not entirely deserved reputation for petulance and iconoclasm, and a shadow of greatness.

It had been years since any Hollywood studio had the courage to give Welles the reins. His reputation for egotism—at times wholeheartedly earned—preceded him, and studio chiefs (rarely perceptive sorts where the film art is concerned) rejected his scripts, denied him the opportunity to direct with a free hand or refused to allow Welles the total creative control he required.

Much like David Lean, who before "A Passage to India" had let slip without a single film almost two decades of what are generally the most productive years of an artist's life, Welles's relative absence from the American cinema is a loss of considerable magnitude.

In her fascinating if occasionally fawning biography, Barbara Leaming reveals the elusive private man as no one else has, and with an almost cinematic force. Here, Welles is candid, reflective, funny, outrageous and wickedly caustic.

Leaming, a professor of theater and film at Hunter College in New York, was the first biographer to have gained Welles's complete cooperation as well as unrestricted access to the man and his personal collection of diaries, letters, and photographs.

Welles spoke openly for the first time about his achievements and the more intimate aspects of his life: his eventful but troubled childhood as a *wunderkind*, world traveler and lonely orphan; his stormy youthful partnership and continuing feud with John Houseman; his first marriage to Chicago socialite Virginia Nicolson; and a cast of characters that is nothing less than a pantheon of the elite of an age—Greta Garbo, John Barrymore, Charles Chaplin, Laurence Olivier, Judy Garland, Delores Del Rio, Marlene Dietrich, Eartha Kitt, Warren Beatty, Prince Aly Khan, Peter Sellers and Franklin and Eleanor Roosevelt.

When Leaming met Welles, she had already spent two years interviewing his loyal and not-so-loyal friends and associates, in addition to performing extensive research in the archives of the Federal Theatre, The Mercury Theatre and such Hollywood studios as RKO.

She chronicles Welles's remarkable range of accomplishments, and tracks the young Welles's ascent to mega-stardom as he staged a string of virtuoso Broadway hits and became the most famous radio actor of his time as Lamont Cranston ("The Shadow") and, above all, with "The War of the Worlds."

Leaming cleverly intersperses the narrative of his life with "interchapters" that allow the reader to eavesdrop on Welles's conversations and follow Leaming's own search for her subject—as flamboyant, engaging and gifted an individual as ever embraced the cinema. Not unexpectedly, this unusual framework was suggested by Welles himself.

Welles was born May 6, 1915 in Kenosha, Wis., and soon demonstrated his famed precociousness. He read at age 2, played the violin for Stravinsky and Ravel at 7, and performed Shakespeare in modern dress at 10. By age 16 he was acting in Dublin, and founded the Mercury Theatre of the Air with Houseman in 1937.

In 1938, Welles adapted H. G. Wells's *The War of the Worlds* for radio, with wildly unexpected results. Listeners were terrified, and in the space of a single day, Welles had earned instant nationwide celebrity and set the tone for a larger-than-life public persona.

Compared with what was to come, however, the radio play was of only passing significance. For at age 25, Welles stunned the motion picture world with "Citizen Kane," his first feature film.

During his uneven but always fascinating career, Welles starred in such classics as "The Third Man," "Lady from Shanghai," "A Man for All Seasons," "Touch of Evil" and other notable films, including two memorable Shakespeare productions: "Falstaff," based on "Henry IV," and "Othello."

Unlike Hitchcock, Hawks, Lubitsch, Chaplin or Ford, whose reputations rest on a great number of impressive films, critical respect for Welles rests primarily with "Kane" and the flawed but extraordinary "The Magnificent Ambersons" (1942).

The greatness of "Kane" can be discussed on several levels: it's unparalleled technical innovation, its structural complexity, its complicated handling of narrative point of view, its controversy as a biography of a famous (or rather, notorious) American, its philosophical search for meaningful human values, its sociological study of the "American Dream," its acting, literacy and individuality.

Welles was invited to bring his Mercury Theatre group—Joseph Cotten and Everett Sloane, among them—to Hollywood in 1941 to make any film he chose. "Kane" would be the first and last film on which he had carte blanche. Like an earlier *enfant terrible* of Hollywood, Erich von Stroheim, Welles insisted on supervising everything himself: acting, directing, writing, editing, set design, even sewing costumes. Also like Stroheim, Welles soon saw the Hollywood lords giving his negative to other hands for slicing and later found the gates to the studios closed to him—undone by his own extravagance and Hollywood's timidity.

Although the movie industry won its battle with "Kane," muzzling and suppressing its creator, it would lose the war. Despite the moguls' attempts to hide it and silence Welles, the picture would become the most influential in American film history after Griffith's "Birth of a Nation." Personal and individual rather than programmed and processed, groundbreaking rather than conventional, daring rather than safe, original rather than formulaic or contrived, bitter rather than sickly sweet, it was a landmark.

Welles received a special (and absurdly belated) Oscar in 1970 for his "superlative artistry and versatility in the creation of motion pictures." In 1975, he was tendered the more meaningful Lifetime Achievement Award of the American Film Institute, and last year was recipient of the Director's Guild's highest honor, the D. W. Griffith Award.

Seeing Welles as Leaming saw him, one suspects he would have traded the lot for just one studio head with patience, foresight and guts.

Whatever one may say of Welles, he was the driving force behind at least three or four of the cinema's finest achievements, generally gave good value as an actor (often memorably), furthered filmed versions of Shakespearean plays even before Olivier, staged several ground-breaking theatrical productions, hatched the most audacious radio program of all time and was what the arts so often craves: a bravura personality. His failures were more interesting than most people's successes.

Exceedingly few people can make any of these claims, much less all of them. And, despite the overweening ego, Welles never once claimed he was a genius. The rest of us did.

October 20, 1985

Medium Raw. By Anthony Bourdain.

Oh, Lucky Man . . . to have survived his worst self-destructive impulses, to have emerged from cocaine and heroin addiction in reasonably good health, to have salvaged a career in decline and rendered it a dream realized.

Anthony Bourdain is astonished that people have treated him so well for so long, that so many of his friendships endure, and that life has bequeathed no end of serendipitous moments when he had done his best to scuttle it. Now, as the foremost documentarian of food and travel television, with the soul of a gadfly and an attitude honed to a katana's edge, he offers this admission:

"Let's face it: I am, at this point in my life, the very picture of the jaded, overprivileged 'foodie' (in the very worst sense of that word) that I used to despise. The kind who's eaten way more than his share of Michelin-starred meals all over the world and is (annoyingly) all too happy to tell you about them."

Granted, but as traveling host of the Travel Channel's series "No Reservations" (and scourge of all things Food Network), the consummate New Yorker also has devoured his share of the unspeakable and inedible in some of the more remote outposts of human gastronomy.

In the appropriately titled *Medium Raw*, Bourdain opens disarmingly, recalling one transcendent, forbidden feast in the company of a lordly aggregate of chefs, each vaguely self-conscious. Then, looking back at how the publication of *Kitchen Confidential: Adventures in the Culinary Underbelly* in 2000 altered the trajectory of his life, Bourdain muses on the notion of having sold out a world whose travails and triumphs he chronicled with such knowing verve.

Bourdain reflects on how the angry, cynical *Kitchen Confidential* propelled him, at age 44, to the life of globe-trotting he long coveted, on who he owes and who he loathes, on how re-marrying and becoming a parent radically shifted the paradigm of his bad-boy style and philosophical outlook.

Medium Raw is also a clear-eyed, if occasionally jaundiced, cook's tour of the New York restaurant scene, past and present, by turns scathing, revelatory and respectful. But, as always, he reserves much of his rancor for the Food Network and its endless array of competition shows, more than ever about spectacle over substance.

Bourdain addresses the schism between "fine dining" and more plebian culinary experiences, how both are legitimate and can be accommodated by a sensible culture which sees through hype and discerns honest value. He champions the viability of a high-grade Asian-style food court/hawker center in U.S. cities—whose freshness and artisanship offer one antidote to the economic downturn that has slammed the restaurant trade and inhibited diners' palettes.

And he asks the never-more salient question: "What does 'authentic' mean, anyway?"

Bourdain holds forth on foodies ("Heroes and Villains") of every stripe, from the reigning and eclipsed godlings of the global chef pantheon to the food writers of various levels of veracity and skill (not excepting his own complicity in the field). He skewers meat-industry horrors on the one hand, then chides vegan extremists and the overwrought reactions of PETA with similar, if not wholly unsympathetic, relish, citing misguided campaigns to stamp out morsels which have become politically incorrect.

He eviscerates the most arrant food fashions, not least the hugely successful con game embodied by Starbucks and its imitators ($5 for a simple cup of Joe), and has little but disdain for the fetishizing of expensive ingredients (meanwhile acknowledging his own part in "exploiting middle-class hopes and insecurities").

The same fate—high-priced creative overkill—that has poisoned coffee may yet befall the hamburger, Bourdain says, provoking a shudder. And yet the same protectiveness he demands for the unadorned, honest-to-goodness burger (medium-rare, of course) is not extended to that other American staple, the hotdog. "We always knew—or assumed—that whatever it was inside that snappy tube, it might contain anything, from 100-percent kosher beef to dead zoo animals or parts missing from Gambino family" members.

On the celebratory side, savor the chapter "Lust," an echo of "No Reservations" with tangy snippets imported from Vietnam, Borneo, Sardinia, Japan, Prague and Greenwich Village, among other ports of call.

Formerly the chef at Les Halles in New York, Bourdain insists the appellation no longer fits. And he adds a caution for others. In the chapter "So You Want to be a Chef," he expresses pity for wannabes with delusions of Food Network stardom and asks: Should they go to culinary school?

"The short answer is 'No.'" Not that culinary school is a bad thing, says Bourdain, himself a grad of the best and most expensive of all such schools, the Culinary Institute of America. But in most cases hopefuls have a better chance of ascending the ladder by getting practical experience.

"You can find yourself $40,000–$60,000 in debt having trained for an industry where—if you're lucky—you make $10 to $12 an hour for the first few years."

Bourdain was in the restaurant business for 28 years (much of that time as an employer). He has met and known a great many students of the trade, but knows that few are cut out for the rigors of "The Life"—particularly, he says, "if you're any kind of normal."

Whatever one may think of the man's personality, *Medium Raw* underscores the fact that Bourdain is a heck of a writer, and not simply of books. His narration for "No Reservations" is as crisp, observant, profane, moral and, at times, poetic, as any. Allowing for the fact that he has handlers, a traveling crew and friends around the world that help grease the wheels, he is a far better reporter in the field than most.

And while he skewers himself in the book, repeatedly, for his own spasms of gloss, Bourdain is as brutally honest about much of what he sees and experiences as he is about his own character. Even from "the softer-edged distance of a far more comfortable life."

Bon appetit.

August 8, 2010

Douglas Fairbanks. By Jeffrey Vance.

On October 6, 1927, the realm ruled by Douglas Fairbanks tottered like an unsteady stage set.

The collapse was not immediate, nor did he abdicate. But his crown as the unassailable king of motion pictures soon would be usurped, not by a rival impresario, but by a technological breakthrough that changed the very nature of an art.

When audiences at the Warner Theatre in New York sat down that evening to witness the first talking picture, *The Jazz Singer*, the writing was on the wall for an industry. The transformation would be brisk, and many could not navigate the transition to sound, which necessitated a radically different approach to filmmaking than the silents.

A master showman, and the most nimble star who ever lived, Fairbanks set the bar as high as could be. So does Jeffrey Vance in his engrossing biography of this icon of early Hollywood, a man of boundless energy and enthusiasm who, as much as directors D. W. Griffith and Sergei Eisenstein, could be called a great artist and pioneer of the cinema. Lavishly illustrated, Vance's painstakingly researched, comprehensive and thoughtful work is a book for buffs to treasure.

Officially, Fairbanks never directed a single one of his seminal costume epics—classics like "Robin Hood" (1922), "The Thief of Baghdad" (1924) and "The Black Pirate" (1926)—but not one frame of one film lacked his unmistakable imprint. He micromanaged every aspect of his (typically) extravagant productions, hiring the finest talent, cultivating new ones, and working tirelessly in concert with them. Yet his sets were joyous, convivial, comparatively low-pressure affairs, generating films that owed as much to literature and dance as to stagecraft and filmic technique.

Fairbanks disdained the coming of sound, but not for the reasons one might suspect. Said his son, actor Douglas Fairbanks Jr., "My father . . . liked to tell a story visually. He thought of his films—silent films—as essentially pantomime and ballet . . . rather than as an actor, he saw himself as an athletic dancer leaping with graceful and visually effective movement across the adventures of history. Sound for his purposes was too literal, too realistic, and too restricting."

And it was, particularly in sound films' awkward beginnings, which Vance so ably chronicles. Though Fairbanks would make more movies, "The Iron Mask" (1929) was undeniably his swan song, arriving at the last glorious gasp of silent pictures with such films as F. W. Murnau's "Sunrise" (1927) and William Wellman's "Wings" (1927).

But Vance underscores his enduring legacy. The stunts Fairbanks devised and executed for his pictures, the gigantic sets whose construction he supervised, the flamboyance and brio with which he performed, are legend. No matter the scale of his pictures, or how opulent the surround, nothing on set could compete, said colleague William Bakewell, "with the towering presence, magnetism and sincerity of purpose of Fairbanks himself."

Every film star of worth should have so gifted a biographer as Vance, a historian, archivist and filmmaker herein aided by his production company partner, Tony Maietta. Naturally, Vance deals with Fairbanks's extraordinary global celebrity—his actress wife, Mary Pickford, was no less iconic, and together they were the first superstar couple—his difficulties in relating to a son whose own ascendance threatened his mantle, and Fairbanks's inevitable decline. It's a warts-and-all bio, but sympathetic in the end, and a riveting read.

March 22, 2009

J. R. R. Tolkien: Author of the Century. By Tom Shippey.

Less charitable critics of the 1940s may have savored the books in private, but for public consumption, they dripped scorn.

As is the case with most writers of fantasy or science fiction, even the most distinguished, J. R. R. Tolkien consistently has been undervalued by highbrow literary critics who regard his work as unworthy of so august an academic. Dismissed possibly because these arbiters of worth were, and are, offended by the ardor of his fans. More likely, it is because this exceedingly influential 20th-century author was, and is, viewed as a challenge to prevailing literary orthodoxies.

The Lord of the Rings series, actually six books collected in three volumes rather than a "trilogy," is, to be sure, immensely entertaining. As Tom Shippey reminds us in *J. R. R. Tolkien: Author of the Century*, it is also complex and fascinating.

Tolkien, who died in 1973, was a professor of Anglo-Saxon, then of English and literature, at Oxford University. The writing of the *Rings* began in 1940, not within some collegiate fastness, but in an Oxford pub named the Eagle and Child, better known to frequenters like Tolkien and friend C. S. Lewis as the Bird and the Baby.

Rather than being discussed to death, as often happens when writers convene in bars, the philologist's tale took flight. Begun as a sequel to his children's book, *The Hobbit*, the little story transformed itself into an epic—17 years in the writing but calling on a lifetime of Tolkien's scholarship.

As his one-time associate, Shippey, writes in his new book, Tolkien's work struck a deep chord with readers not only because of its great imaginative power, but because it "articulates some of the deepest and most specific concerns of the 20th century—concerns such as industrialized warfare, the temptations of power, the origins of evil, the failure of good intentions and righteous causes."

Concerns just as present in the 21st century. With Wednesday's upcoming debut of "The Fellowship of the Ring," the first installment of Peter Jackson's three-film adaptation, it seems an appropriate time to reflect on Tolkien as something more than an antiquarian writer who produced a ripping good yarn with imperishable characters.

Shippey, who held the same positions at the University of Leeds and Oxford that Tolkien once did, says Tolkien "opened up a new imaginative space—he would have said it was an OLD imaginative space—which had been walled off, that of traditional legend and fairy-tale." But Tolkien supplied his world of dwarfs, elves, trolls and wizards with a vividly drawn schematic, "a consistent history and geography which feels as if it is infinitely extendable." He not only reinvented fantasy, he made it respectable.

That helps explain why there have been so many successors to Tolkien, among the most notable being Charleston's own Robert Jordan, a writer of similarly impressive imagination who has defined the "medieval" fantasy genre for his own era. But it's more than that. Tolkien, whose major work was not even published until he was 62, addressed the same sort of questions we're asking today in the aftermath of September 11. Not simply on the age-old battle of good vs. evil, which lends itself to caricature, but on the true nature of evil and how the 19th century's hope for "moral progress and freedom from want" were dashed by the horrors of the 20th century.

A veteran of World War I, Tolkien's experience made him want to restate traditional images rather than discard them. Particularly, says Shippey, he wanted to forge a new way of representing heroes and heroism. Tolkien knew the old social and political strategies all too well, and that they would no longer work. Instead of yielding to the allure of cynicism, he refused to abandon the effort. For his optimistic outlook, he has been subjected to the same sort of sneering derision aimed at "Star Trek" and its hopeful, sometimes thoughtful view of the human future.

Today, he may seem quaintly Victorian, certainly a Luddite. Yet Tolkien wrote an enduring and wonderful series of books—a serious body of literature—much of it revealing characters setting aside ancient prejudices for the common good. At more than 1,000 pages, the books are not for the casual reader. But it's worth the effort, many times over. So is Shippey's not-quite biography.

The author does a splendid job of lending perspective to Tolkien and his canon, if we may be permitted the term. And he benefits from information that has come to light since Humphrey Carpenter's authorized biography in 1977. We know a good deal more about the manner in which Tolkien worked and wrote, amplified by the release of a number of volumes of his early drafts, as well as pieces not published in his lifetime. Shippey helps us see Tolkien and his inner anxieties. He also succeeds in his principal aim of making a potent case for Tolkien being the past century's most influential writer of fiction—although many would opt for Hemingway in this regard—and not simply because of the millions of books Tolkien sold.

How many writers have the confidence or literary background to invent whole new poetic traditions? Not many. And none possesses the mythic and imaginative dimensions of Tolkien's work.

December 16, 2001

Less Than Glory. By Norman Gelb.

As schoolchildren we learn those dates that mark the signal events of the American Revolution. Throughout our lives, Independence Day is commemorated with fireworks displays, family picnics, fife and drum parades and, less admirably, with wholesale commercialism.

But should July 4 *be* a day of celebration? Was the American Revolution the unassailably glorious and noble endeavor extolled in our textbooks, and so unquestioningly embraced by our people?

In this era of resurgent patriotism, it may be heresy even to think along these lines, much less articulate one's doubts. But historians of a revisionist bent are producing unorthodox and highly provocative reassessments of this hallowed ground.

Add to their number journalist and author Norman Gelb, London correspondent for The New Leader. In *Less Than Glory*, Gelb marshals a body of evidence—sometimes persuasive, sometimes not—which is designed to strip away much of the "red, white and blue rhetoric of the revolution" and reveal what are, allegedly, some of the more unsavory truths about the struggle for independence.

Gelb chronicles a nightmarish period of soaring inflation, discredited currency, squalid scrounging, political infighting, naked avarice, and the miseries of a bitter, always hungry army that was inadequately led.

Gelb also portrays, and documents, the tragedy of the Loyalist exodus: the tens of thousands of Americans who so vehemently opposed the revolution that they abandoned their homes and positions to resettle under the King's dominion, or remained to suffer persecution before and after the British defeat.

Gelb concludes that the radical colonists' initial achievement—a gruesome war—was anything but glorious. Thousands deserted due to appalling conditions (the deserters' numbers at times equaled the number in the ranks).

The Revolutionary War also bore aspects of a civil conflict. Families, including those of Benjamin Franklin, Gen. Henry Knox and John Hancock, were divided by allegiances. There were 50 Loyalist regiments and battalions and at least 30,000 men who volunteered to fight with the British. Astonishingly, during two of the most bitter engagements of the war—Hanging Rock, S.C., and Ramsour's Mill, N.C.—not a single British soldier was present.

The Declaration of Independence itself, as interpreted by Gelb, seems drenched in hypocrisy, assuring freedom for all even as blacks slaved in the fields, Indians were slaughtered for land and women remained subordinate.

In light of British misdeeds that Gelb terms "vexations at worst, or botherations having only marginal impact on the way of life or the prosperity of the American colonies," it seems unlikely that the rebellion should have occurred at all. What made the war inevitable, Gelb says, was political manipulation by moneyed aristocrats and the impassioned rhetoric of the radical element.

Moreover, Gelb contends that the United States might be a far richer and more powerful nation had the revolution not occurred, or if independence had been achieved later and peacefully, as in Australia and Canada.

This, of course, is purely speculative.

Suited to more concrete analysis is the emergence of revisionist history itself, which has turned the harsh light of scrutiny not merely upon the individuals we lionize, but on the ideals they have come to represent.

Such questions sit poorly on the palate. Few desire to have their most deep-seated beliefs and basic assumptions so vigorously challenged. What science has done to superstition and to fundamentalist religious doctrine, revisionist history may do to the public mind. It undermines the scaffolding of tradition, erecting new and sometimes painful models of thought, of interpretation and of reality. We may resent this force for disillusionment, but it's here, undermining cherished images like a burrowing mole until they collapse of their own weight.

Of course, conscientious historians always have revised the narrative as new information and insights have come to light. That's the job of a professional.

Still, illusion dies hard. Though Americans are by no means unique in this regard, we have been spoon-fed all manner of fictions: the mythology of the Old West, Manifest Destiny, the conquest of the "savage" Indian, the motives for the Mexican and Spanish-American wars, the promise of equal justice under the law.

Yet the most insidious fable, born in the heady, ambitious days of the 18th century, remains that of our noble adventure westward.

"The more common reflex, that of the real American he-man upon being confronted with wild vistas, was to shoot anything that moved, chop down anything that grew, and salivate over the profits to be grubbed from the primeval soil," wrote Ezra Bowen in *The High Sierra.*

A broad brushstroke to be sure, but there is no denying that, hearing the seductive whisper of gold dust and the entreaty of free land, we came west by the thousands, slaughtering animals by the millions, dredging and damming streams, killing Indians and each other, and generally making a mess of whatever we touched. All this under the banner of civilization.

The vistas of revision are without boundary, though the impulse comes in two forms. One at least purports to seek the truth. The other, in a self-conscious attempt to offend no one, winds up obscuring it.

The latter variety was attacked in Frances FitzGerald's seminal *America Revisited.* Published in 1979, it focused on how adult America goes about indoctrinating its young. In FitzGerald's view, a complex of publishers, educators and groups with axes to grind has struck an uneasy alliance accommodating ideology, profits and careers, with history as the victim.

Many of today's texts have no discernable authors. They are not so much written as "developed" by teams of anonymous consultants, editors and designers. Texts are expected to be up to date: pictures must show a liberal sprinkling of races, neither patronizing nor demeaning. The same holds true for the sexes.

"Class conflict is inadmissible," writes FitzGerald. "The books also must stroke the school boards, most of which still stand watch for the local business community. So our economy is never called 'capitalist,' which might be construed as criticism."

We get a lot of social-scientific psychobabble. But old-fashioned questions such as "Have we a national identity?" or "What kind of society are we?" rarely get raised. And they need to be, now more than ever.

Gelb's form of revisionism has its place. But it likewise bears potential for excess. A stubborn refusal to re-evaluate has its converse. The risks of a debilitating cynicism are equally present.

In the course of 200 years, Americans have proved themselves to be among the most tolerant and generous of peoples in world history. Altruism does exist. But we are also human. It must be remembered that history, by whomever it is written or revised, is a ship carrying living memories into the future. One can not expect that this ship, in times past and in times to cone, will not have erred in its course, or left wreckage on the shoals.

August 19, 1984

American Beat. By Bob Greene.

It has been said that water covers two thirds of the earth, and that Bob Greene covers the rest.

Intentional hyperbole in this case, but not without a measure of veracity. This much is known: Greene niggles at the mind. His insightful, broadly entertaining columns for years have challenged readers to peer into the world with the same unvarnished, but sympathetic vision.

In prose as spare as polished bone, Greene can incite us to fury, pillory us with wit or elicit a roar of laughter. His singular gift is that of making a syndicated column consumed by millions seem like a one-to-one conversation. At his best, Green can bring tears to your eyes: in commiseration, in his evocation of the simplest joys and, among his fellow writers, in bald-faced envy.

"I am neither a pundit or a political philosopher," he writes. "I try to be a storyteller. I try to go out and explore something that interests me, and then—after hanging around and watching and listening and asking questions—I try to give the reader some sense of what it was like to be there."

Indeed, there is an almost palpable quality to his presence on the scene, be it the blood-stained barbarity of a Toughman contest, a suburban shopping mall, or Hugh Hefner's living room. Greene is that rare talent, an exceptionally sensitive observer and interpreter of symbols who, although maintaining a dispassionate eye, gives voice to the voiceless. And he put you *there*, with them.

This collection of 88 short pieces was compiled from columns originally published in The Chicago Sun-Times, The Chicago Tribune and Esquire magazine's "American Beat." Though at times uneven, and occasionally without apparent point, as a whole they are a vivid reflection of experiences which defy categories and labels.

In the words of one critic, Greene " . . . brings back instant snapshots from America's heartland . . . sudden, clear images that reveal the small, aching truths and needs of people pursuing, finding and losing their dreams."

This is a powerful ability, but Greene makes it appear effortless.

Few writers are at once utterly merciless in their dissection of individual folly, and so generously understanding of human failure. In "Miss McNichol Will See You Now," Greene strips the manufactured veneer from a spoiled pop star who delights in using, then summarily discarding, those close to her. He does this not with invective, but with straightforward reportage: the film idol's crassness, egomania and psychic gluttony are betrayed by her own words and actions; ultimately, she hangs herself.

Later, in "He Was No Bum," Greene sympathetically chronicles the last days in the life of a shell-shocked war veteran, a helpless, childlike man who finds not only a home in a city fire department but a brand of loyalty long thought dead. Greene finds a parable in these telling friendships. And he finds something else—a secret of the human heart.

Greene is not our foremost journalistic or literary figure. Greene is not a genius, though he is often possessed of it. He hasn't the majestic imagery, the conceptual and stylistic artifice, or the compulsive singleness of mind owned by the great novelists.

Yet he has one distinct advantage. Research completed, the novelist typically distances himself from people; isolation is a necessary characteristic the fiction writer's process. Not so with Greene, whose thirst is for mixing it up cheek to jowl. His reach extends from cocktails with Prince Charles to warm beer at a seedy tavern.

His narratives are real and present. And, in a time when our media and publicity organs alternately reduce or elevate everything to the same level of "significance," so is his value.

January 15, 1984

Sean Connery: From 007 to Hollywood Icon. By Andrew Yule.

Within a year of his debut as an extra in a touring company of "South Pacific" in 1954, young Thomas Connery had devoured the works of Ibsen, all 12 daunting volumes of Marcel Proust's *Remembrance of Things Past*, Tolstoy's *War and Peace*, Turgenev's *Fathers and Sons*, Joyce's *Ulysses* and *Finnegans Wake*, Wolfe's *Look Homeward, Angel*, the collected works and letters of George Bernard Shaw, all of Shakespeare's plays and Stanislavski's *An Actor Prepares* and *My Life in Art.*

Biographer Andrew Yule recalls this sudden, ravenous literary hunger by a largely untutored Scottish laborer to underscore the dedication to learning and craft Connery always has exhibited, then and now.

The man the world knows as Sean Connery is a skilled, thoughtful, aggressively professional actor who at last has shed the mantle of James Bond to be accepted as a versatile and durable star. On screen, he is also the quintessential man's man/ladies' man, this era's Clark Gable.

Although there is little new to be garnered here of the character of the man that has not been revealed elsewhere, Yule captures Connery's persistent restiveness, his inexorable drive and ambition to improve himself, with considerably greater resonance.

Herein, the now-familiar Connery story is more vividly drawn, from his impoverished youth in a drab working-class sector of Edinburgh to the innumerable false starts, his early struggles as an actor, the catapult to international renown as 007, his battles with studios over money, the maddening costs of fame, his loves and lasting friendships.

Suffusing the book is the simultaneously larger-than-life, yet curiously down-to-earth Connery persona: unflinching candor and honesty, loyalty, a dual fiscal nature (half pinch-penny, half generous benefactor), an endearing if troublesome naiveté about other's motives, and a saving propensity to suffer fools not at all, much less gladly.

Often moody and cantankerous, Connery is not always the most agreeable of men on the set. But Yule convincingly demonstrates that his exacting professionalism and collaborative acumen are the equal of anyone in the business, as are his vigor and unselfconsciousness.

Connery's formidable temper, unsoothed by a long string of commercial flops in the 1970s, fortunately is balanced by a playful sense of humor.

Yule packs his book with intriguing detail, some of it telling, some trivial. We learn that the name "Sean" was adopted as a bastardized version of the film title "Shane," that Connery's boyhood idol was Roy Rogers, that he turned down the offer of a lead role in TV's "Maverick," that Lana Turner and Shelly Winters were among his early boosters (and romances), that he was selected to play Bond only after Cary Grant, James Mason and Patrick McGoohan each declined a four-film package, that Ursula Andress replaced Julie Christie as the first "Bond girl" when the latter's bust failed to meet producer's specifications, that Noel Coward was originally cast as Dr. No, how touched Connery was by the reaction of his peers when he won an Oscar for "The Untouchables," and so forth.

Interviews with those closest to Connery, including Michael Caine, Sidney Lumet, ex-wife Diane Cilento, son Jason, brother Neil and current spouse Micheline Roquebrune, lend the book an expansive tone.

Yule has done a creditable job. But leave it to writer William McIllvanney to place Connery in his milieu so succinctly: "An interested hand-knitted commodity in an industry of synthetic fibers."

November 8, 1992

An Urchin in the Storm. By Stephen Jay Gould.

Skepticism often seems a malicious perversity to the naïve, for whom all things are possible—not least trance channeling, harmonic convergences, griffons and unicorns.

Into this lexicon of lunacy rides Stephen Jay Gould, wielding that most nefarious of illusion-bashers, the unfettered human brain.

Confronting the conjectural drivel that is the soul of the "New Age" fringe, Gould states the problem succinctly: "In this climate, beleaguered rationalism needs its skilled debaters—writers who can combine wit, penetrating analysis, sharp prose and sweet reason into an expansive view that expunges nonsense without stifling innovation, and that presents the excitement and humanity of science in a positive way."

One could find no more apt description for Gould's own incisive, important work.

But take heart, all ye reincarnated and astrally projected, the gentleman is not without some modicum of tolerance and understanding. And he reserves arrows aplenty for the demons born of hubris and hidebound "rationality."

Gould, a professor of biology, geology and the history of science at Harvard University, is as likely to invoke Voltaire or Alexander Pope as he is a member of the scientific pantheon in *An Urchin in the Storm: Essays on Books and Ideas,* a collection of his writings originally appearing in The New York Times Review of Books.

Gould considers 18 recent books and their subjects in a manner that is as elegant and original as it is learned. In so doing, he gifts the reader with a heightened critical perception—the review as expository essay.

Herein are engaging meditations on the possibility of artificial intelligence and the nature of geologic time; portraits of four distinguished biologists, among them fellow author and physician Dr. Lewis Thomas; and cogent attacks both on the delirium tremens of pseudo-science and the polemical scaffolding of deterministic thought.

Consider "Nurturing Nature," Gould's review of *Not in Our Genes: Biology, Ideology and Human Nature* by R. C. Lewontin, Steven Rose and Leon J. Kamin.

Gould is both a defender of Darwinian principles—one who views evolution as "the quintessential science of history"—as well as a scourge of those who misinterpret or subvert it; those, to be specific, who would explain every creature's traits strictly in terms of survival or reproductive imperatives.

To that vexing body, ideologue and scientist alike, who have chosen to ignore the synthesis of influences embodied in biology and culture while insisting on a polar division between nature and nurture, between genetic programming and environment, Gould replies:

"The view that human culture cancels biology . . . is equally fallacious (and equally cruel and restrictive). Biological determinism has limited the lives of millions by misidentifying their socioeconomic disadvantages as inborn deficiencies, but cultural determinism can be just as cruel in attributing severe congenital diseases—autism, for example—to psychobabble about too much parental love, or too little."

Gould is one of an exceedingly small group of contemporary thinkers who understand that science doesn't exist in a social or cultural vacuum. In the same review he eviscerates the view of science as a wholly impartial, linear advancement of knowledge, devoid of human emotional or motivational "contaminants."

Years ago, Sir Henry Hallett Dalt wrote, "Any science, we should insist, better than any other discipline, can hold up to its students and followers an ideal of patient devotion to the search for objective truth, with vision unclouded by personal and political motive."

Would that it were so.

"After all," writes Gould, who manages to evince a more plausible message, "isn't science supposed to be a cool, passionless, absolutely objective exploration of an external reality?

"But we scientists are no different than anyone else. We are passionate human beings, enmeshed in a web of personal and social circumstances . . . unless scientists understand their hopes and engage in vigorous self-scrutiny, they will not be able to sort unacknowledged preference from nature's weak and imperfect message."

Still, in our culture, the scientific method is the paradigm of all impartial knowledge. Science may well be the only construct of the human species that is self-correcting, given time. Its only sacred truth, to paraphrase Carl Sagan, is that there are no sacred truths.

Given this, science is among our most valuable tools. As for Gould, an exemplar of the method, we need as many like him as we can get.

January 17, 1988

The New Biographical Dictionary of Film. By David Thomson.

Allowing for devotees of the writings of the late Pauline Kael, who sometimes seem to regard her as the Oracle, there are three principal books on motion pictures that should grace any serious film buff's library.

James Agee's *On Film* offers as concise, witty and individual a look at the medium as any book yet written. And it still feels fresh. Though somewhat dated now, *The Filmgoer's Companion* by the late British historian and critic Leslie Halliwell remains indispensable, a warm and observant personal tribute to the movies that makes up in enthusiasm and encyclopedic knowledge what it may lack in intellectual rigor.

Then there's the latest (fifth) edition of David Thomson's *The New Biographical Dictionary of Film*, less a reference book than a compendium of highbrow biographical essays. Addictive, mercilessly honest and sometimes maddening, it is also invaluable, a wellspring for countless debates.

Thomson's judgments are not immutable; with each new edition he reconsiders and revises his analyses of filmmakers in light of their latest work in the case of active figures, or as new thoughts emerge with regard to luminaries of the past.

The British-born resident of San Francisco, now pushing 70, can write with incomparable flair. He is uncommonly probing, insightful and well-versed as well as unsparing, oft favoring a contrarian view and never given to following mere fashion. Few writers are as persuasive (see the author's critiques of Cary Grant and Robert Mitchum as the greatest of film actors) or as conversant in the ways all the arts impinge on film.

Though Thomson seldom slips into sentimentality, he can stir you with a generous remark or dazzle with an accumulation of critical detail. He also can be infuriatingly dismissive about someone whose work you've admired for decades. Opinionated? Excruciatingly so at times, delightfully so at others.

On the acknowledgments page, Thomson again lists his three favorites of all time: Howard Hawks's 1940 screwball jewel, "His Girl Friday"; Francois Truffaut's 1969 Cornell Woolrich adaptation, "Mississippi Mermaid"; and Jacques Rivette's 1974 meditation on magic and memory, "Celine and Julie Go Boating."

Eccentric tastes? Not at all. But characteristic of the man and his wide-ranging though definable tastes.

With more than 20 books to his credit, Thomson is no less substantial for being prolific. He has just as keen an appreciation for the nuances of comedy as the gravitas of drama. He is an unabashed lover of motion pictures and one of the most trenchant writers we have.

January 30, 2011

Adventures in Porkland. By Brian Kelly.

"Thank you, boys."

Conductor Lawrence Welk's liltingly familiar nod to his orchestra might well be echoed by the townsfolk of Yankton, S.D., site of a pointless congressional farrago known as the Lawrence Welk Museum, funded by the largesse of you and me, the American taxpayer.

The fact that even Welk, known for his popular if sleep-inducing music, was appalled at the idea seemed not to deter North Dakota Sen. Quentin Burdick, architect of this costly absurdity.

If this homage to desultory art is not the paradigm of congressional pork barreling, criminally wasteful spending that has cost taxpayers as much as $100 billion in a single year, it is certainly emblematic of the laughable extremes.

This, even as deficits soar into the stratosphere. The Welk silliness, and countless others, is in large measure a product of the Fiscal 1991 Budget Summit Accord, a.k.a., the Omnibus Budget Reconciliation Act (OBRA), a deal cut between the White House and Congress.

But pork's recent past is just as illuminating.

"In the past few years," writes journalist Brian Kelly in *Adventures in Porkland*, "Congress has funded studies on the sexual habits of Japanese quail and how long it takes to cook breakfast eggs. A $7 million grant went to study jet lag and a half-million dollars to build a 10-story replica of the Pyramid of Cheops and an 800-foot model of the Great Wall of China in Bedford, Ind."

Enormous sums have been spent on pork-barrel projects which share one overriding similarity: their utter uselessness. We've "invested" tens of millions to explore why people fall in love, the causes of rudeness, more efficient ways to can mackerel, why people cheat and lie on tennis courts, the likelihood of Belgian endive taking root in Massachusetts soil and, for the kingly sum of $19 million alone, a study on the causes and nature of cow flatulence.

Hands down the crowning nonpartisan achievement of late is the ridiculous Steamtown USA, an $80-million national railroad museum in Scranton, Pa., that no one deigns to visit. That it looks more like an abandoned factory yard than a museum may have something to do with why visitors bypass the site.

It is what Kelly terms "a classic case study of how pork is dispensed." Thank Rep. Joseph McDade (R, Pa.), one of Congress's shadiest characters, for this boondoggle.

Drawing on his years of observing the Washington moil, Kelly, political editor of The Washington Post "Style" section, has compiled a rogue's gallery of porkers.

The most egregious exponents of the practice include the unchallenged Pope of Pork, Sen. Robert C. Byrd (D, W.Va.), who garnered $700 million from the 1991 OBRA for special projects above and beyond normal federal spending for his state—including superhighways on which almost no one travels.

"My list starts with Byrd, a Hall of Famer even for connoisseurs of the Sam Rayburns and Lyndon Johnsons," said Kelly in a telephone interview with The Post and Courier. "Also high on the list is Rep. Jamie Whitten (D, Miss.), who's already rebuilt the Mississippi River. He controls the whole world of farm pork."

An overwhelming number of these colossal public works projects such as the Mississippi River nonsense are undertaken not because of need or practicality, but for the purposes of currying favor or engaging in the usual *quid pro quo.* Not to mention the psychic reward of wielding power.

The most successful porkers, Kelly said, are characterized by "awesome tenacity."

"All of them exhibit this quality, from John Murtha of Pennsylvania (who got $13 million as a down payment to begin transforming a string of abandoned factories into an "America's Industrial Heritage" theme park) to McDade."

President Bush is not immune to the lure, or the political expediency of pork.

"I find the Supercollider being built in Texas to be especially outrageous because of the involvement of President Bush. It's the President's own pork. It clearly sends a message that he is willing to play the backroom game like everyone else in Congress, and he abdicates his moral authority when that happens. He's not a man serious about reducing spending or curbing the deficit."

The numbers are so vast that the eye begins to glaze over. Yet how much of this can be tolerated by a nation already bleeding from an open and festering fiscal wound?

"I guess I'm as cynical as the next reporter who has covered these stories," said Kelly, "but I'm optimistic that people are more engaged by the subject than before. They are not as naïve. It's an incremental process, I realize. But we are going in that positive direction.

"Some politicians have had the fear of God struck into them. There have been some pretty surprising victories in the areas of apportionment, grandfathering of campaign contributions, etc. And it's not over. You've got to try to cut through that frustration and the sense that things won't change."

Distinguishing between worthwhile local projects and those that go "oink" is not so simple a matter as it may seem, but Kelly insists it behooves us to educate ourselves.

"First, people must realize that none of this stuff is free. You're paying for your bacon, and everyone else's, too. It's the special interests that petition for this stuff, but the average taxpayer who has to foot the bill.

"As taxpayers, we have to say 'I'm prepared to forgo this shortsighted small gain in favor of concentrating on the bigger problems."

Kelly has provided the primer, superior to P. J. O'Rourke's otherwise amusing *Parliament of Whores* in that it names names and is mercifully devoid of the latter's heavy-handed ideological slant and smug tone.

Kelly's year in the life of piggery is an engrossing travelogue through the fields of political folly, and one book that should not be missed in this election year, or any other.

August 23, 1992

Fishing in the Tiber. By Lance Morrow.

If the 1970s rescued the American short story from the precipice of irrelevancy, injecting its shriveled carcass with robust new life, might the 1980s be remembered for resurrecting the floundering American essay?

They just might, thanks in large measure to such apostles of the form as Lance Morrow, senior writer and columnist for Time magazine.

A literary standby long in decline in the United States, the essay—at its best—is trenchant, insightful, well-turned. It is less an editorial than a compact rumination. In Morrow's nimble prose, it is this and more.

From meditations on the decay and collapse of oratory to a balanced consideration of abortion and the unfairness of life, Morrow helps us see conventional perspectives and doctrinal points of view in decidedly new lights. His essays are very much journeys of rediscovery on the human landscape, by turns clever, rollicking and dead serious.

Chief among them, perhaps, is a moving vision of the tragedy that is Lebanon, once a geographic and cultural crossroads of Middle Eastern civilization—the Paris of its region—now a nation steeped only in rubble. Stark, lyrical, heartbreaking, it is writing for the ages, imbued with outrage and profound sadness, the product of a distinctly moral mind.

William F. Buckley, Jr., though of a markedly different political camp, avers that "An essay by Lance Morrow is a literary tropism. One needs to advance on it, peer at it, wonder over it, feel it even, meditate on it. His is a striking descriptive power governed by a mind of engaging inquisitiveness; that and a reticulative flair that feels out, and feels, the connection of apparently disparate things. A blessing that we should have now a collection of these fleeted essays."

As exceptional as *Fishing in the Tiber* undoubtedly is, the collection is not without the occasional descent into frivolity—sometimes amusing, more often superfluous—or even a bit of injudicious padding. On the other hand, an uneven quality is rather typical of such compilations.

Taken together, Morrow's essays fulfill all the requirements. They edify, entertain, provoke, and impel us to *see*.

August 26, 1988

A Literary Feast. Edited by Lilly Golden.

Yves Mirande is a corpulent Caravaggio of the dinner table, a "round-the-clock gastronome" whose gustatory prowess rivals the generous girth of his belly. As the unabashed hero of A. J. Liebling's delightful "A Good Appetite," a fictionalized memoir of Paris, circa 1955, he is a merry avatar of the gourmet's hedonistic obsessions.

Inveighing against the contemporary preoccupation with "moderation," and knowing full well that it leads to both culinary and existential ruin, Mirande, an author of farces and musical comedies, steadfastly eschews the new caution in favor of the old recklessness.

Liebling, his frequent companion at table, recounts several of their more elaborate meals (and philosophical musings), not excluding one conspicuously consumptive foray:

"Mirande . . . dazzled his juniors, French and American, by dispatching a lunch of raw Bayonne ham and fresh figs, a hot sausage in crust, spindles of filleted pike in a rich rose *sauce Nantua,* a leg of lamb larded with anchovies, artichokes on a pedestal of foie gras, and four or five kinds of cheese, with a good bottle of Bordeaux and one of champagne, after which he would call for the Armagnac."

"A Good Appetite" serves the same purpose as the ham and figs, to set the table, as it were, for editor Lilly Golden's delectable anthology *A Literary Feast.*

By turns luxuriant and spare, coarse and refined, caustic and whimsical, this fine coupling of food and literature—a time-honored recipe—offers an epicurean extravaganza of great writing. The 27 selections are very much a smorgasbord, including short stories, essays and excerpts from the works of Somerset Maugham, Virginia Woolf, V. S. Pritchett, Jorge Luis Borges, Isaac Bashevis Singer, Elizabeth Bowen, James Joyce, Isak Dinesen, Ernest Hemingway, Hortense Calisher and numerous others.

Especially succulent are Peter Mayle's "January" (a chapter drawn from *A Year in Provence*), M. F. K. Fisher's wry "Define This Word," and Robin Hemley's piquant "All You Can Eat."

Our intimate relationships with our repasts could not have been more tantalizingly explored, served with discerning and brio by Ms. Golden.

Dig in.

January 24, 1994

www.ingramcontent.com/pod-product-compliance
Lightning Source LLC
Chambersburg PA
CBHW060808310726
48980CB00002B/275

* 9 7 8 1 6 1 1 1 7 4 4 1 0 *